ETHICS, THE HEART OF LEADERSHIP

Edited by
Joanne B. Ciulla

Foreword by James MacGregor Burns

Westport, Connecticut
London

The Library of Congress has cataloged the hardcover edition as follows:

Ethics, the heart of leadership/ edited by Joanne B. Ciulla ; foreword
  by James MacGregor Burns.
      p.   cm.
    Includes bibliographical references and index.
    ISBN 1-56720-175-X (alk. paper).
    1. Business ethics.   2. Leadership—Moral and ethical aspects.
  I. Ciulla, Joanne B.
  HF5387.E875   1998
  174'.4—dc21   97-13410

British Library Cataloguing in Publication Data is available.

A hardcover edition of *Ethics, the Heart of Leadership* is available
from Quorum Books, an imprint of Greenwood Publishing Group, Inc.
(ISBN 1-56720-175-X).

Library of Congress Catalog Card Number: 97-13410
ISBN: 0-275-96120-6

First published in 1998

Praeger Publishers, 88 Post Road West, Westport, CT 06881
An imprint of Greenwood Publishing Group, Inc.
www.praeger.com
Printed in the United States of America

The paper used in this book complies with the
Permanent Paper Standard issued by the National
Information Standards Organization (Z39.48-1984).

10 9 8 7

For James MacGregor Burns

Contents

Foreword

If you're teaching a class in leadership and wish to start up a lively discussion, try posing that old chestnut of a question—"Was Adolf Hitler a leader?" The last time I tried this, in an honors course at the University of Maryland, a woman student vehemently answered "YES." Bad as he was, she said, he mirrored the hopes and hates of the German people, he won elections, and he fulfilled his promises by changing Germany along the lines his followers wanted. How could he not be called a leader? She had the class all but convinced—and almost me. Almost.

It was not, of course, that she was in any way pro-Hitler, who stands as the most universally detested man in history. The problem was not confusion about Hitler but about the true nature of leadership. One of the many virtues of this excellent collection of working papers is Joanne Ciulla's confrontation at the outset of the question, What constitutes a good leader? This central question raises further questions about ethical and moral leadership. The problem for this book, and for many others on leadership, is that the richness and heterogeneity of the field of leadership have led to great confusion about the difference between ethical and moral leadership; some use the terms interchangeably in this volume and elsewhere.

I discern three types of leadership values: *ethical* values—"old-fashioned character tests" such as sobriety, chastity, abstention, kindness, altruism, and other "Ten Commandments" rules of personal conduct; *modal* values such as honesty, integrity, trustworthiness, reliability, reciprocity, and accountability; and *end* values such as order (or security), liberty, equality, justice, and community (meaning brotherhood and sisterhood, replacing the traditional term "fraternity").

Each of these types of leadership values has implications for styles and strategies of leadership itself. "Status-quo" leaders, presiding over relatively stable communities, are dependent on rules of personal behavior, such as tolerance and altruism, that make for harmonious communal relationships. "Modal values" are crucially important to transactional leaders, whether in politics or education or other fields, who must depend on partners, competitors, clients, and others to live up to promises and understandings, as they must themselves. Responsibility and accountability are the tests here. "End values" lie at the heart of transforming leadership, which seeks fundamental changes in society, such as the enhancement of individual liberty and the expansion of justice and of equality of opportunity.

Wouldn't it be lovely, in this fragmented world, if these three sets of values, and hence all these forms of leadership, could exist in happy harmony? Alas, it cannot be. The more that a community embraces ethical values of mutual helpfulness, the more it is likely to come into conflict with the ethical values of other communities—for example, in the treatment of women and children, or in religious dogma and behavior. Modal values too tend to be culture-based and hence diverse. One society's honesty is another society's incivility; one society's reciprocity is another society's corruption.

Consider the question of manipulation—"managing" other persons' motives—which is so crucial to transactional leadership. Over three decades ago, in the April 1965 *Journal of Social Issues*, Herbert Kelman, recognizing increasing concern over ethical problems in the study of behavioral change, saw a basic dilemma: "On the one hand, for those of us who hold the enhancement of man's freedom of choice to be a fundamental value, any manipulations of the behavior of others constitutes a violation of their essential humanity. . . . On the other hand, effective behavior change inevitably involves some degree of manipulation and control, and at least an implicit imposition of the change agent's values on the client or the person he is influencing." In short, a dilemma.

Of my three sets of values, I would guess that ethical values are most diverse from culture to culture. Although modal values have had far more relevance to modern market societies than to Third or Fourth

World "traditional" cultures, transactional leadership values may become more universal as markets and privatization become more global.
What about end values? One might assume, in this ideologically torn
world, with its fierce religious and secular conflicts, that end values
might be the most multifarious of all.

I believe, however, that the people of the world, even under diverse
leaders, have been—slowly, gropingly, tortuously—shaping and rank-
ordering sets of meaningful end values. I believe that the Enlightenment values of liberty, equality, and fraternity (community) are still
evocative and controlling for vast numbers of people in the East as well
as the West. I believe that life, liberty, and the pursuit of happiness
dominate not only the American "mass mind" but also that of many
other societies. Despite numerous violations of its terms, the U.N.
"Universal Declaration of Human Rights" continues as a moral standard for most nations of the world.

Values are not only standards by which we measure our character,
our transactions, our policies, and programs. They may also contain
enormously evocative and revitalizing ideas, for which men and
women fight and die. Hence values can serve as transforming forces.
But much depends on a crucial step—to translate ideals into action,
promises into outcomes, "to walk the talk." Joanne Ciulla wrote to me
(March 1997): "You have to make a lot of assumptions to make a value
do something. You have to assume that because people value something
they act accordingly, but we know this isn't the case. Value articulations
of ethics often leave the door open for hypocrisy. Many people sincerely
value truth, but often lie. People can also tell the truth, but not value
it." The test lies in *outcomes*—real, intended, and durable change.

And what is the relationship of all these values to *vision*? We think of
vision as an overarching, evocative, energizing, moralizing force, ranging from broad, almost architectural plans for a new industry, say, to an
inspirational, spiritual, perhaps morally righteous evocation of future
hopes and expectations for a new political movement. Visions are often
projected by charismatic leaders, calling for mass mobilization and
action over the long run on many fronts, perhaps even for a revolution.
To the extent that vision is transformational—that is, calls for real
change—must it not embody supreme values in some kind of hierarchy? Otherwise would not vision be a kind of loose cannon, lurching
back and forth as the visionary leaders follow their own guiding stars?

Another question posed by visionary leadership is the balance of
cognitive and affective forces in change decisions. That visionary leadership embraces much that is spiritual and even emotional its proponents do not deny—they assert it. They like to point to Thomas
Jefferson's famed dialogue between "the Head and the Heart" as proof

that even that great Enlightenment rationalist understood the place of sentiment in the affairs of state as well as the affairs of people.

So was Adolf Hitler a leader, measured by those three levels of values? He was a terrible mis-leader: personally cruel and vindictive, politically duplicitous and treacherous, ideologically vicious and anni-hilative in his aims. A leader of change? Yes, he left Germany a smoking devastated land. My student may have Hitler—I'll take Gandhi, Mandela, and King.

JAMES MACGREGOR BURNS

Acknowledgments

Over the past four years most of the contributors to this volume have been engaged in dialogue with each other about leadership. James MacGregor Burns brought us together as a part of the Kellogg Leadership Studies Project (KLSP), of which he was the project scholar. The KLSP was funded by a W. K. Kellogg Foundation grant given to the Center for Political Leadership and Participation (recently renamed the James MacGregor Burns Academy of Leadership) at the University of Maryland, College Park. The essays by Gini, Solomon, and Wren and my essay "Leadership and the Problem of Bogus Empowerment" came out of the focus group on ethics and leadership, which I convened as a part of this project. They were first published in a set of working papers by the KLSP. Bass's article was also part of a KLSP focus group on transformational leadership. Many thanks to the Kellogg Foundation for its support of the KLSP and to Larraine R. Matusak, its Leadership Program officer. I also am grateful to Georgia J. Sorenson, the Director of the Center for Political Leadership and Participation; Bruce Adams, the KLSP Project Director; and Scott W. Webster, the Assistant KLSP Project Director; for making the conversations and working papers that led to this book possible.

The articles by Hollander and Keeley and my article "Leadership Ethics: Mapping the Territory" were first published in *Business Ethics Quarterly* (Vol. 5, No. 1, January 1995). A special thanks goes to David C. Smith, who edited this extraordinary issue on ethics and leadership, and Al Gini, the managing editor of *Business Ethics Quarterly*.

I am indebted to my friend and former colleague James MacGregor Burns, not just for his work on this book and the KLSP but for the many years of conversation and correspondence that we have had on ethics and leadership. Though we don't always agree on things, we both share in the passionate belief that ethics and morality are at the heart of leadership.

I also want to thank all contributors to this volume. It was an honor and a pleasure to work with them. And last but not least, I am grateful to my husband, René Kanters, who prepared the manuscript for publication, and my acquisitions editor, Alan Sturmer, for enthusiastically undertaking this book project.

Introduction

Some people become leaders because they have or develop certain talents and dispositions, or because of their wealth, military might, or position. Others lead because they possess great minds and ideas or they tell compelling stories. And then there are people who stumble into leadership because of the times or circumstances in which they find themselves. No matter how people get to be leaders, no one is a leader without willing followers. Managers and generals can act like playground bullies and use their power and rank force to force their will on people, but this is coercion, not leadership. Leadership is not a person or a position. It is a complex moral relationship between people, based on trust, obligation, commitment, emotion, and a shared vision of the good. Ethics, then, lies at the very heart of leadership. The essays in this volume explore the ethical intricacies of leadership.

I dedicate this book to James MacGregor Burns, because his theory of transforming leadership rests on the on-going moral relationship of leaders and followers. In his book, *Leadership*, Burns describes transforming leadership as a relationship in which leaders and followers morally elevate each other. Leadership for Burns is about change and sharing common purpose and values. The transforming leader helps people change for the better and make their lives better. It is fitting that this collection begins with Burns's Foreword and closes with an essay by Bernard M. Bass. Bass is well known for his theory and research on transformational leadership. Transformational and transforming leadership are similar in many ways; however, Bass's work concentrates on the psychological and emotional elements of leadership, such as charisma, whereas Burns's theory rests on values.

Like leadership studies, this collection is interdisciplinary. Three contributors are philosophers, two are industrial psychologists, one is a historian, and one a management scholar. All cast their ideas about ethics in slightly different terms, which allows us to understand the issues in different ways. In the Foreword, Burns laments that the authors in this volume do not make a crisp distinction between ethical and moral leadership and use the terms consistently. Oddly enough, we philosophers, who never miss a chance to make a distinction, tend to use the words moral and ethical interchangeably. Even if we were to accept Burns's categories of values, I'm not sure that it would make things clearer. Burns's ethical, modal, and end values—like most ethical concepts—are general and straightforward. But with ethics, the devil is in the details, and that's what this book is about. What do all of these values mean and how do they play out in the relationship of leaders to followers?

In the beginning, I said you can't be a leader without willing followers. Most people agree that coercion is not leadership, but what is a willing follower? How do we draw the moral line between free will and subtle forms of manipulation, deception, and the pressure that the norms of a group place on the individual? Similarly, few would argue with Burns's idea that the leadership relationship should be one that morally elevates both parties, but here again, the details matter. Elevate from what to what? Who determines which moral values are better and what is the criteria for better? What if people don't want to be elevated or incorrectly understand the common good? All the chapters in this collection raise these questions in different ways.

The first section of the book provides two overviews of the subject. In the first chapter I argue that a greater understanding of ethics will improve our understanding of leadership. Debates about the definition of leadership are really debates over what researchers think constitutes good leadership. The word *good* refers to both ethics and competence. Leadership scholars know quite a bit about the psychology of leadership but very little about the moral relationship of leadership. Al Gini's chapter explores the intersection of business ethics and leadership studies. He provides an excellent profile of the issues and literature in both fields. Gini emphasizes the role that "the witness of moral leadership" plays in improving the standards of business and everyday life.

In the second section, noted researcher Edwin P. Hollander takes us into the psychological and moral depths of leadership. He describes the leader-follower relationship as a unified, interdependent relationship held together by loyalty and trust, and rooted in the leader's commitment to principles of justice, equity, responsibility, and accountability in the exercise of authority and power. Hollander examines the moral hazards of leaders who feel the need to maintain power and distance and become detached from how followers feel about them and their actions. He says that this pattern can be especially damaging to teamwork when leaders continue to receive disproportionate rewards despite their poor performance, especially when coupled with organizational downsizing and layoffs.

My chapter on "bogus empowerment" is about honesty and the distribution of power in the leader-follower relationship. Burns's theory of transforming leadership emphasizes the importance of morally improving followers so that they can lead themselves. This too is a very good idea, but what does it really mean to give followers power? I examine the failure of empowerment schemes in the workplace over the past fifty years, and I argue that empowerment that attempts to change workers without changing leaders or empowerment that is aimed at making people feel good but not at giving them resources and real discretion is bogus. Authentic empowerment requires honesty and a full understanding of how the redistribution of power changes the leader-follower relationship.

Robert C. Solomon's chapter analyzes the role of emotions in the leader-follower relationship. He begins by exploding what he calls the myth of charisma. According to Solomon, charisma is not a quality of a leader's character nor is it an essential element of leadership, rather it is a general and vacuous way of talking about the complex emotional relationship of leaders to followers that is empty of moral content. He believes that trust is the emotional core of the leader-follower relationship and that we can better understand this relationship by looking at how the leaders and the led give and get trust.

The third section of the book is about the conflict between factional interests of followers and the common good. Popular media, communitarian writers, and recent management literature suggest that communities and organizations are rent by social interest groups who pursue their own selfish interests without regard for the common good. Some people think that transformational leadership offers a solution to this problem because it refocuses people's attention on higher goals and collective interests. Michael Keeley believes that this is a dangerous solution, one that James Madison and the Constitutional Convention of 1787 sought to thwart. Using examples from the organizational literature as well as history, Keeley argues that it is better to accommodate factions and individual interests by building them into the leader-follower relationship. For Keeley, a system of checks and balances is ethically better than transforming people so that they share the same higher collective goals. In his chapter, Keeley explains the implications of this approach for leadership in organizations and political theory.

The next two chapters offer a defense of transformational leadership. J. Thomas Wren criticizes Keeley for getting Madison wrong. He argues that Keeley failed to take into account all of Madison's writings, which over his lifetime show that Madison himself was ambivalent about the way to deal with factions and the common good. Madison believed in the common good, but he worried that followers would misunderstand it. His solution, which Wren says is the legitimate precursor to transformational leadership, is to find leaders capable of helping followers understand the common good. Wren believes that Burns's theory of transformational leadership "may have done Madison one better" because it creates a place in the leader-follower relationship where followers' desires intersect with the common good.

Bernard M. Bass's chapter defends transformational leadership from the charges of its critics who say that it leads to moral puffery and impression management; that it lacks checks and balances; that it is antithetical to organizational learning and development, shared learning, equality, consensus, and participatory decision making; that it leads followers to put off self-interest for a common good; and that it manipulates people and causes them harm. This is a tall order, and Bass draws on his own long career of research to answer these claims. In the end Bass says that the real test of transformational leadership is in the eyes of the beholder. Some leaders fool followers into believing that they have their interests at heart. Bass believes that these are not transformational leaders, they are pseudotransformational leaders, who are self-aggrandizing and immoral. By the end of Bass's chapter, the differences between Bass's transformational theory and Burns's transforming leadership seem significantly narrower than they have in the past.

What is clear from all of these essays is that the morality of leadership depends on the particulars of the relationship. It matters who the leaders and the followers are and how well they understand and feel about themselves and each other. It depends on whether they are honest and trustworthy, and most importantly, what they do and what they value. Behind all of these things are broad philosophic questions such as What is the common good? and Do people have free will? These are eternal questions that have kept generations of philosophers up late at night. This book is written at a more practical level. It offers the reader an insight into the moral dynamics of the heart that gives leadership its life everyday.

Part I

The Scope of
the Issues

1

Leadership Ethics:
Mapping the Territory

Joanne B. Ciulla

We live in a world where leaders are often morally disappointing. Even the greats of the past, such as Martin Luther King, Jr., and George Washington, are diminished by probing biographers who document their ethical shortcomings. It's hard to have heroes in a world where every wart and wrinkle of a person's life is public. Ironically, the increase in information that we have about leaders has increased the confusion over the ethics of leadership. The more defective our leaders are, the greater our longing to have highly ethical leaders. The ethical issues of leadership are found not only in public debates, they also lie embedded below the surface of the existing leadership literature.

Most scholars and practitioners who write about leadership genuflect at the altar of ethics and speak with hushed reverence about its importance to leadership. Somewhere in almost any book devoted to the subject, there are either a few sentences, paragraphs, pages, or even a chapter on how integrity and strong ethical values are crucial to leadership. Yet, given the central role of ethics in the practice of leadership, it's remarkable that there has been little in the way of sustained and systematic treatment of the subject by scholars. A literature search of 1,800 article abstracts from psychology, business, religion, philosophy, anthropology, sociology, and political science yielded only a handful of articles that offered any in-depth discussion of ethics and leadership.[1] Articles on ethics and leadership are either about a particular kind of leadership (for example, business leadership or political leadership), or a particular problem or aspect of leadership, or they are laudatory articles about the importance of honesty and integrity in leadership. There are also a number of studies that measure the moral development of managers.[2] The state of research on leadership ethics is similar to the state of business ethics twenty years ago. For the most part, the discussion of ethics in the leadership literature is fragmented, there is little reference to other works on the subject, and one gets the sense that most authors write as if they were starting from scratch.

In this chapter I map the place of ethics in the study of leadership. I argue that ethics is located in the heart of leadership studies and not in an appendage. This chapter consists of three parts. In the first part, I discuss the treatment of ethics within existing research in leadership studies. In the second part I look at some discussions concerning the definition of leadership and locate the place of ethics in those discussions. In the third part I examine two normative leadership theories and use them to illustrate how more rigorous work in the area of leadership ethics will give us a more complete understanding of leadership itself.

Throughout the chapter I use the term *leadership ethics* to refer to the study of the ethical issues related to leadership and the ethics of leadership. The study of ethics generally consists of the examination of right, wrong, good, evil, virtue, duty, obligation, rights, justice, fairness, and so on, in human relationships with each other and other living things. Leadership studies, either directly or indirectly, tries to understand what leadership is and how and why the leader-follower relationship works (What is a leader and what does it mean to exercise leadership? How do leaders lead? What do leaders do? and Why do people follow?).[3] Because leadership entails very distinctive kinds of human relationships with distinctive sets of moral problems, I thought it appropriate to refer to the subject as *leadership ethics*; however, my main reason for using the term is that it is less awkward than using expressions like *leadership and ethics*.

PART I: TREATMENT OF ETHICS IN LEADERSHIP STUDIES

Ethics without Effort

Ethics is one of those subjects that people rightfully feel they know about from experience. Most people think of ethics as practical knowledge, not theoretical knowledge. One problem that exists in applied ethics is that scholars sometimes feel that their practical knowledge and common sense (and exemplary moral character) are adequate for discussion of ethics in their particular field. The results of research that uses this approach are sometimes good, sometimes awful, but most of the time just not very informative. Philosophic writings on ethics are frequently (and understandably) ignored or rejected because they appear obtuse and irrelevant to people writing about ethics in their own area of research or practice.[4]

What is striking about leadership studies is not the absence of philosophic writings on ethics, but the fact that authors expend so little energy on researching ethics from any discipline. To some extent this is even true of Joseph Rost's book, *Leadership for the Twenty-First Century*, which contains one of the best critiques of the field of leadership studies. I frequently comment on Rost's book in this chapter because it is an important new contribution to the field. It is extensively researched and contains a terrific twenty-four-page bibliography. However, the chapter on ethics stands out because of its paucity of references. After a very quick run through utilitarian, deontic, relativistic, and contractarian ethics, Rost concludes that "none of the ethical systems is particularly valuable in helping leaders and followers make decisions about the ethics of the changes they intend for an organization or society."[5] He condemns all ethical theories as useless, using only two books, James Rachels's *The Elements of Moral Philosophy* and Mark Pastin's *The Hard Problems of Management*.[6,7]

Scholars who either reject or ignore writings on ethics usually end up either reinventing fairly standard philosophic distinctions and ethical theories or doing without them and proceeding higgledy-piggledy with their discussion. Rost concludes his chapter on ethics by saying, "Clearly, the systems of ethical thought people have used in the past and that are still in use are inadequate to the task of making moral judgments about the content of leadership."[8] Citing the work of Robert Bellah et. al., William Sullivan, and Alasdair MacIntyre, Rost proposes "a new language of civic virtue to discuss and make moral evaluations of the changes they [leaders] intend."[9] After dismissing ethical theory, he goes on to say that out of this new language there will "evolve a new ethical framework of leadership content, a system of ethical thought applied to the content of leadership, that actually works."[10] Rost does not really tell us what will take the place of all the theories that he has dismissed, but rather he assures us that a new system of ethics will emerge. At least Rost pays some attention to the literature in ethics; however, he spends most of his time throwing it out and then runs out of steam when it comes to offering anything concrete in regard to leadership, except for some form of communitarianism.

Another more significant example of the paucity of research energy expended on ethics is *Bass & Stogdill's Handbook of Leadership*, hailed by reviewers as "the most complete work on leadership" and "encyclopedic."[11] This is considered the source book on the study of leadership. The text is 914 pages long and contains a 162-page bibliography. There are 37 chapters in this book, none of which treats the question of ethics in leadership. If you look up ethics in the index, 5 pages are listed. Page 569 contains a brief discussion of different work ethics, page 723 is a reference to the gender differences in values, and page 831 refers to a question raised about whether sensitivity training is unethical. The reader has to go to the last chapter of the book, called "Leadership in the Twenty-First Century," to get to the 2-page exposition on ethics. What we are treated to on the first page of the handbook is a meager grabbag of empirical studies and one fleeting reference to the argument of James MacGregor Burns that transformational leaders foster moral virtue.[12]

The empirical studies include a 1988 Harris poll of 1,031 office workers that revealed that 89 percent of employees thought it was important for managers to be, for example, honest and upright; J. Weber's study of 37 managers, which led to the conclusion that managers reasoned to conform to majority opinion rather than universal rules;[13] and Kuhnert and Lewis's discussion of how transformational leaders develop and move up Kohlberg's scale from concern for personal goals to higher levels of values and obligations.[14] Final references are to a study of seven mainland Chinese factories, hospitals, and agencies, which included, among many other questions, survey questions on the character function of leadership and moral character.[15] The last part of this subsection on ethics contains a paragraph on how professional associations such as the American Psychological Association set standards of ethical behavior.

The second section on ethics, "A Model for Ethical Analysis," sounds more promising. Bass, the author, defines ethics as a "creative searching for human fulfillment and choosing it as good and beautiful." He goes on to argue that professional ethics focuses too much on negative vices and not on the good things. Bass's definition of ethics and sole reference on ethics in this section is taken from *The Paradox of Poverty: A Reprisal of Economic Development Policy* by P. Steidlmeier.[16] The model for ethical analysis that it suggests is one that "determines the connection between moral reasoning and moral behavior and how each depends on the issue involved."[17] After reading these two pages, one gets little information about the area of ethics and leadership.[18] What is most remarkable about this section of the book is that it offers little insight into what the questions are in this area. It is not surprising that the standard reference work on leadership does not carry much information on ethics, in part because there isn't much research on it.[19] Nonetheless, for all the research that went into his book, Bass seems to wing it when it comes to talking about ethics.

Leadership and the Rosetta Stone

As Rost points out in his book, one of the problems with leadership studies is that most of the work has been done from one discipline and a large part of the research rests on what he calls the industrial paradigm, which views leadership as good management.[20] (Bass and Stogdill are both management scholars.) Rost also criticizes the field for overemphasis on things that are peripheral to leadership such as traits, group facilitation, effectiveness, or the content of leadership, which includes the things that leaders must know in order to be effective.[21] This is clearly the case if you look at the contents of Bass and Stogdill. The largest section in the book is on the personal attributes of leaders.

Marta Calas and Linda Smircich also offer a provocative critique of the field that indirectly helps to explain why there has been little work on ethics in leadership studies. Along with Rost, they point out the positivist slant in much of the leadership research (particularly research on leadership in psychology and business). According to Calas and Smircich, the "saga" of leadership researchers is to find the Rosetta stone of leadership and break its codes. They argue that because the research community believes that society puts a premium on science, researchers' attempts to break the Rosetta stone have to be "scientific." Hence the "scientists" keep breaking leadership into smaller and smaller pieces until the main code has been lost and can't be put back together.[22] This fragmentation accounts for one of the reasons why Rost urges us to focus on the essence of leadership, and it also explains why there is so little work on ethics and leadership. Ethical analysis generally requires a broad perspective on a practice. For example, in business, ethical considerations of a problem often go hand in hand with taking a long-term view of a problem and the long-term interests of an organization.

Calas and Smircich also observe that the leadership literature seems irrelevant to practitioners, whereas researchers don't feel like they are getting anywhere—nobody seems happy. They believe that leadership researchers are frustrated because they are trying to do science but they know that they aren't doing good science. The researchers are also trying to do narrative, but the narrative is more concerned with sustaining the community of researchers instead of helping explicate leadership. Calas and Smircich, like Rost, point to the necessity of a multidisciplinary approach to leadership. All three scholars emphasize the importance of narratives, such as case studies, mythology, and biography, in understanding leadership.

It is interesting to note that the two most respected and quoted figures in leadership studies, John W. Gardner and James MacGregor Burns, both do take a somewhat multidisciplinary approach to the subject. John W. Gardner's book, *On Leadership*, is a simple and readable outline of the basic issues in leadership studies. Gardner writes as a practitioner. He has held many distinguished posts in the government and in business and currently teaches at Stanford University. He offers a good, common-sense discussion of ethics and leadership in his chapter "The Moral Dimension." It is interesting to note that the phrase, "the moral dimension of leadership," is now frequently used in the leadership literature; a recent conference on ethics and leadership used this phrase as its title. The conceptualization of morality as a dimension of leadership rather than a part or element is significant in that it implies that it is another way of seeing the whole of leadership rather than simply investigating a part of it.[23]

Gardner's chapter on ethics is a thoughtful piece that uses examples from several disciplines. One reason why it is often quoted is because he is a talented wordsmith, he uses engaging examples, and he offers wisdom that comes from experience. Gardner lines up the usual suspects of evil leadership, such as Hitler and the Ku Klux Klan, and peppers his discussion with a diverse set of examples from history and politics. For the most part, his discussion of ethics is hortatory. He says that we should hope that "our leaders will keep alive values that are not so easy to embed in laws—our feeling about individual moral responsibility, about caring for others, about honor and integrity, about tolerance and mutual respect, and about human fulfillment within a framework of values."[24] Gardner offers some good advice on ethics, but that's about all.

James MacGregor Burns's book *Leadership* is considered by many to be the best book to date on leadership. Burns, a political scientist, historian, and biographer, is probably the most referenced author in leadership studies. Burns's theory of transforming leadership is one that is built around a set of moral commitments. I discuss Burns's work later in this chapter because his work is central to my contention that ethics is at the heart of leadership.

In this section, I have discussed some representative examples of the ways in which ethics has been treated in the leadership literature. Most of what is considered leadership literature comes from the social sciences of psychology, business, and political science. The scarcity of work done on leadership in the humanities is another reason why there is little done on ethics. Burns, the most quoted scholar in the field, takes a multidisciplinary approach to leadership. However, it is not the number of disciplines that makes Burns's work compelling—it is the fact that he tries to understand leadership as a whole and not as a combination of small fragments.

Paradigm, Shifting Paradigm, or Shifty Paradigm?

For an investigation into leadership ethics to be meaningful and useful, it has to be embedded in the study of leadership. Again, it is worthwhile to make an analogy to business ethics. If courses and research on business ethics ignored existing business research and practice, then the subject of ethics would become a mere appendage, a nice but not a crucial addition to our knowledge about business and a business school curriculum. Research and teaching in areas like business ethics and leadership ethics should aim not only at making businesspeople and leaders more ethical but also at reconceptualizing the way that we think about the theory and practice of business and leadership. This is why both areas of applied ethics have to embed themselves into their respective fields.[25]

Using Thomas Kuhn's analysis in *The Structure of Scientific Revolutions,* one might argue that there exists a paradigm of leadership studies, based primarily on the work done in business and psychology.[26] Kuhn says that one way you can tell if a paradigm has been established is if scientists enhance their reputations by writing journal articles that are "addressed only to professional colleagues, the men whose knowledge of a shared paradigm can be assumed." Prior to the establishment of a paradigm, writing a textbook would be prestigious, because you would be making a new contribution to the field.[27,28] Using Kuhn's criteria, there is evidence for the existence of a paradigm of leadership studies: Bass and Stogdill's handbook (now in its third edition), various symposia on leadership,[29] the kinds of leadership articles that are accepted to journals, and the literature that is cross-referenced in these journals.

According to Kuhn, when a paradigm is established and researchers engage in "normal science," there is little discussion of rules or definitions because they become internalized by researchers working in that paradigm. Kuhn says, "lack of a standard interpretation or of an agreed reduction to rules will not prevent a paradigm from guiding research."[30] He points out that over time the meaning of important terms can shift along with theories, which seems to be what has happened in leadership studies. Kuhn believes that scientific progress would be impeded if the meanings of terms were overly rigid.

Rost criticizes some research in leadership studies because researchers don't define leadership. But as Kuhn points out, this sort of definition is not really necessary if researchers are working in a paradigm, because definitions are internalized and unarticulated. Rost's second charge is that researchers all have different definitions of leadership and that the field cannot progress unless there is a shared definition of leadership.[31] If Rost is correct and researchers have radically different definitions of leadership (meaning that leadership denotes radically different things), then either there never was a well-formed paradigm (so leadership studies is in a pre-paradigm phase), or there exists a paradigm, and that paradigm is shifting. In both cases, there would be considerable debate over definitions. However, if there is a paradigm of sorts and researchers are still arguing over definitions, then there is a paradigm of leadership studies but it is a shifty one. By this I mean that scholars don't really trust this paradigm, but they nonetheless stick to it and keep doing research in the same old way.[32]

PART II: LOCATING ETHICS

What Do the Definitions Really Tell Us?

Leadership scholars have spent a large amount of time and trouble worrying about the definition of leadership. Rost analyzes 221 definitions to make his point that there is not a common definition of leadership. What Rost does not make clear is what he means by a definition. Sometimes he sounds as if a definition supplies necessary and sufficient conditions for identifying leadership. He says, "neither scholars nor the practitioners have been able to define leadership with precision, accuracy, and conciseness so that people are able to label it correctly when they see it happening or when they engage in it."[33] He goes on to say that the various publications and the media all use leadership to mean different things that have little to do with what leadership really is.[34] In places Rost uses the word *definition* as if it were a theory or perhaps a paradigm. He says that a shared definition implies that there is a "school" of leadership. When the definition changes, there is a "paradigm shift."[35]

Rost's claim that what leadership studies needs is a common definition of leadership is off the mark for two reasons. One would be hard-pressed to find a group of sociologists or historians who shared the exact same definition of sociology or history. It is also not clear that the various definitions that Rost examines are that different in terms of what they denote. I selected the following definitions from Rost's book on the basis of what Rost says are definitions most representative of each particular era. We need to look at these definitions and ask, Are these definitions so different that there is no family resemblance between them, that is, would researchers be talking about different things?[36] Lastly I look at what these definitions tell us about the place of ethics in leadership studies.

1920s [Leadership is] the ability to impress the will of the leader on those led and induce obedience, respect, loyalty, and cooperation.[37]

1930s Leadership is a process in which the activities of many are organized to move in a specific direction by one.[38]

1940s Leadership is the result of an ability to persuade or direct men, apart from the prestige or power that comes from office or external circumstance.[39]

1950s [Leadership is what leaders do in groups.] The leader's authority is spontaneously accorded him by his fellow group members.[40]

1960s [Leadership is] acts by a person that influence other persons in a shared direction.[41]

1970s Leadership is defined in terms of discretionary influence. Discretionary influence refers to those leader behaviors under control of the leader which he may vary from individual to individual.[42]

1980s Regardless of the complexities involved in the study of leadership, its meaning is relatively simple. Leadership means to inspire others to undertake some form of purposeful action as determined by the leader.[43]

1990s Leadership is an influence relationship between leaders and followers who intend real changes that reflect their mutual purposes.[44]

If we look at the sample of definitions from different periods, we see that the problem of definition is not that scholars have radically different meanings of leadership. Leadership does not denote radically different things for different scholars. One can detect a family resemblance between the different definitions. All of them talk about leadership as some kind of process, act, or influence that in some way gets people to do something. A roomful of people, each holding one of these definitions, would understand each other.

Where the definitions differ is in their connotation, particularly in terms of their implications for the leader-follower relationship. In other words, how leaders get people to do things (impress, organize, persuade, influence, and inspire) and how what is to be done is decided (obedience, voluntary consent, determined by the leader, and reflection of mutual purposes) have normative implications. So perhaps what Rost is really talking about is not definitions, but theories about how people lead (or how people should lead) and the relationship of leaders and those who are led. His critique of particular definitions is really a critique of the way they do or don't describe the underlying moral commitments of the leader-follower relationship.[45]

If the above definitions imply that leadership is some sort of relationship between leaders and followers in which something happens or gets done, then the next question is How do we describe this relationship? For people who believe in the values of a democratic society such as freedom and equality, the most morally unattractive definitions are those that appear to be coercive and manipulative and disregard the input of followers. Rost clearly dislikes the theories from the 1920s, 1970s, and 1980s, not because they are inaccurate, but because he rejects the authoritarian values inherent in them.[46] Nonetheless, theories such as the ones from the 1920s, 1970s, and 1980s may be quite accurate if we were observe the way some corporate and world leaders behave.

The most morally attractive definitions hail from the 1940s, 1950s, 1960s, and Rost's own definition from the 1990s. They imply a noncoercive, participatory, and democratic relationship between leaders and followers. There are two morally attractive elements of these theories. First, rather than induce, these leaders influence, which implies that leaders recognize the autonomy of followers. Rost's definition uses the word *influence*, which carries an implication that there is some degree of voluntary compliance on the part of followers. In Rost's chapter on ethics he says, "The leadership process is ethical if the people in the relationship (the leaders and followers) *freely* agree that the intended changes fairly reflect their mutual purposes."[47] For Rost consensus is an important part of what makes leadership leadership, and it does so because free choice is morally pleasing. The second morally attractive part of these definitions is that they imply recognition of the beliefs, values, and needs of the followers. Followers are the leader's partner in shaping the goals and purposes of a group or organization.

The morally attractive definitions also speak to a distinction frequently made between leadership and headship (or positional leadership). Holding a formal leadership position or position of power does not necessarily mean that a person exercises leadership. Furthermore, you do not have to hold a formal position in order to exercise leadership. Leaders can wield force or authority using only their position and the resources and power that come with it.[48] This is an important distinction, but it does not get us out of "the Hitler problem." The Hitler problem is answering the question, "Is Hitler a leader?" Under the morally unattractive definitions he is a leader, perhaps even a great leader, albeit an immoral one. Ron Heifetz argues that under the great man and trait theories of leadership you can put Hitler, Lincoln, and

Gandhi in the same category because the underlying value of the theory is that leadership is influence over history.[49] However, under the morally attractive theories, Hitler is not a leader at all. He's a bully or tyrant or simply the head of Germany.

To muddy the waters even further, according to one of Warren Bennis's and Burt Nanus's characterizations of leadership, "The manager does things right and the leader does the right thing," one could argue that Hitler is neither unethical nor a leader, he is a manager.[50] Bennis and Nanus are among those management writers who talk as if all leaders are wonderful and all managers morally flabby drones. However, what appears to be behind this in Bennis and Nanus's work is the idea that leaders are morally a head above everyone else.[51]

So what does this all mean? It looks like we are back to the problem of definition again. The first and obvious meaning is that definitions of leadership have normative implications (the old "there is no such thing as a value-free social science"). Leadership scholars such as Bennis and Nanus are sloppy about the language they use to describe and prescribe. Though it is true that researchers have to be clear about when they are describing and when they are prescribing, the crisp fact/value distinction will not in itself improve our understanding of leadership.

Leadership scholars who worry about constructing the ultimate definition of leadership are asking the wrong question but inadvertently trying to answer the right question. As we have seen from the examination of definitions, the ultimate question in leadership studies is not "What is the definition of leadership?" The ultimate point of studying leadership is What is good leadership?" The use of the word *good* here has two senses, morally good and technically good or effective. These two senses form a logical conjunction. In other words, in order for the statement "She is a good leader" to be true, it must be true that she is effective and that she is ethical.[52] The question of what constitutes a good leader lies at the heart of the public debate on leadership. We want our leaders to be good in both ways. It's easy to judge if they are effective, but more difficult to judge if they are ethical, because there is some confusion over what factors are relevant to making this kind of assessment.

Ethics and Effectiveness

The problem with the existing leadership research is that few studies investigate both senses of good, and when they do, they usually do not fully explore the moral implications of their research questions or their results. The research on leadership effectiveness touches indirectly on the problem of explicitly articulating the normative implications of descriptive research. The Ohio Studies and the Michigan Studies both measured leadership effectiveness in terms of how leaders treated subordinates and how they got the job done. The Ohio Studies measured leadership effectiveness in terms of consideration, the degree to which leaders act in a friendly and supportive manner, and initiating structure, or the way that leaders structure their own role and the role of subordinates in order to obtain group goals.[53] The Michigan Studies measured leaders on the basis of task orientation and relationship orientation.[54] These two studies spawned a number of other research programs and theories, including the situational leadership theory of Hersey and Blanchard, which looks at effectiveness in terms of how leaders adapt their leadership style to the requirements of a situation. Some situations require a task orientation, others a relationship orientation.[55]

Implicit in all these theories and research programs is an ethical question. Are leaders more effective when they are nice to people, or are leaders more effective when they use certain techniques for structuring and ordering tasks?[56] One would hope that the answer is both, but that answer is not conclusive in the studies that have taken place over the last three decades.[57] The interesting question is What if this sort of research shows that you don't have to be kind and considerate of other people to run a country or a profitable organization? Would scholars and practitioners draw an *ought* from the *is* of this research?[58] It's hard to tell, when researchers are not explicit about their ethical commitments. The point is that no matter how much empirical information we get from the "scientific" study of leadership, it will always be inadequate if we neglect the moral implications. The reason why leadership scholarship has not progressed very far is that most of the research focuses on explaining leadership, not on understanding it.[59]

The discussion of definition is intended to locate where some of the ethical problems are in leadership studies. As we have seen, ethical commitments are central to how scholars define leadership and shape their research. Leadership scholars do not need to have one definition of leadership in order to understand each other, they just need to be clear about the values and normative assumptions that lie behind the way that they go about researching leadership.[60] By doing so, we have a better chance of understanding the relationship between what leadership is and what we think leadership ought to be.[61] This state of affairs would represent a marked shift in the existing Bass/Stogdill-type paradigm (and maybe finally put to rest the pretensions of value-free social science).

PART III: THE NORMATIVE THEORIES

Transforming Leadership

So far we have located the place of leadership ethics in definitions and in some of the empirical research on leadership. Now we look at two normative leadership theories.

James MacGregor Burns's theory of transforming leadership is compelling because it rests on a set of moral assumptions about the relationship between leaders and followers.[62] Burns's theory is clearly a prescriptive one about the nature of morally good leadership. Drawing from Abraham Maslow's work on needs, Milton Rokeach's research on values development, and research on moral development from Lawrence Kohlberg, Jean Piaget, Erik Erickson, and Alfred Adler, Burns argues that leaders have to operate at higher need and value levels than those of followers.[63] A leader's role is to exploit tension and conflict within people's value systems and play the role of raising people's consciousness.[64]

On Burns's account, transforming leaders have very strong values. They do not water down their values and moral ideals by consensus, but rather they elevate people by using conflict to engage followers and help them reassess their own values and needs. This is an area where Burns is very different from Rost. Burns writes that "despite his [Rost's] intense and impressive concern about the role of values, ethics and morality in transforming leadership, he underestimates the crucial importance of these variables." Burns goes on to say, "Rost leans towards, or at least is tempted by, consensus procedures and goals that I believe erode such leadership."[65]

The moral questions that drive Burns's theory of transforming leadership come from his work as a biographer and a historian.[66] When biographers or historians study a leader, they struggle with the question of how to judge or keep from judging their subject. Throughout his book, Burns uses examples of a number of incidents where questionable means, such as lying and deception, are used to achieve honorable ends or where the private life of a politician is morally questionable.[67] If you analyze the numerous historical examples in Burns's book, you find that two pressing moral questions shape his leadership theory. The first is the morality of means and ends (and this also includes the moral use of power), and the second is the tension between the public and private morality of a leader. His theory of transforming leadership is an attempt to characterize good leadership by accounting for both of these questions.

Burns's distinction between transforming and transactional leadership and modal and end values offers a way to think about the question

"What is a good leader?" in terms of the relationship to followers and the means and ends of actions. Transactional leadership rests on the values found in the means of an act. These are called modal values, which are things like responsibility, fairness, honesty, and promise keeping. Transactional leadership helps leaders and followers reach their own goals by supplying lower-level wants and needs so that they can move up to higher needs. Transforming leadership is concerned with end values, such as liberty, justice, and equality. Transforming leaders raise their followers up through various stages of morality and need.[68] They turn their followers into leaders, and the leader becomes a moral agent.

As a historian, Burns is very concerned with the ends of actions and the change that they initiate. In terms of his ethical theory, at times he appears to be a consequentialist, despite his acknowledgment that "insufficient attention to means can corrupt the ends."[69] However, because Burns does not really offer a systematic theory of ethics in the way that a philosopher might, he is difficult to categorize. Consider for example, Burns's two answers to the Hitler question. In the first part of the book, he says quite simply that after Hitler gained power and crushed all opposition, he was no longer a leader. He was a tyrant.[70] Later in the book, he offers three criteria for judging how Hitler would fare before "the bar of history." Burns says that Hitler would probably argue that he was a transforming leader who spoke for the true values of the German people and elevated them to a higher destiny. First, he would be tested by modal values of honor and integrity or the extent to which he advanced or thwarted the standards of good conduct in humanity. Second, he would be judged by the end values of equality and justice. Lastly, he would be judged on the impact that he had on the well-being of the people whom he touched.[71] According to Burns, Hitler would fail all three tests. Burns doesn't consider Hitler a leader or a transforming leader, because of the means that he used, the ends that he achieved, and the impact of Hitler as a moral agent on his followers during the process of his leadership.[72]

By looking at leadership as a process and not a set of individual acts, Burns's theory of good leadership is difficult to pigeonhole into one ethical theory and warrants closer analysis. The most attractive part of Burns's theory is the idea that a leader elevates his or her followers and makes them leaders. Near the end of his book, he reintroduces this idea with an anecdote about why President Johnson did not run for re-election in 1968. Burns tells us, "Perhaps he did not comprehend that the people he had led—as a part of the impact of his leadership—have created their own fresh leadership, which was now outrunning his." All the people that Johnson helped—the sick, the blacks, and the poor—now had their own leadership. Burns says, "Leadership begat leadership and hardly recognized its off-spring." "Followers had become leaders."[73]

Burns's theory has spawned a number of descriptive studies on transformational leadership. For example, Bernard Bass studies transformational leadership in terms of the impact of leaders on their followers. In sharp contrast to Burns, Bass removes Burns's condition that leaders have to appeal to higher-order needs and values. So, Bass is willing to call Hitler a transformational leader.[74] There are a number of other researchers writing about transformational leadership, including Judith Rosner, who uses transformational leadership as a means for understanding how women lead.[75]

The other area of research related to transformational leadership is charismatic leadership. Charismatic leaders, according to Jay Conger, "hold certain keys to transformational processes within organizations."[76] Bass believes that charismatic leadership is a necessary ingredient of transformational leadership.[77] The research on charismatic leadership opens up a wide range of ethical questions because of the powerful emotional and moral impact that charismatic leaders have on followers.[78] Charismatic leadership can be the best and the worst kind of leadership depending on whether you are looking at a Gandhi or a Charles Manson.[79] Leadership ethics clearly finds a place in this literature where the moral problems are near the surface, but not explicitly explored.

Servant Leadership

The second example of a normative theory of leadership is servant leadership. Robert K. Greenleaf's book, *Servant Leadership: A Journey into the Nature of Legitimate Power and Greatness,* presents a view of how leaders ought to be. However, the best way to understand servant leadership is to read *Journey to the East,* by Hermann Hesse.[80] Hesse's story is about a spiritual journey to the East. On the journey a servant named Leo carries the bags and does the travelers' chores. There is something special about Leo. He keeps the group together with his presence and songs. When Leo mysteriously disappears, the group loses its way. Later in the book the main character, HH, discovers that the servant, Leo, was actually the leader. The simple but radical shift in emphasis is from followers serving leaders to leaders serving followers.

Servant leadership has not gotten as much attention as transformational leadership in the literature, but students and businesspeople often find this a compelling characterization of leadership. According to Greenleaf, the servant leader leads because he or she wants to serve others.[81] People follow servant leaders freely because they trust them.

Like the transforming leader, the servant leader elevates people. Greenleaf says a servant leader must pass this test: "Do those served grow as persons? Do they, *while being served*, become healthier, wiser, freer, more autonomous, more likely themselves to become servants?" He goes on and adds a Rawlsian proviso, "*And*, what is the effect on the least privileged in society?"[82] As normative theories of leadership, both servant leadership and transforming leadership are areas of leadership ethics that are open to ethical analysis and provide a rich foundation of ideas for developing future normative theories of leadership.

CONCLUSION: ETHICS AT THE HEART OF LEADERSHIP

In this chapter I have mapped the territory of ethics in leadership studies. I argued that the definition question in leadership studies is not really about the question "What is leadership?" but about the question "What is good leadership?" By *good*, I mean morally good and effective. This is why I think it's fair to say that ethics lies at the heart of leadership studies. Researchers in the field need to get clear on the ethical elements of leadership in order to be clear on what the term *leadership* connotes.

Existing theories and empirical literature have strong normative implications that have not been fully developed by their authors. A second place for ethics in leadership studies is expanding the ethical implications of these theories and research findings. Normative theories of leadership, such as transforming leadership and servant leadership, are not well-developed in terms of their philosophic implications. They need more analysis as ethical theories and more empirical testing. One reason why the body of research on transformational leadership looks promising is because it contains empirical research on a theory that was constructed to address some of the basic moral problems of leadership. It offers a richer understanding of leadership than theories that are just about ethics or just about leader behavior.

Leadership ethics can also serve as a critical theory that opens up new kinds of dialogues among researchers and practitioners. Business ethics has certainly played this role in business studies and practice. Lastly, work in leadership ethics should generate different ways of conceptualizing leadership and new ways of asking research questions. To some extent, the ideas of servant leadership and transforming leadership have done this.

In conclusion, the territory of ethics lies at the heart of leadership studies and has veins in leadership research. Ethics also extends to territories waiting to be explored. As an area of applied ethics, leadership ethics needs to take into account research on leadership, and it should be responsive to the pressing ethical concerns of society. Today the most important and most confusing public debate is over what ethical issues are relevant in judging whether a person should lead and whether a person is capable of leadership. Research into leadership ethics should not only help us with questions like "What sort of person should lead?" and "What are the moral responsibilities of leadership?" It should also give us a better understanding of the nature of leadership.

NOTES

This chapter was originally published by *Business Ethics Quarterly* (Vol. 5, No. 1).

1. The best of these articles will be discussed in a separate annotated bibliography. I owe a debt of gratitude to Litt Maxwell, a University of Richmond librarian, for helping to execute this literature search.

2. These Kohlberg-type studies can be interesting for leadership ethics if you put all these studies together. However, taken one by one, they give a very small snapshot of a group. Kohlberg's work on moral development also has the problems that Carol Gilligan has articulated. A number of philosophers also have problems with Kohlberg's description of the highest stage of development. Nonetheless, some of the most fascinating research that uses this approach is cross-cultural. For example, see Sara Harkness, Carolyn Pope Edwards, and Charles M. Super, "Social Roles and Moral Reasoning, A Case Study in a Rural African Community," in *Developmental Psychology* 17, no. 5 (1981): 595–603. Also see Anne Marie Tietjen and Lawrence J. Walker, "Moral Reasoning and Leadership among Men in a Papua New Guinea Society," *Developmental Psychology* 21, no. 6 (1985): 982–92.

3. Many areas of leadership literature from psychology focus on different types of relationships. For example contingency theories focus on the relationship of the leader and the group in a given situation. See Fred Feidler, *A Theory of Leadership Effectiveness* (New York: McGraw-Hill, 1967) and Victor H. Vroom and Paul W. Yetton, *Leadership and Decision-Making* (Pittsburgh: University of Pittsburgh Press, 1973). The vertical dyad linkage model focuses on dyads such as the relationship between leaders and managers. See Fred Dansereau, Jr., George Graen, and William J. Haga, "Vertical Dyad Linkage Approach to Leadership within Formal Organizations: A Longitudinal Investigation of the Role Making Process," *Organizational Behavior and Human Performance* 13 (1975): 46–78.

4. Some of the most frequently cited ethics texts in leadership articles and books are from business ethics. The reasons for this might be that researchers are often in business schools, business ethics texts are written for a broad audience, and the content of business ethics research into managerial ethics and organizational ethics is relevant to leadership.

5. Joseph Rost, *Leadership for the Twenty-First Century* (New York: Praeger, 1991), 172.

6. James Rachels, *The Elements of Moral Philosophy* (New York: Random House, 1986). Mark Pastin, *The Hard Problems of Management: Gaining the Ethics Edge* (San Francisco: Jossey-Bass, 1986). I am not arguing about the quality of these books but rather the quantity of research done by Rost.

7. The chapter also contains pronouncements and generalizations that are not well supported. For example, he says, "The first thing that I want to emphasize is that the ethics of what is intended by leaders and followers in proposing changes may not be the same as the ethics of those changes once they have been implemented. This troubling distinction is not often developed in books on professional ethics, but it does turn up time and time again in real life" (Rost, 168). A number of Kantians who write about professional ethics would take issue with this claim.

8. Rost, 177.

9. Ibid., 77. The works cited in his argument are Robert Bellah et al., *Habits of the Heart* (New York: Harper and Row, 1985); William M. Sullivan, *Reconstructing Public Philosophy* (Berkeley: University of California Press, 1986); and Alasdair MacIntyre, *After Virtue* (Notre Dame, Ind.: University of Notre Dame Press, 1984). Rost seems to miss the point that all three of these books are reapplications of older traditions of ethics. Bellah et al. and Sullivan make this point clear in their books. Rost does not discuss virtue ethics in this chapter, so it is not clear whether he means to discard this too when he rejects "ethical theory."

10. Ibid., 177.

11. Bernard M. Bass, *Bass & Stogdill's Handbook of Leadership*, 3rd edition (New York: The Free Press, 1990). The quotes are taken from the back jacket of the book.

12. From James MacGregor Burns's book, *Leadership* (New York: Harper, 1978).

13. J. Weber, "Managers and Moral Meaning: An Exploratory Look at Managers' Responses to Moral Dilemmas," *Proceedings of the Academy of Management* (Washington, D.C.: Academy of Management, 1989), 333–37.

14. K. W. Kuhnert and C. J. Lewis, "Transactional and Transformational Leadership: A Constructive/Developmental Analysis," *Academy of Management Review* 12 (1987): 648-57.

15. M. F. Peterson, R. L. Phillips, and C. A. Duran, "A Comparison of Chinese Performance Maintenance Measures with U.S. Leadership Scales," *Psychologia—An International Journal of Psychology in the Orient* 32 (1989): 58–70.

16. P. Steidlmeier, *The Paradox of Poverty: A Reprisal of Economic Development Policy* (Cambridge, Mass.: Ballinger, 1987).

17. Bass, 906.

18. This is not to say that the articles cited in Bass and Stogdill are not good, but rather that they are focused studies that taken together would not give the reader much of a perspective on ethics as it pertains to leadership.

19. For example, John Gardner is well known in the leadership area. His leadership paper, "The Moral Aspect of Leadership," was published in 1987. Burns's book was published in 1978 and contained a wealth of references that might have been useful.

20. Rost, 27.

21. Ibid., 3.

22. Marta Calas and Linda Smircich, "Reading Leadership as a Form of Cultural Analysis," in James G. Hunt, B. Rajaram Baliga, H. Peter Dachler, and Chester A. Schriesheim, eds., *Emerging Leadership Vistas* (Lexington, Mass.: Lexington Books, 1988), 222–26.

23. For example, see Thomas Sergiovanni, *Moral Leadership* (San Francisco: Jossey-Bass, 1992), xiii. Sergiovanni argues that "rich leadership practice cannot be developed if one set of values or one basis of authority is simply substituted for

another. What we need is an expanded theoretical and operational foundation for leadership practice that will give balance to a full range of values and bases of authority." He refers to this expanded foundation as the moral dimension in leadership.

24. John Gardner, *On Leadership* (New York: Free Press, 1990), 77.

25. Because most of my work has been in business ethics, I use that field as an example. Few philosophers would attempt to write about a topic in business ethics without doing research into that area of business, yet a number of business scholars over the years have felt no discomfort over writing about business ethics without doing research into ethics. If you look at what is considered the best work in business ethics, you do not find research that is only business or only philosophic ethics. A good example of the ideal mix is Ed Freeman's and Dan Gilbert's *Ethics and Strategy* (Englewood Cliffs, N.J.: Prentice Hall, 1988).

26. Extensive work has been done on leadership in political science, but this research is not well integrated into the business/psychology literature. One might argue that because the discussion of leadership is so much a part of political science, it is not noticeable as a separate field, except perhaps for Presidential Studies. It is, however, interesting to note that Barbara Kellerman's anthology on political leadership is interdisciplinary. See Barbara Kellerman, ed., *Political Leadership: A Source Book* (Pittsburgh: University of Pittsburgh Press, 1986). It draws from political science, philosophy, economics, history, sociology. Yet if one looks at the references in Bass and Stogdill, the lion's share of them are from management and psychology and very few from political science or other fields. Extensive work has also been done on leadership in military academies. For example, see Howard Prince and Associates, eds., *Leadership in Organizations*, 3rd edition (West Point, N.Y.: United States Military Academy, 1985).

27. Thomas Kuhn, *The Structure of Scientific Revolutions* (Chicago: University of Chicago Press, 1970), 20.

28. A recent example of a leadership textbook is Richard Hughes, Robert Ginnett, and Gordon J. Curphy, *Leadership: Enhancing the Lessons of Experience* (New York: Irwin, 1993).

29. James G. Hunt has published eight collections of symposia papers on leadership. Note the language in the titles of these books, "Current Developments," "Leadership Frontiers," "The Cutting Edge," "Beyond Establishment Views," and "Emerging Vistas." One senses that Hunt is trying to capture something that keeps falling through scholars' fingers like sand.

E. A. Fleishman and J. G. Hunt, eds., *Current Developments in the Study of Leadership* (Lexington, Mass.: Lexington Books, 1973).

J. G. Hunt and L. L. Larson, eds., *Contingency Approaches to Leadership* (Lexington, Mass.: Lexington Books, 1974).

J. G. Hunt and L. L. Larson, eds., *Leadership Frontiers* (Kent, Ohio: Kent State University Press, 1975).

J. G. Hunt and L. L. Larson, eds., *Leadership: The Cutting Edge* (Lexington, Mass.: Lexington Books, 1977).

J. G. Hunt and L. L. Larson, eds., *Crosscurrents in Leadership* (Lexington, Mass.: Lexington Books, 1979).

J. G. Hunt, U. Sekaran, and C. A. Schriesheim, eds., *Leadership: Beyond Establishment Views* (Lexington, Mass.: Lexington Books, 1982).

J. G. Hunt, D. M. Hosking, C. A. Schriesheim, and R. Stewart, eds., *Leaders and Managers: International Perspectives on Managerial Behavior and Leadership* (Lexington, Mass.: Lexington Books, 1984).

James G. Hunt, B. Rajaram Baliga, H. Peter Dachler, and Chester A. Schriesheim, eds., *Emerging Leadership Vistas* (Lexington, Mass.: Lexington Books, 1988).

30. Kuhn, 20.
31. Rost, 6–7.
32. In J. G. Hunt's symposia (see note 29) and in other articles on leadership, scholars constantly lament that they have done so much studying and know so little about leadership. Yet these same scholars who lament this fact do little to change the way that they do research.
33. Rost, 6.
34. Ibid.
35. Ibid., 99.
36. The theory of meaning that I have in mind is from Ludwig Wittgenstein, *Philosophical Investigations*, translated by G. E. M. Anscomb, 3rd edition (New York: Macmillan, 1968), 18–20, 241.
37. Rost, 47, from B. V. Moore, "The May Conference on Leadership," *Personnel Journal* 6 (1927): 124.
38. Rost, 47, from E. S. Bogardus, *Leaders and Leadership* (New York: Appleton-Century, 1934), 5.
39. Rost, 48, from Reuter (1941), 133.
40. Rost, 50. The bracket part is Rost's summary of the definition from C. A. Gibb, "Leadership," in G. Lindzey, ed., *Handbook of Social Psychology* 2 (1954): 877–920.
41. Rost, 53, from M. Seeman, *Social Status and Leadership* (Columbus: Ohio State University Bureau of Educational Research, 1960), 127.
42. Rost, 59, from R. N. Osborn and J. G. Hunt, "An Adaptive Reactive Theory of Leadership," in J. G. Hunt and L. L. Larson, eds., *Leadership Frontiers* (Kent, Ohio: Kent State University Press, 1975), 28.
43. Rost, 72. From S. C. Sarkesian, "A Personal Perspective," in R. S. Ruch and L. J. Korb, eds., *Military Leadership* (Beverly Hills, Calif.: Sage, 1979), 243.
44. Rost, 102.
45. Burns criticizes leadership studies for bifurcating literature on leadership and followership. He says that the leadership literature is elitist, projecting heroic leaders against the drab mass of powerless followers. The followership literature, according to Burns, tends to be populist in its approach, linking the masses with small overlapping circles of politicians, military officers, and businesspeople. See Burns, 3.
46. One's choice of a definition can be aesthetic and/or moral and/or political (if you control the definitions, you control the research agenda).
47. Rost, 161.
48. Leaders carry their own normative baggage in their definitions. For example:

• "A leader is a man who has the ability to get other people to do what they don't want to do, and like it." (Harry Truman)

• "Clean examples have a curious method of multiplying themselves." (Gandhi)

- "Whatever goal man has reached is due to his originality plus his brutality." (Adolf Hitler)

- "If we do not win, we will blame neither heaven nor earth, only ourselves." (Mao)

These examples are from G. D. Paige's book, *The Scientific Study of Political Leadership*, 66. They are taken from Barbara Kellerman, *Leadership: Multidisciplinary Perspectives* (Pittsburgh: University of Pittsburgh Press, 1986), 71–72.

49. This is from Ron Heifetz's book manuscript *Leadership without Easy Answers* (Cambridge, Mass.: Belknap/Harvard University Press, 1994), 17–18.

50. See Warren Bennis and Burt Nanus, *Leaders: Strategies for Taking Charge* (New York: Harper Collins, 1985), 45.

51. The leader/manager distinction is a troublesome one in the leadership literature. One problem is that *leadership* is a hot word these days and the current trend is to put leadership in the title of books on traditional management subjects. If we look at the formal positions of leaders and managers in organizations, the leader's job requires a broader perspective on the operation and on the moral significance of policies and actions of the organization (this is part of the "vision thing"). The manager's domain of perspective is usually more narrowly defined as people whose job is to ensure that a set of tasks is completed. In ethical terms this element of leadership boils down to thinking about actions in terms of how they impact on the organization as a whole and in the long run. In the ethics seminars that I have run for corporate managers, I have noticed that the managers who tend to take a big picture view of particular ethical problems are most often the ones who have been identified as having the greatest leadership potential. So Bennis and Nanus do seem to be right. However, it is not that managers are unethical, but rather that they have a narrower moral perspective that is in part dictated by the way in which they respond to the constraints and pressures of their position. Managers are also subject to Kant's old adage that "ought implies can."

52. Here Aristotle's discussion of excellence (areté) would be useful. Aristotle says that excellent actions must be good in themselves and good and noble. See the argument in Aristotle, *Nichomachean Ethics*, Book I, sections 6–8 (1096a12–1098b8). Later in Book II, sections 13–16 (31104b), Aristotle argues that a virtuous person has appropriate emotions along with dispositions to act the right way. Virtue then is being made happy by the right sort of thing.

53. See E. A. Fleishman, "The Description of Supervisory Behavior," *Personnel Psychology* 37: 1–6.

54. Results from the earlier and later Michigan Studies are discussed in R. Leikert, *New Patterns of Management* (New York: McGraw-Hill, 1961) and *The Human Organization: Its Management and Value* (New York: McGraw-Hill, 1967).

55. See P. Hersey and K. H. Blanchard, *The Management of Organizational Behavior*, 5th edition (Englewood Cliffs, N.J.: Prentice Hall, 1993).

56. It would be worthwhile to look at some of the studies and ask how the subjects with high/high orientations solve ethical problems. Do they tend to find themselves trapped in between deontic and consequentialist approaches to the problem? Are people who score high on the task scale consequentialists when it comes to approaching ethical problems? and so on.

57. According to Gary Yukl, the only consistent findings that have come from this research is that considerate leaders usually have more satisfied followers. See

Gary Yukl, *Leadership in Organizations*, 2nd edition (Englewood Cliffs, N.J.: Prentice Hall, 1989), 96.

58. Old metaethical problems, such as David Hume's problem of drawing an *ought* from G. E. Moore's naturalistic fallacy, and more recent discussions of ethical realism take on a certain urgency in applied ethics. I find that the more work that I do in applied ethics, the more I lean towards the position that moral discourse is cognitive in that it expresses propositions that have truth value. However, I am still uncomfortable with drawing moral prescriptions from "scientific" studies of leadership. I have not really worked out a coherent position on these points of moral epistemology. For a good discussion of these issues see Geoffrey Sayre-McCord, ed., *Essays on Moral Realism* (Ithaca, N.Y.: Cornell University Press, 1988). I find David Wiggins's and Geoffrey Sayre-McCord's articles on ethical realism to be particularly compelling.

59. This is the argument that the sciences provide explanation and the humanities understanding. See Chapter 1 of G. H. von Wright, *Explanation and Understanding* (Ithaca: Cornell University Press, 1971).

60. In most journal articles, authors, including this one, offer stipulative definitions. These definitions make clear how concepts are being used in the paper. They are not meant to be universal definitions.

61. We need a better picture of what a leader ought to be in order to educate and develop leaders in schools and organizations.

62. Burns uses the terms *transforming* and *transformational* in his book. However, he prefers to refer to his theory as *transforming* leadership.

63. I think that Burns is sometimes overly sanguine about the universal truth of these theories of human development.

64. Burns, 42–43.

65. Rost, xii.

66. I am very grateful to Professor Burns for the discussions that we have had on the ethics of leadership. Burns's reflections on his work as a biographer have lead me to this conclusion.

67. For example, see Burns's discussion of Franklin D. Roosevelt's treatment of Joseph Kennedy, 32–33.

68. One of the problems with using the values approach to ethics is that it requires a very complicated taxonomy of values. The word *value* is also problematic because it encompasses so many different kinds of things. The values approach requires arguments for some sort of hierarchy of values that would serve to resolve conflicts of values. In order to make values something that people do rather than just have, Milton Rokeach offers a very awkward discussion of the ought character of values. "A person phenomenologically experiences 'oughtness' to be objectively required by society in somewhat the same way that he perceives an incomplete circle as objectively requiring closure." See Milton Rokeach, *The Nature of Human Values* (New York: The Free Press, 1973), 9.

69. Burns, 426.

70. Ibid., 3.

71. Ibid., 426.

72. The third test has an Aristotelian twist to it. The relationship of leaders and followers and the ends of that relationship must rest on *eudaimonia* or happiness,

which is understood as human flourishing or, as Aristotle says, "living well and faring well with being happy." Aristotle, *Nicomachean Ethics*, Book I (1095a19), from Jonathan Barnes, ed., *The Complete Works of Aristotle*, vol. II (Princeton: Princeton University Press, 1984), 1730.

73. Burns, 424.

74. Bernard Bass, *Leadership and Performance Beyond Expectations* (New York: Free Press, 1985).

75. Judith Rosner, "Ways Women Lead," in *Harvard Business Review* (November-December 1990), 99–125.

76. Jay Conger, *The Charismatic Leader: Behind the Mystique of the Exceptional Leader* (San Francisco: Jossey-Bass, 1989), xiv.

77. Bass, *Leadership and Performance*, 31.

78. For example, see Robert J. House, William D. Spangler, and James Woycke's "Personality and Charisma in the U.S. Presidency," *Administrative Science Quarterly* 36, no. 3 (September 1991), 334–96. Their study looks at charisma in terms of the bond between leaders and followers and in terms of actual behavior of the presidents (366). The questions that lurk in the background are Is this relationship, in Burns's terms, morally uplifting? Is the behavior ethical? and Does the process that takes place in the relationship between these charismatic presidents and their followers humanly enriching?

79. For a very provocative account of charismatic leadership from an anthropological point of view see Charles Lindholm, *Charisma* (Cambridge, Mass.: Basil Blackwell, 1990). Lindholm includes several case studies, including ones on Charles Manson and Jim Jones.

80. Greenleaf takes his theory from Hesse. See Robert K. Greenleaf, *Servant Leadership: A Journey into the Nature of Legitimate Power and Greatness* (New York: Paulist Press, 1977); and Hermann Hesse, *The Journey to the East* (New York: Farrar, Straus and Giroux, 1991).

81. The Robert K. Greenleaf Center in Indianapolis works with companies to implement this idea of leadership in organizations. The Robert K. Greenleaf Center, 1100 W. 42nd St., Suite 321, Indianapolis, IN 46208.

82. Greenleaf, 13–14.

2

Moral Leadership and Business Ethics

Al Gini

Those who really deserve praise are the people who, while human enough to enjoy power, nevertheless pay more attention to justice than they are compelled to do by their situation.

—Thucydides

Conventional wisdom has it that two of the most glaring examples of academic oxymorons are the terms "business ethics" and "moral leadership." Neither term carries credibility in popular culture, and when conjoined, they constitute a "null-set" rather than just a simple contradiction in terms. The reason for this is definitional, but only in part. More significant is that we have so few models of businesses and leaders operating on ethical principles. Simply put, the cliché persists because of the dearth of evidence to the contrary. At best, both these terms remain in the lexicon as wished-for ideals rather than actual states of being.

A *New York Times*/CBS News Poll conducted in 1985 revealed that 55 percent of the American public believe that the vast majority of corporate executives are dishonest, and 59 percent think that executive white-collar crime occurs on a regular basis. A 1987 *Wall Street Journal* article noted that one-fourth of the 671 executives surveyed by a leading research firm believed that ethics can impede a successful career, and that over one-half of all the executives they knew bent the rules to get ahead.[1] Most recently, a 1990 national survey published by Prentice Hall concluded that the standards of ethical practice and moral leadership of business leaders merit at best a C grade. Sixty-eight percent of those surveyed believed that the unethical behavior of executives is the primary cause of the decline in business standards, productivity, and success. The survey further suggested that because of the perceived low ethical standards of the executive class, workers feel justified in responding in kind—through absenteeism, petty theft, indifference, and a generally poor performance on the job. Many workers openly admitted that they spend more than 20 percent (eight hours a week) of their time at work totally goofing off. Almost half of those surveyed admitted to chronic malingering on a regular basis. One in six of the workers surveyed said that he or she drank or used drugs on the job. Three out of four workers reported that their primary reason for working was "to keep the wolf from the door"; only one in four claimed to give his or her "best effort" to the job. The survey concluded that the standards equation of the American workplace is a simple one: American workers are as ethical/dutiful in doing their jobs as their bosses and companies are perceived to be ethical/dutiful in leading and directing them.[2]

Sadly, ample evidence suggests that this mutually reinforcing thesis often starts long before one enters the confines of the workplace. Recently one of the teacher-coaches in the Chicago public school system not only encouraged his high school students to cheat in the citywide Academic Decathlon contest, he fed them the answers. According to the eighteen-year-old student captain of the team: "The coach gave us the answer key. . . . He told us everybody cheats, that's the way the world works and we were fools to just play by the rules."[3] Unfortunately, just as workers often mirror the standards set by their bosses, these students followed the guidance of their teacher.

As a student of business ethics, I am convinced that without the continuous commitment, enforcement, and modeling of leadership, standards of business ethics cannot and will not be achieved in any organization. The ethics of leadership—whether they be good or bad, positive or negative—affect the ethos of the workplace and thereby help to form the ethical choices and decisions of the workers in the workplace. Leaders help to set the tone, develop the vision, and shape the behavior of all those involved in organizational life. The critical point to understand here is that, like it or not, business and politics serve as the metronome for our society. And the meter and behavior established by leaders set the patterns and establish the models for our behavior as individuals and as a group. Although the terms "business ethics" and "moral leadership" are technically distinguishable, in fact, they are inseparable components in the life of every organization.

The fundamental principle that underlies my thesis regarding leadership and ethical conduct is age-old. In his *Nichomachean Ethics*, Aristotle suggested that morality cannot be learned simply by reading a treatise on virtue. The spirit of morality, said Aristotle, is awakened in the individual only through the witness and conduct of a moral person. The principle of the "witness of another," or what we now refer to as "patterning," "role modeling," or "mentoring," is predicated on a four-step process, three of which follow:

(1) As communal creatures, we learn to conduct ourselves primarily through the actions of significant others.

(2) When the behavior of others is repeated often enough and proves to be peer-group positive, we emulate these actions.

(3) If and when our actions are in turn reinforced by others, they become acquired characteristics or behavioral habits.

According to B. F. Skinner, the process is now complete. In affecting the actions of individuals through modeling and reinforcement, the mentor in question (in Skinnerean terms, "the controller of the environmental stimuli") has succeeded in reproducing the type of behavior sought after or desired. For Skinner the primary goal of the process need not take into consideration either the value or worth of the action or the interests or intent of the reinforced or operant-conditioned actor. From Skinner's psychological perspective, the bottom line is simply the response evoked.[4] From a philosophical perspective, however, even role modeling that produces a positive or beneficial action does not fulfill the basic requirements of the ethical enterprise at either the descriptive or normative level. Modeling, emulation, habit, results—whether positive or negative—are neither the sufficient nor the final goal. The fourth and final step in the process must include reflection, evaluation, choice, and conscious intent on the part of the actor, because ethics is always "an inside-out proposition" involving free will.[5]

John Dewey argued that at the precritical, prerational, preautonomous level, morality starts as a set of culturally defined goals and rules that are external to the individual and are imposed or inculcated as habits. But real ethical thinking, said Dewey, begins at the evaluative period of our lives, when, as independent agents, we freely decide to accept, embrace, modify, or deny these rules. Dewey maintained that every serious ethical system rejects the notion that one's standard of conduct should simply and uncritically be an acceptance of the rules of the culture we happen to live in. Even when custom, habit, convention, public opinion, or law are correct in their mandates, to embrace them without critical reflection does not constitute a complete and formal ethical act and might be better labeled "ethical happenstance" or "ethics by virtue of circumstantial accident." According to Dewey, ethics is essentially "reflective conduct," and he believed that the distinction between custom and reflective morality is clearly marked. The former places the standards and rules of conduct solely on habit, the latter appeals to reason and choice. The distinction is as important as it is definite, for it shifts the center of gravity in morality. For Dewey, ethics is a two-part process; it is never enough simply to do the right thing.[6]

In claiming that workers/followers derive their models for ethical conduct from the witness of leaders, I am in no way denying that workers/followers share responsibility for the overall conduct and culture of an organization. The burden of this chapter is not to exonerate the culpability of workers but rather to explain the process involved: The witness of leaders both communicates the ethics of our institutions and establishes the desired standards and expectations leaders want and often demand from their fellow workers and followers. Although it would be naive to assert that employees simply and unreflectively absorb the manners and mores of the workplace, it would be equally naive to suggest that they are unaffected by the modeling and standards of their respective places of employment. Work is how we spend our lives, and the lessons we learn there, good or bad, play a part in the development of our moral perspective and the manner in which we formulate and adjudicate ethical choices. As a business ethicist, I believe that without the active intervention of effective moral leadership, we are doomed to forever wage a rear-guard action. Students of organizational development are never really surprised when poorly managed, badly lead businesses wind up doing unethical things.

ETHICS AND BUSINESS

Jean-Paul Sartre argued that, like it or not, we are by definition moral creatures because our collective existence "condemns" us continuously to make choices about "what we ought to do" in regard to others.[7] Ethics is primarily a communal, collective enterprise, not a solitary one. It is the study of our web of relationships with others. When Robinson Crusoe found himself marooned and alone on a tiny Pacific atoll, all things were possible. But when Friday appeared and they discovered pirates burying treasure on the beach, Crusoe was then involved in the universe of others, an ethical universe. As a communal exercise, ethics is the attempt to work out the rights and obligations we have and share with others. What is mine? What do I owe you?

According to John Rawls, given the presence of others and our need of these others both to survive and to thrive, ethics is elementally the pursuit of justice, fair play, and equity. For Rawls, building on the cliché that "ethics is how we decide to behave when we decide we belong together," the study of ethics has to do with developing standards for judging the conduct of one party whose behavior affects another. Minimally, "good behavior" intends no harm and respects the rights of all affected, and "bad behavior" is willfully or negligently trampling on the rights and interests of others.[8] Ethics, then, tries to find a way to protect one person's individual rights and needs against and alongside the rights and needs of others. Of course, the paradox and central tension of ethics lie in the fact that although we are by nature communal and in need of others, at the same time we are by disposition more or less egocentric and self-serving.[9]

If ethics is a part of life, so too are work, labor, and business. Work is not something detached from the rest of human life, but rather "man is born to labor, as a bird to fly."[10] What are work and business about? Earning a living? Yes. Producing a product or service? Sure. Making money or profit? Absolutely. In fact, most ethicists argue that business has a moral obligation to make a profit. But business is also about people—the people you work for and work with. Business is an interdependent, intertwined, symbiotic relationship. Life, labor, and business are all of a piece. They should not be seen as separate "games" played by different "rules." The enterprise of business is not distinct from the enterprise of life and living because they share the same bottom line—people. Therefore, as in the rest of life, business is required to ask, "What ought to be done in regard to others?"

Although no one that I am aware of would argue seriously against the notion of ethics in our private lives, many would have it that ethics and business don't or can't mix. That is, many people believe that "business is business" and that the stakes and standards involved in business are simply different from, more important than, and perhaps even antithetical to the principles and practices of ethics. Ethics is something we preach and practice at home in our private lives, but not at work. After all, it could cost us prestige, position, profits, and success.

Theologian Matthew Fox maintains that we lead schizophrenic lives because we either choose or are forced to abandon our personal beliefs and convictions "at the door" when we enter the workplace. The "destructive dualism" of the workplace, says Fox, separates our lives from our livelihood, our personal values from our work values, our personal needs from the needs of the community. Money becomes the sole reason for work, and success becomes the excuse we use to justify the immoral consequences of our behavior.[11] This "dualism" produces and perpetuates the kind of "occupational schizophrenia" recently articulated by nationally known jurist Alan Dershowitz: "I would never do many of the things in my personal life that I have to do as a lawyer."[12]

According to ethicist Norman E. Bowie, the disconnection between business and ethics and the dualism of the workplace stem from the competing paradigms of human nature of economists and ethicists. Economics is the study of the betterment of self. Most economists, says Bowie, have an egoistic theory of human nature. Their analyses focus on how an individual rationally pursues desired tastes, wants, or preferences. Within the economic model, individuals behave rationally when they seek to strengthen their own perceived best interests. Individuals need only take the interests of others into account when and if such considerations work to their advantage. Economics, Bowie claims, is singular and radically subjective in its orientation. It takes all tastes, wants, and desires as simply given and does not evaluate whether the economic actor's preferences are good or bad. The focus remains on how the individual can achieve his/her wants and desires.

Ethics, on the other hand, is nonegoistic or pluralistic in nature. Its primary paradigm of evaluation is always self in relation to others. The ethical point of view, says Bowie, requires that an actor take into account the impact of his/her action on others. If and when the interests of the actor and those affected by the action conflict, the actor should at least consider suspending or modifying his/her action and, by so doing, recognize the interests of the other. In other words, ethics requires that on occasion we "ought to act" contrary to our own self-interest and that on occasion a person "ought to" act actively on behalf of the interests of another. Economists ask, "What can I do to advance my best interests against others?" Ethicists ask, "In pursuing my best interests, what must I do, what 'ought' I do, in regard to others?" Whereas economics breeds competition, ethics encourages cooperation.[13]

For R. Edward Freeman, these competing paradigms are firmly entrenched in our collective psyches and give rise to what he calls "The Problem of the Two Realms." One realm is the realm of business. It is the realm of hard, measurable facts: market studies, focus groups, longitudinal studies, production costs, managed inventory, stock value, research and development, profit and loss statements, quantitative analysis. The other realm is the realm of philosophy/ethics. This is the soft realm, says Freeman. This is the realm of the seemingly ineffable: myth, meaning, metaphor, purpose, quality, significance, rights, values. Whereas the realm of business can be easily dissected, diagnosed, compared, and judged, the realm of philosophy is not open to precise interpretation, comparison, and evaluation. For Freeman, in a society that has absorbed and embraced the Marcusian adage "the goods of life are equal to the good life," these two realms are accorded separate but unequal status. Only in moments of desperation, disaster, or desire does the realm of business solicit the commentary and insights of the realm of ethics. Otherwise, the realm of business operates under the dictum of legal moralism: Everything is allowed that is not strictly forbidden.

For Freeman the assertion that "business is business" and that ethics is what we try to do in our private lives simply does not hold up to close scrutiny. Business is a human institution, a basic part of the communal fabric of life. Just as governments come to be out of the human need for order, security, and fulfillment, so too does business. The goal of all business, labor, and work is to make life more secure, more stable, more equitable. Business exists to serve more than just itself. No business can view itself as an isolated entity, unaffected by the demands of individuals and society. As such, business is required to ask, "What ought to be done in regard to the others we work with and serve?" For Freeman, business ethics, rather than being an oxymoron, a contradiction in terms, is really a pleonasm, a redundancy in terms.[14] As Henry Ford, Sr., once said: "For a long time people believed that the only purpose of industry is to make a profit. They are wrong. Its purpose is to serve the general welfare."[15]

What business ethics advocates is that people apply in the workplace those commonsensical rules and standards learned at home, from the lectern, and from the pulpit. The moral issues facing a person are age-old, and these are essentially the same issues facing a business—only writ in large script.[16] According to Freeman, ethics is "how we treat each other, every day, person to person. If you want to know about a company's ethics, look at how it treats people—customers, suppliers, and employees. Business is about people. And business ethics is about how customers and employees are treated."[17]

What is being asked of the business community is neither extraordinary nor excessive: a decent product at a fair price; honesty in advertisements; fair treatment of employees, customers, suppliers, and competitors; a strong sense of responsibility to the communities it inhabits and serves; and a reasonable profit for the financial risk-taking of its stockholders and owners. In the words of General Robert Wood Johnson, founder of Johnson and Johnson: "The day has passed when business was a private matter—if it even really was. In a business

society, every act of business has social consequences and may arouse
public interest. Every time business hires, builds, sells or buys, it is
acting for the . . . people as well as for itself, and it must be prepared to
accept full responsibility."[18]

LEADERSHIP

According to Georges Enderle, business leadership would be relatively simple if corporations only had to produce a product or service,
without being concerned about employees; if management only had
to deal with concepts, structures, and strategies, without worrying
about human relations; if businesses just had to resolve their own
problems, without being obligated to take the interests of individuals
or society into consideration.[19] But such is not the case. Leadership
is always about self and others. Like ethics, labor, and business
leadership is a symbiotic, communal relationship. It's about leaders,
followers-constituencies, and all stakeholders involved. And, like
ethics, labor and business leadership seems to be an intrinsic part of
the human experience. Charles DeGaulle once observed that men can
no longer survive without direction than they can without eating,
drinking, or sleeping. Putting aside the obvious fact that DeGaulle
was a proponent of "the great-person theory" of leadership, his point
is a basic one. Leadership is a necessary requirement of communal
existence. Minimally, it tries to offer perspective, focus, appropriate
behavior, guidance, and a plan by which to handle the seemingly
random and arbitrary events of life. Depending on the type of
leadership/followership involved, it can be achieved by consensus,
fiat, or cooperative orchestration. But whatever techniques are employed, leadership is always, at bottom, about stewardship—"a per-
son(s) who manages or directs the affairs of others . . . as the agent
or representative of others." To paraphrase the words of St. Augustine,
regardless of the outcome, the first and final job of leadership is the
attempt to serve the needs and the well-being of the people led.

What is leadership? Although the phenomenon of leadership can and
must be distinguishable and definable separately from our understanding of what and who leaders are, I am convinced that leadership can
only be known and evaluated in the particular instantiation of a leader
doing a job. In other words, even though the terms "leadership" and
"leader" are not strictly synonymous, the reality of leadership cannot
be separated from the person of the leader and the job of leadership.
Given this caveat, and leaning heavily on the research and insights of
Joseph C. Rost,[20] we can define leadership as follows: Leadership is a
power- and value-laden relationship between leaders and follow-

ers/constituents who intend real changes that reflect their mutual purposes and goals. For our purposes, the critical elements of this definition that need to be examined are, in order of importance: followership, values, mutual purposes, and goals.

Followership

As Joseph Rost has pointed out, perhaps the single most important thesis developed in leadership studies in the last twenty years has been the evolution and now almost universal consensus regarding the role of followers in the leadership equation. Pulitzer prize–winning historian Garry Wills argues that we have long had a list of the leader's requisites—determination, focus, a clear goal, a sense of priorities, and so on. But until recently, we overlooked or forgot the first and all-encompassing need. "The leader most needs followers. When those are lacking, the best ideas, the strongest will, the most wonderful smile have no effect."[21] Followers set the terms of acceptance for leadership. Leadership is a "mutually determinative" activity on the part of the leader and the followers. Sometimes it's cooperative, sometimes it's a struggle, and often it's a feud, but it's always collective. Although "the leader is one who mobilizes others toward a goal shared by leaders and followers," leaders are powerless to act without followers. In effect, Wills argues, successful leaders need to understand their followers far more than followers need to understand leaders.[22]

Leadership, like labor and ethics, is always plural; it always occurs in the context of others. E. P. Hollander has argued that even though the leader is the central and often the most vital part of the leadership phenomenon, followers are important and necessary factors in the equation.[23] All leadership is interactive, and all leadership should be collaborative. In fact, except for the negative connotation sometimes associated with the term, perhaps the word "collaborator" is a more precise term than either "follower" or "constituent" to explain the leadership process.[24] But whichever term is used, as James MacGregor Burns wrote, one thing is clear, "leaders and followers are engaged in a common enterprise; they are dependent on each other, their fortunes rise and fall together."[25]

From an ethical perspective, the argument for the stewardship responsibilities of leadership is dependent upon the recognition of the roles and rights of followers. Followership argues against the claim of Louis XIV, "L'état c'est moi!" The principle of followership denies the Machiavellian assertions that "politics and ethics don't mix" and that the sole aim of any leader is "the acquisition of personal power." Followership requires that leaders recognize their true role within the commonwealth. The choices and actions of leaders must take into consideration the rights and needs of followers. Leaders are not independent agents simply pursuing personal aggrandizement and career options. Like the "Guardians" of Plato's *Republic*, leaders must see their office as a social responsibility, a trust, a duty, and not as a symbol of their personal identity, prestige, and lofty status.[26] In more contemporary terms, James O'Toole and Lynn Sharp-Paine have separately argued that the central ethical issue in business is the rights of stakeholders and the obligation of business leaders to manage with due consideration for the rights of all stakeholders involved.[27]

In his cult classic *The Fifth Discipline*, management guru Peter Senge has stated that of all the jobs of leadership, being a steward is the most basic. Being a steward means recognizing that the ultimate purpose of one's work is others and not self; that leaders "do what they do" for something larger than themselves; that their "life's work" may be the "ability to lead," but that the final goal of this talent or craft is "other directed."[28] If the real "business of business" is not just to produce a product/service and a profit but to help "produce" people, then the same claim/demand can be made of leadership. Given the reality of the "presence of others," leadership, like ethics, must by definition confront the question, What ought to be done with regard to others?

Values

Ethics is about the assessment and evaluation of values, because all of life is value laden. As Samuel Blumenfeld emphatically pointed out, "You have to be dead to be value-neutral."[29] Values are the ideas and beliefs that influence and direct our choices and actions. Whether they are right or wrong, good or bad, values, both consciously and unconsciously, mobilize and guide how we make decisions and the kinds of decisions we make. Reportedly, Eleanor Roosevelt once said, "If you want to know what people value, check their checkbooks!"

I believe that Tom Peters and Bob Waterman were correct when they asserted, "The real role of leadership is to manage the values of an organization."[30] All leadership is value laden. And all leadership, whether good or bad, is moral leadership at the descriptive if not the normative level. To put it more accurately, all leadership is ideologically driven or motivated by a certain philosophical perspective, which upon analysis and judgment may or may not prove to be morally acceptable in the colloquial sense. All leaders have an agenda, a series of beliefs, proposals, values, ideas, and issues that they wish to "put on the table." In fact, as Burns has suggested, leadership only asserts itself, and followers only become evident, when there is something at stake—ideas to be clarified, issues to be determined, values to be adjudicated.[31] In the words of Eleanor's husband, Franklin D. Roosevelt: "The Presidency is . . . preeminently a place of moral leadership. All our great Presidents were leaders of thought at times when certain historic ideas in the life of the nation had to be clarified."[32]

Although we would prefer to study the moral leadership of Lincoln, Churchill, Gandhi, and Mother Teresa, like it or not, we must also evaluate Hitler, Stalin, Saddam Hussein, and David Koresh within a moral context.

All ethical judgments are in some sense a values-versus-values or rights-versus-rights confrontation. Unfortunately, the question of what we ought to do in relation to the values and rights of others cannot be reduced to the analogue of a simple litmus test. In fact, I believe that all of ethics is based on what William James called the "will to believe." That is, we choose to believe, despite the ideas, arguments, and reasoning to the contrary, that individuals possess certain basic rights that cannot and should not be willfully disregarded or overridden by others. In "choosing to believe," said James, we establish this belief as a factual baseline of our thought process for all considerations in regard to others. Without this "reasoned choice," says James, the ethical enterprise loses its "vitality" in human interactions.[33]

If ethical behavior intends no harm and respects the rights of all affected, and unethical behavior willfully or negligently tramples on the rights and interests of others, then leaders cannot deny or disregard the rights of others. The leader's worldview cannot be totally solipsistic. The leader's agenda should not be purely self-serving. Leaders should not see followers as potential adversaries to be bested but rather as fellow travelers with similar aspirations and rights to be reckoned with.

How do we judge the ethics of a leader? Clearly, we cannot expect every decision and action of a leader to be perfect. As John Gardner has pointed out, particular consequences are never a reliable assessment of leadership.[34] The quality and worth of leadership can only be measured in terms of what a leader intends, values, believes in, or stands for—in other words, character. In *Character: America's Search for Leadership*, Gail Sheehy argues, as did Aristotle before her, that character is the most crucial and most elusive element of leadership. The root of the word "character" comes from the Greek word for engraving. As applied to human beings, it refers to the enduring marks or etched-in factors in our personality, which include our inborn talents as well as the learned and acquired traits imposed upon us by life and experience. These engravings define us, set us apart, and motivate behavior.

In regard to leadership, says Sheehy, character is fundamental and prophetic. The "issues [of leadership] are today and will change in time. Character is what was yesterday and will be tomorrow."[35] Character establishes both our day-to-day demeanor and our destiny. Therefore, it is not only useful but essential to examine the character of those who desire to lead us. As a journalist and longtime observer of the political scene, Sheehy contends that the Watergate affair of the early 1970s serves as a perfect example of the links between character and leadership. As Richard Nixon demonstrated so well, says Sheehy, "The Presidency is not the place to work out one's personal pathology."[36] Leaders rule us, run things, wield power. Therefore, says Sheehy, we must be careful about whom we choose to lead, because whom we chose is what we shall be. If, as Heraclitus wrote, "character is fate," the fate our leaders reap will also be our own.

Putting aside the particular players and the politics of the episode, Watergate has come to symbolize the failings and failures of people in high places. Watergate now serves as a watershed, a turning point, in our nation's concern for integrity, honesty, and fair play from all kinds of leaders. It is not a mere coincidence that the birth of business ethics as an independent, academic discipline can be dated from the Watergate affair and the trials that came out of it. No matter what our failings as individuals, Watergate sensitized us to the importance of ethical standards and conduct from those who direct the course of our political and public lives. What society is now demanding, and what business ethics is advocating, is that our business leaders and public servants should be held accountable to an even higher standard of behavior than we might demand and expect of ourselves.

Mutual Purposes and Goals

The character, goals, and aspirations of a leader are not developed in a vacuum. Leadership, even in the hands of a strong, confident, charismatic leader remains, at bottom, relational. Leaders, good or bad, great or small, arise out of the needs and opportunities of a specific time and place. Leaders require causes, issues, and—most important—a hungry and willing constituency. Leaders may devise plans, establish an agenda, bring new and often radical ideas to the table, but all of them are a response to the milieu and membership of which they are a part. If leadership is an active and ongoing relationship between leaders and followers, then a central requirement of the leadership process is for leaders to evoke and elicit consensus in their constituencies and conversely for followers to inform and influence their leaders. This is done through the uses of power and education.

The term "power" comes from the Latin *posse*: to do, to be able, to change, to influence or effect. To have power is to possess the capacity to control or direct change. All forms of leadership must make use of power. The central issue of power in leadership is not Will it be used? but rather Will it be used wisely and well? According to James MacGregor Burns, leadership is not just about directed results; it is also about offering followers a choice among real alternatives. Hence, leadership assumes competition, conflict, and debate, whereas brute power denies it.[37] "Leadership mobilizes," said Burns, "naked power coerces."[38] But power need not be dictatorial or punitive to be effective. Power can also be used in a noncoercive manner to orchestrate, direct, and guide members of an organization in the pursuit of a goal or series of objectives. Leaders must engage followers, not merely direct them. Leaders must serve as models and mentors, not martinets. Or to paraphrase novelist James Baldwin, power without morality is no longer power.

For Peter Senge, teaching is one of the primary jobs of leadership.[39] The "task of leader as teacher" is to empower people with information, offer insights, new knowledge, alternative perspectives on reality. The "leader as teacher" is not just about "teaching" people how "to achieve their vision." Rather, it is about fostering learning, offering choices, and building consensus.[40] Effective leadership recognizes that in order to build and achieve community, followers must become reciprocally coresponsible in the pursuit of a common enterprise. Through their conduct and teaching, leaders must try to make their fellow constituents aware that they are all stakeholders in a conjoint activity that cannot succeed without their involvement and commitment. Successful leadership believes in and communicates some version of the now famous Hewlett Packard motto: "The achievements of an organization are the results of the combined efforts of each individual." In the end, says Abraham Zaleznik, "leadership is based on a compact that binds those who lead with those who follow into the same moral, intellectual and emotional commitment."[41] However, as both Burns and Rost warn us, the nature of this "compact" is inherently unequal because the influence patterns existing between leaders and followers are not equal. Responsive and responsible leadership requires, as a minimum, that democratic mechanisms be put in place that recognize the right of followers to have adequate knowledge of alternative options, goals, and programs, as well as the capacity to choose among them. "In leadership writ large, mutually agreed upon purposes help people achieve consensus, assume responsibility, work for the common good, and build community."[42]

STRUCTURAL RESTRAINTS

There is, unfortunately, a dark side to the theory of the "witness of others." Howard S. Schwartz, in his radical but underappreciated managerial text *Narcissistic Process and Corporate Decay*,[43] argues that corporations are not bastions of benign, other-directed ethical reasoning; nor can corporations, because of the demands and requirements of business, be models and exemplars of moral behavior. The rule of business, says Schwartz, remains the "law of the jungle," "the survival of the fittest," and the goal of survival engenders a combative "us-against-them mentality" that condones the moral imperative of getting ahead by any means necessary. Schwartz calls this phenomenon "organizational totalitarianism": Organizations and the people who manage them create for themselves a self-contained, self-serving worldview, which rationalizes anything done on their behalf and which does not require justification on any grounds outside of themselves.[44] The psychodynamics of this narcissistic perspective, says Schwartz, impose Draconian requirements on all participants in organizational life: Do your work; achieve organizational goals; obey and exhibit loyalty to your superiors; disregard personal values and beliefs; obey the law when necessary, obfuscate it whenever possible; and deny internal or external discrepant information at odds with the stated organizational worldview. Within such a "totalitarian logic," neither leaders nor followers, rank nor file, operate as independent agents. To "maintain their place," to "get ahead," all must conform. The agenda of "organizational totalitarianism" is always the preservation of the status quo. Within such a logic, like begets like, and change is rarely possible. Except for extreme situations in which "systemic ineffectiveness" begins to breed "organization decay," transformation is never an option.

In *Moral Mazes*, Robert Jackall parallels much of Schwartz's analysis of organizational behavior, but from a sociological rather than a psychological perspective. According to critic and commentator Thomas W. Norton, both Jackall and Schwartz seek to understand why and how organizational ethics and behavior are so often reduced to either dumb loyalty or the simple adulation and mimicry of one's superiors. Whereas Schwartz argues that individuals are captives of the impersonal structural logic of "organizational totalitarianism," Jackall contends that "organizational actors become personally loyal to their superiors, always seeking their approval and are committed to them as persons rather than as representatives of the abstractions of organizational authority." But in either case, both authors maintain that organizational operatives are prisoners of the systems they serve.[45]

For Jackall, all American business organizations are examples of "patrimonial bureaucracies" wherein "fealty relations of personal loyalty" are the rule and the glue of organizational life. Jackall argues that all corporations are like fiefdoms of the Middle Ages, wherein the lord of the manor (CEO, president) offers protection, prestige, and status to his vassals (managers) and serfs (workers) in return for homage (commitment) and service (work). In such a system, advancement and promotion are predicated on loyalty, trust, politics, and personality as much as, if not more than, on experience, education, ability, and actual accomplishments. The central concern of the worker/minion is to be known as a "can-do guy," a "team player," being at the right place at the right time and master of all the social rules. That's why in the corporate world, asserts Jackall, 1,000 "atta-boys" are wiped away with one "oh, shit!"

Jackall maintains that, as in the model of a feudal system, employees of a corporation are expected to become functionaries of the system and supporters of the status quo. Their loyalty is to the powers that be; their duty is to perpetuate performance and profit; and their values can be none other than those sanctioned by the organization. Jackall contends that the logic of every organization (place of business) and the collective personality of the workplace conspire to override the wants, desires, and aspirations of the individual worker. No matter what a person believes off the job, said Jackall, on the job all of us to a greater or lesser extent are required to suspend, bracket, or only selectively manifest our personal convictions: "What is right in the corporation is not what is right in a man's home or his church. What is right in the corporation is what the guy above you wants from you."[46]

For Jackall the primary imperative of every organization is to succeed. This logic of performance, what he refers to as "institutional logic," leads to the creation of a private moral universe, a moral universe that by definition is totalitarian (self-sustained), solipsistic (self-defined), and narcissistic (self-centered). Within such a milieu, truth is socially defined, and moral behavior is determined solely by organizational needs. The key virtues, for all alike, become the virtues of the organization: goal preoccupation, problem solving, survival/success, and—most important—playing by the house rules. In time, says Jackall, those initiated and invested in the system come to believe that they live in a self-contained world that is above and independent of outside critique and evaluation.

For both Schwartz and Jackall, the logic of organizational life is rigid and unchanging. Corporations perpetuate themselves, both in their strengths and weakness, because corporate cultures clone their own. Even given the scenario of a benign organizational structure that produces positive behavior and beneficial results, the etiology of the problem and the opportunity for abuse that it offers represent the negative possibilities and inherent dangers of the "witness of others" as applied to leadership theory. Within the scope of Schwartz's and Jackall's allied analyses, "normative" moral leadership may not be possible. The model offered is both absolute and inflexible, and only "regular company guys" make it to the top. The maverick, the radical, and the reformer are not long tolerated. The "institutional logic" of the system does not permit disruption, deviance, or default.

The term "moral leadership" often conjures up images of sternly robed priests, waspishly severe nuns, carelessly bearded philosophers, forbiddingly strict parents, and something ambiguously labeled the "moral majority." These people are seen as confining and dictatorial. They make us do what we should do, not what we want to do. They encourage following the "superego" and not the "id." A moral leader is someone who supposedly tells people the difference between right and wrong from on high. But there is much more to moral leadership than merely telling others what to do.

The vision and values of leadership must have their origins and resolutions in the community of followers, of whom they are a part, and whom they wish to serve. Leaders can drive, lead, orchestrate, and cajole, but they cannot force, dictate, or demand. Leaders can be the catalyst for morally sound behavior, but they are not, by themselves, a sufficient condition. By means of their demeanor and message, leaders must be able to convince, not just tell others, that collaboration serves the conjoint interest and well-being of all involved. Leaders may offer a vision, but followers must buy into it. Leaders may organize a plan, but followers must decide to take it on. Leaders may demonstrate conviction and willpower, but followers, in the new paradigm of leadership, should not allow the leader's will to replace their own.[47]

Joseph C. Rost has argued, both publicly and privately, that the ethical aspects of leadership remain thorny. How, exactly, do leaders and collaborators in an influence relationship make a collective decision about the ethics of a change that they want to implement in an organization or society? Some will say, "option A is ethical," some others will say, "option B is ethical." How are leaders and followers to decide? As I have suggested, ethics is what "ought to be done" as the preferred mode of action in a right-versus-right, values-versus-values confrontation. Ethics is an evaluative enterprise. Judgments must be made in regard to competing points of view. Even in the absence of a belief in the existence of a single universal, absolute set of ethical rules, basic questions can still be asked: How does it affect the self and others? What are the consequences involved? Is it harmful? Is it fair? Is it equitable? Perhaps the best, but by no means most definitive, method suited to the general needs of the ethical enterprise is a modified version of the scientific method: A) *Observation*, the recognition of a problem or conflict; B) *Inquiry*, a critical consideration of facts and issues involved;

C) *Hypothesis*, the formulation of a decision or plan of action consistent with the known facts; D) *Experimentation and Evaluation*, the implementation of the decision or plan in order to see if it leads to the resolution of the problem. There are, of course, no perfect answers in ethics or life. The quality of our ethical choices cannot be measured solely in terms of achievements. Ultimately and ethically, intention, commitment, and concerted effort are as important as outcome: What/why did leader/followers try to do? How did they try to do it?

Leadership is hard to define, and moral leadership is even harder. Perhaps, like pornography, we only recognize moral leadership when we see it. The problem is, we so rarely see it. Nevertheless, I am convinced that without the "witness" of moral leadership, standards of ethics in business and organizational life will neither emerge nor be sustained. Leadership, even when defined as a collaborative experience, is still about the influence of individual character and the impact of personal mentoring. Behavior does not always beget like behavior in a one-to-one ratio, but it does establish tone, set the stage, and offer options. Although to achieve ethical behavior, an entire organization, from top to bottom, must make a commitment to it, the model for that commitment has to originate from the top.[48] Labor Secretary Robert Reich recently stated, "The most eloquent moral appeal will be no match for the dispassionate edict of the market."[49] Perhaps the "witness" of moral leadership can prove to be more effective.

NOTES

1. Maynard M. Dolecheck and Carolyn C. Dolecheck, "Ethics: Take It from the Top," *Business* (January-March 1989): 13.
2. James Patterson and Peter Kim, *The Day America Told the Truth* (New York: Prentice Hall Press, 1991), 1, 20, 21, 22.
3. "Quotable Quotes," *Chicago Tribune Magazine*, January 1, 1996, p. 17.
4. B. F. Skinner, *Beyond Freedom and Dignity* (New York: Alfred A. Knopf, 1971), 107, 108, 150, 214, 215.
5. Stephen R. Covey, *The Seven Habits of Highly Effective People* (New York: A Fireside Book, 1990), 42, 43.
6. John Dewey, *Theory of the Moral Life* (New York: Holt, Rinehart and Winston, 1960), 3–28.
7. Jean-Paul Sartre, *Existentialism and Human Emotions* (New York: The Wisdom Library, ND), 23, 24, 32, 33, 39, 40, 43, 44.
8. John Rawls, "Justice as Fairness: Political not Metaphysical," *Philosophy and Public Affairs* 14 (1985): 223–51.
9. The academic issue of which system of ethics best answers "what we ought to do" is a moot point and may in fact be an artificial one. However, the reality is, whichever way one decides to answer the question, "what we ought to do" is an endemic requirement of the human condition.

10. Pope Pius XI, "Quadragesimo Anno (On Reconstructing the Social Order)," in David M. Byers, ed. *Justice in the Marketplace: A Collection of the Vatican and U.S. Catholic Bishops on Economic Policy, 1891–1984* (Washington, D.C.: United States Catholic Conference, 1985), 61.

11. Matthew Fox, *The Reinvention of Work* (San Francisco: Harper San Francisco, 1994), 298, 299.

12. "Tempo" section, *Chicago Tribune*, February 1, 1995, p. 2.

13. Norman E. Bowie, "Challenging the Egoistic Paradigm," *Business Ethics Quarterly* 1, no. 1 (1991): 1–21.

14. R. Edward Freeman, "The Problem of the Two Realms," speech given at Loyola University Chicago, The Center for Ethics, Spring 1992.

15. Henry Ford, Sr., quoted by Thomas Donaldson, *Corporations and Morality* (New Jersey: Prentice Hall, Inc., 1982), 57.

16. Ibid., 14.

17. Freeman, "The Problem of the Two Realms."

18. General Robert Wood Johnson, quoted by Frederick G. Harmon and Gary Jacobs, "Company Personality: The Heart of The Matter," *Management Review* (October 1985e): 10, 38, 74.

19. Georges Enderle, "Some Perspectives of Managerial Ethical Leadership," *Journal of Business Ethics* 6 (1987): 657.

20. Joseph C. Rost, *Leadership for the Twenty-First Century* (Westport, Conn.: Praeger, 1993).

21. Garry Wills, *Certain Trumpets* (New York: Simon and Schuster, 1994), 13.

22. Ibid., 17.

23. E. P. Hollander, *Leadership Dynamics* (New York: The Free Press, 1978), 4, 5, 6, 12.

24. In a recent article, Joseph Rost made a change in his use of the word *followers*: "I now use the word *followers* when I write about leadership in the industrial paradigm. I use the word *collaborators* when I write about leadership in the postindustrial paradigm. This is a change from *Leadership for the Twenty-First Century*, in which I use the word *followers* all the time. The reason for the change is the unanimous feedback I received from numerous professionals throughout the nation. . . . After trying several alternative words, I settled on the word *collaborators* because it seemed to have the right denotative and connotative meanings. In other words, *collaborators* as a concept fits the language and values of the postindustrial paradigm and so its usage should not be a problem to those who want to articulate a new paradigm of leadership." See Rost, "Leadership Development in the New Millennium," *The Journal of Leadership Studies* 1, no. 1 (1993): 109, 110.

25. James MacGregor Burns, *Leadership* (New York: Harper Torchbooks, 1979), 426.

26. Al Gini, "Moral Leadership: An Overview," *Journal of Business Ethics*, forthcoming.

27. James O'Toole, *Leading Change* (San Francisco: Jossey-Bass, 1994); Lynn Sharp-Paine, "Managing for Organizational Integrity," *Harvard Business Review* (March-April 1994): 106–17.

28. Peter M. Senge, *The Fifth Discipline* (New York: Double/Currency Books, 1990), 345–52.

29. Christina Hoff Sommers, "Teaching the Virtues," *Chicago Tribune Magazine*, September 12, 1993, p. 16.

30. Thomas J. Peters and Robert H. Waterman, Jr., *In Search of Excellence* (New York: Harper and Row, 1982), 245.

31. Burns, chapters 2, 5.

32. Ibid., xi.

33. William James, *The Will to Believe* (New York: Dover Publications, Inc., 1956), 1–31, 184–215.

34. John W. Gardner, *On Leadership* (New York: The Free Press, 1990), 8.

35. Gail Sheehy, *Character: America's Search for Leadership* (New York: Bantam Books, 1990), 311.

36. Ibid., 66.

37. Burns, 36.

38. Ibid., 439.

39. For Senge the three primary tasks of leadership include: leader as designer; leader as steward; leader as teacher.

40. Senge, 353.

41. Abraham Zaleznik, "The Leadership Gap," *Academy of Management Executives* 4, no. 1 (1990): 12.

42. Rost, *Leadership for the Twenty-First Century*, p. 124.

43. Howard S. Schwartz, *Narcissistic Process and Corporate Decay* (New York: New York University Press, 1990).

44. Howard S. Schwartz, "Narcissistic Project and Corporate Decay: The Case of General Motors," *Business Ethics Quarterly* 1, no. 3 (1991): 250.

45. Thomas W. Norton, "The Narcissism and Moral Mazes of Corporate Life: A Commentary on the Writings of H. Schwartz and R. Jackall," *Business Ethics Quarterly* 2, no. 1 (1991): 76.

46. Robert Jackall, *Moral Mazes* (New York: Oxford University Press, 1988), 6.

47. Wills, 13.

48. Dolecheck and Dolecheck, 14.

49. William Pfaff, "It's Time for a Change in Corporate Values," *Chicago Tribune*, January 16, 1996, p. 17.

Part II

Leaders and Followers:
A Difficult Relationship

3

Ethical Challenges in the Leader-Follower Relationship

Edwin P. Hollander

Various streams of thought have converged on the concept of leadership as a process rather than a person or state. This process is essentially a shared experience, a voyage through time, with benefits to be gained and hazards to be surmounted by the parties involved. A leader is not a sole voyager, but a key figure whose actions or inactions can determine others' well-being and the broader good. It is not too much to say that communal social health, as well as achieving a desired destination, are largely influenced by a leader's decisions and the information and values upon which they are based.

The leadership process is therefore especially fraught with ethical challenges. Hodgkinson (1983) considers leadership to be "intrinsically valuational," as "philosophy-in-action." He says, "Logic may set limits for and parameters within the field of value action but value phenomena determine what occurs within the field. They are indeed the essential constituents of the field of executive action. . . . If this were not true then leadership behaviour could be routinized and, ultimately, computerized" (p. 202). Gardner (1990), too, sees values as part of "the moral framework that permits us to judge some purposes as good and others as bad" in leadership (pp. 66–67). Rost (1991) stresses the place of ethics in leadership regarding both process and ends.

THE CENTRALITY OF THE LEADER-FOLLOWER RELATIONSHIP

Evidence continues to accumulate about the importance of relational qualities in the unity of leadership-followership (for example, Hollander 1992a,b). A major component of the leader-follower relationship is the leader's perception of his or her self relative to followers, and how they in turn perceive the leader. This self-other perception implicates important ethical issues concerning how followers are involved, used, or abused, especially in a relationship favoring a leader's power over them. Within this dominance motif, followers are essentially seen to be compliant and manipulable in the extreme. An instance of this is a corporate CEO who said that "leadership is confirmed when the ability to inflict pain is demonstrated" (Menzies 1980). Clearly such abuse of power runs counter to the idea of mutual dependency in a shared enterprise and the value of maintaining personal dignity. Hurting people is usually not the way to get the best from them. Further, abuse deprives a leader of honest information and judgments from cowed subordinates. This can fuel the self-absorption and self-deception that are pitfalls of arbitrary power.

Nevertheless, the leader role is still seen as preeminent, often as power over others, rather than as a stewardship, or even as a service to others (see, for example, DePree 1989). Not least there is the very real problem of what Drucker (1988) calls "misleaders" who are dysfunctional. From a ten-year perspective, DeVries (1992) estimates that the base rate for executive incompetence is at least 50 percent. Hogan, Raskin, and Fazzini (1990) found that organizational climate studies from the mid-1950s onward show 60 percent to 75 percent of organizational respondents reporting their immediate supervisor as the worst or most stressful aspect of their job.

Management performance decrements also can have calamitous consequences to the organization and to others, but not necessarily to the rewards given to these managers. Responsibility for performance is somehow detached from them. A corporation head like Roger Smith, chairman of General Motors from 1981 to 1990, is a good example. He presided over a phenomenal drop of almost 20 percent of his company's share of the U.S. market. For many there and elsewhere, Smith was considered to be rigid and unresponsive to the challenges of consumer needs and foreign competition. Asked by *Fortune* magazine to explain what went wrong, he replied, "I don't know. It's a mysterious thing." Commenting on this statement, Samuelson (1993) says, "As a society, we have spent the past decade paying for mistakes like Smith's" (p. 55). Yet the organization continued its reward pattern: On his retirement the

GM board increased his already generous pension to over a million dollars a year.

This dysfunctional system contrasts with one that shows the discipline and unity of purpose represented in "teamwork" aimed at clear performance goals (see, for example, Hackman 1989; Katzenbach and Smith 1993). Achieving teamwork demands a concern for maintaining responsibility, accountability, authenticity, and integrity in the leader-follower relationship. Indeed, the oft mentioned "crisis of leadership" usually reveals an absence of these elements (Hollander 1978b). This normative position has distinctly functional value as a universal perspective applicable to the political and organizational spheres. Though this position comes out of a democratic ethos, its generality is evident in the organizational psychology literature on leadership (see, for example, Gardner 1990; Hollander 1978a; Manz and Sims 1989).

HISTORICAL CONTEXT

Followership is periodically rediscovered as important to leadership, despite a long tradition of usage. The term is variously employed by those who come upon it and declare anew that leadership cannot exist without followership. But the essence of the matter is to recognize that a leader-centric focus is inadequate to understanding the interdependence of leadership and active followership (see, for example, Hollander and Offermann 1990; Kelley 1988; Vanderslice 1988).

In sixth century B.C. China, Lao Tzu wrote about the "wise leader" in his *Tao Te Ching* (Schmidt 1975). His philosophy makes a major contribution to the theme of sharing leadership with followers: "The wise leader settles for good work and then lets others have the floor. The leader does not take all the credit for what happens and has no need for fame" (Heider, p. 162). Similarly, Hegel taught in the eighteenth century that the good leader must incorporate the experience and qualities of the follower, and demonstrate followership in leading.

The late-nineteenth-century European social philosophers showed recognition that leading involves a relational process with followers. Interest in crowd behavior, imitation, and the group mind were central to an ethos expressed most notably in the writings of Tarde (1890/1903) and LeBon (1896/1922) in France. Both were influenced by Charcot, who drew to Paris such later eminences as Freud and Prince to study with him. Indeed, Prince called his *Journal of Abnormal and Social Psychology* by that name because he saw the two fields as inextricably linked, through his belief in Charcot's idea of the parallel between hypnotic states and the susceptibility of a mob to social influence. It was LeBon, however, who also reported the story of a man chasing after a crowd of protesters saying he had to catch them because he was their leader.

From otherwise different perspectives, Freud (1921/1960) and Floyd Allport (1924) criticized LeBon's view of crowd behavior and, indirectly, Charcot's conception behind it. In *Group Psychology and the Analysis of the Ego* (1921) Freud developed his conception of the followers' identification with the leader as a shared ego-ideal. A significant disciple, Fromm (1941), extended this conception in personality terms, in his contention that "the psychology of the leader and that of his followers, are, of course, closely linked with each other" (p. 65). Erikson (1975) made an associated point about this linkage in asserting that followers "join a leader and are joined together by him" (p. 153).

CHARISMA AND ITS EFFECTS

Contemporary with Freud's conception of the ego-ideal was the idea of the "charismatic leader," to whom followers are drawn by a special quality. Max Weber (1921), the famous German sociologist of bureaucracy, advanced the concept to account for the loyalty and devotion of followers who are emotionally tied to a leader, especially in a time of crisis (House and Shamir 1993).

Charisma is not an unmixed good. Hodgkinson (1983) says, "Beware charisma" (p. 187), and Howell and Avolio (1992) have observed the need to distinguish between ethical and unethical charismatic leaders. In the organizational sphere, they cite the dubious ethical standards associated with Robert Campeau, John DeLorean, and Michael Milken, all of whom were acknowledged to have charisma for many of their followers. Unethical leaders are more likely to use their charisma to enhance power over followers, directed toward self-serving ends, usually in a calculated, manipulable way. Ethical leaders are considered to use their charisma in a socially constructive way to serve others.

When Burns (1978) advanced his concept of the "transforming leader," who changes the attitudes and behavior of followers, he regarded this as having a moral basis yielding beneficial ends. Yet, charisma is *the* quality often imputed to such leaders, though Burns says it "is so overburdened as to collapse under close analysis" (p. 243). Still, charisma has by now become a favored term of almost general approval. In the corporate world, as well as in politics, charismatic leaders are often sought as saviors. But they also may present difficulties, such as tendencies toward narcissism (Post 1986) as well as unethical behavior.

Weber (1946) conceived charisma to be one part of acceptance by followers of a leader's various bases for claiming legitimacy, and said, "if his leadership fails to benefit followers, it is likely that his charisma will disappear" (p. 360). Barnard (1938) dealt with this issue in his "acceptance theory of authority," stating conditions that permitted a follower to judge an order as authoritative, thus raising the issue of legitimacy of power (see Hollander 1993).

THE CONTRAST BETWEEN POWER AND IDENTIFICATION

In his classic conception of powerholding, Kipnis (1976) identified four corrupting influences of power affecting the powerholder and those in a relationship with that individual. Briefly these "metamorphic effects" are: (1) Power becomes desired as an end in itself, to be sought at virtually any cost; (2) holding power tempts the individual to use organizational resources for self-benefit, even illegally; (3) creates the basis for false feedback and an exalted sense of self-worth; (4) and a corresponding devaluation of others' worth, with a desire to avoid close contact with them. Mulder (1981) has extended the last point especially in his concept of "power distance." Such distance heightens the gap between leader and followers that exists because of disparities in available information or resources. This gap will be smaller where processes of identification and sharing occur.

Because well-being is at stake, other important features of this relationship are equity, equality, and need, with the potential for perception of injustice (see Deutsch 1975). These issues are especially salient in a condition where one person depends on another with a great power difference between them. On this point, Emerson (1962) said that the explicit recognition of dependence by a lower-power person on one of higher power can promote resentment by the former. This effect can undermine mutual efforts, though it has not received as much attention as more-tangible rewards, such as markedly different economic benefits (see Bok 1993). Clearly, the element of trust may be undercut by a leader's self-serving activity, especially the lack of accountability when he or she is manifestly failing.

SELF-SERVING BIASES

Given their traditional superordinate role, leaders may be prone to self-serving biases beyond those that exist in other social relationships. In his analysis of some key psychological processes involved, Greenwald (1985) has presented an interpretation of how the leader's ego or self incorporates several distinctive cognitive biases. These include the self as focus of knowledge; "beneffectance" as the perception of responsibility for desired, but not undesired, outcomes; and resistance to change.

These tendencies are further enhanced by power over others and a sense of being different, with accompanying social distance, and potential manipulation of them as objects. A necessary corrective is for the leader to be attuned to the needs of followers, their perceptions, and expectancies. However, the narcissism associated with leaders who draw on the affection of followers, as in "charismatic leadership," often deprives them of this corrective (see Post 1986). As a counterpart, followers may be vulnerable to perceptual distortions as a feature of the self-serving bias and identification with the leader that can bolster the self (see Hollander 1992b).

MUTUAL IDENTIFICATION

An alternative view, more in keeping with responsive participation, considers the leader-follower relationship within a mutual identification motif. This includes the prospect of two-way influence, and the perception and counterperception of leader and followers. Cantril (1958) has said that the leader must be able to perceive the reality worlds of followers and have sensitivity to guide intuitions, if a common consensus and mutual trust rather than "mere power, force, or cunning" are to develop and prevail (p. 129).

Identification with the leader is exemplified in Freud's (1921) concept of the leader as a shared "ego-ideal" with whom members of a group mutually identify. They have a common bond on which life itself may depend, as in the military. For instance, according to military historians Gabriel and Savage (1978), inadequate and inattentive leadership were found to be responsible for the failure to maintain "unit cohesion" in the U.S. Army serving in Vietnam. They say, "The officer corps grew in inverse proportion to its quality ... [and] could be described as both bloated in number and poorer in quality ... One result was My Lai. Even the staunchest defenders of the Army agree that in normal times a man of Lieutenant Calley's low intelligence and predispositions would never have been allowed to hold a commission. .... The lowering of standards was a wound that the officer corps inflicted on itself" (p. 10). They also detail the way that the senior officer corps successfully managed to put themselves farther to the rear of action than before.

By contrast, this identification process is enhanced in those production firms where managers have closer contact with their work force on the shop floor, and in the cafeteria, often wearing the same company uniform. This pattern illustrates the opposite of distancing employees.

JOINING OR DISTANCING FOLLOWERS

In April 1992, the first page of the *New York Times* Business Section (Hicks 1992) featured a story about the CEO of U.S. Steel, Thomas Usher. He took the unusual step of unexpectedly going to the offices of the United Steelworkers at the company's largest mill in Gary, Indiana. What he said there was not as interesting as the fact of his being there. While acknowledging that, Usher commented that "Our long-term interests are exactly the same. Whether you are a manager or a member of the union, everyone wants to do a good job. . . . I think there is a growing realization that we are not going to make it without the union and the union . . . without us" (p. D3).

The Usher view is evidently uncommon among corporate executives, or it would not be so newsworthy. Indeed, the founder of Total Quality Management (TQM), W. Edwards Deming, believed that the enormous financial incentives corporate executives receive have destroyed teamwork at many American companies (1992).

Some leaders have become so removed from followers' perceptions and needs that they may cease to be aware of how their actions affect the "team" they wish to foster. A pertinent example of this is seen in the issue of high compensation packages given to American CEOs (see Byrne et al. 1991; Crystal 1991). *Business Week, Forbes,* and *Fortune* are among the major business publications that recently featured articles on this issue.

Criticisms have centered on how these sums greatly exceed the pay of the average worker, as compared to foreign competitors, despite manifestly poor outcomes for some American firms. "In Japan, the compensation of major CEOs is 17 times that of average workers; in France and Germany, 23–25 times; in Britain, 35 times; in America, between 85 and 100-plus times. In 1990, CEO pay rose 7 percent while corporate profits fell 7 percent. . . . United Airlines' CEO . . . received $18.3 million (1,200 times what a new flight attendant makes) [though] United's profits fell 71 percent" (Will 1991).

Such disparities may produce even more alienation of followers from their leaders. Though leaders are recognized as needed, they also may be resented for having a position of authority that accords them special benefits, as seen now for instance in the contempt many hold for members of Congress. Least of all, leaders whose performance is substandard, but who remain well-rewarded, are unable to encourage good followership by gaining and retaining loyalty and trust. Indeed, it is quite to the contrary, in part due to the inability to show concern for equity to followers.

On the same day that the *New York Times* (March 31, 1993) reported major layoffs of even longtime employees at IBM, it also indicated the pay package for IBM's new CEO. It included $5 million as a bonus for signing, a basic annual salary of $2 million, plus other incentives that would be worth millions more. The article revealed the personal devastation of the employees leaving the company and the likely psychological toll on those who survived this round of cuts.

Signs of off-the-scale executive compensation exist not only in the private sector but also in the political realm. Congressional salaries have grown from $30,000 in 1967 to $130,000 in 1991, when they were most recently raised. In that same interval, the average private sector salary has increased from $5,296 to $18,425 (*USA Today*, June 12, 1992, p. 1). Based on the salary differential between the Congress and the public, the distance gap (expressed in absolute dollars) increased disproportionately from $24,704 to $111,575 in less than twenty-five years.

This pattern is observed to extend widely (see, for example, Bok 1993). It is even seen in some charitable and nonprofit organizations, and among some university presidents. In the first category is the well-publicized case of the president of United Way of America, whose annual salary and benefits, apart from other perquisites, approximated half a million dollars (Hevesi 1992). Not long after these revelations, he reluctantly agreed to resign, at his board's urging. Other disclosures were made about his self-dealing activities, including the appointment he created for his son as president of a spin-off firm to market United Way products. Then came word that the most recent president of the largest affiliate of United Way, the Tri-State (New York, New Jersey, Connecticut) division, had resigned in 1989 with a $3.3 million pension payment from that affiliate's funds. Its constituent groups voiced considerable displeasure when that fact surfaced, but much after the payment was made.

In 1991, the president of the University of Pittsburgh retired with a pension plan that included a multimillion dollar package plus a guaranteed annual salary of $309,000 for life. When members of the Pennsylvania legislature, the primary funding source for the university, learned about it through the press, they expressed outrage at the scale of these payments and at having been bypassed by the trustees, who approved this package (Reeves 1991). More pointedly, the campus community was understandably upset over the considerable sum of money given up from institutional funds, which engendered a great loss of confidence in the trustees and their judgment.

LEADER PERFORMANCE

As Drucker (1988) has long noted, leadership *is* performance. The central question is What earns a favorable judgment on a leader's performance? Obviously one important answer has to do with success in achieving group goals. But such goals may be set by the leader who thereby defines—and may redefine—the criteria for judgment within the system. In the political sphere, notably the macro-leadership of the presidency, this is "setting the agenda" and frequently involves a process of "getting on the right side on an issue." This usually requires *value expression*, particularly in what the leader says about what is desirable and to be sought. The element of trust also contributes to allowing the leader latitude for action (see Hollander 1992b).

Other things being equal, positive or negative outcomes are more likely to be attributed to the leader, so that when things go wrong, he or she is more readily faulted and even removed. In Pfeffer's (1977) causal attribution terms, leaders are symbols who can be fired to convey a sense of rooting out the basis for the problem. For Sartre, "To be a leader is to be responsible," but the reality too often is that responsibility and accountability are lacking.

One effect of the attributional view is to make even more explicit the significance of how followers and others perceive the leader, not least regarding expectations about leader competence and motivation. A pointed example of this is shown in the work on "derailment" by McCall, Lombardo, and Morrison (1988) with four hundred promising managers, seen to be on a fast track. Those who failed to reach their expected potential were more often found to lack skills in relating to others, but not technical skills. Other research by Kouzes and Posner (1987), with a sample of 3,400 organizational respondents, dealt with qualities they admired in their leaders, and also found the relational realm significant. Renewed interest in charisma, and now in transformational leadership (Bass 1985), makes the followers' view even more appropriate for understanding these phenomena.

Hollander and Kelly (1990, 1992) used critical incidents, open-ended questions, and rating scales to study responses to good and bad leadership. This research was done with 280, mainly organizationally based, respondents, half male and half female. It affirmed the major point that relational qualities were emphasized in reports and evaluations distinguishing good from bad leadership. Most notably, these included providing personal and professional support, communicating clearly as well as listening, taking needed action, and delegating.

Although this research is organizationally based, it has larger implications at the societal level and resonates with ideas about the effects of power and distance. One point clearly is that leader characteristics have an effect on followers by shaping their perceptions and responses. Indeed, this link between perceptions and behavior tests the ethics of a leader's actions and other attributes as perceived by followers, and their response to those attributes (see, for example, Lord and Maher 1990).

How the leader's self-presentation is perceived by followers has broader ethical and performance consequences. These include obvious instances of unfairness, self-seeking at others' expense, weakness, vacillation, and outright misconduct, all of which detract from the leader's standing with followers. Emler and Hogan (1991) say, "There is no inbuilt tendency to use power responsibly. You cannot randomly allocate leadership responsibility and expect the interests of justice or society to be well served. Those in charge have a responsibility to make moral decisions greater than those they command . . . [and] those differences become more consequential the further up the hierarchy one goes" (p. 86).

CONCLUSIONS

Clearly there are ethical challenges in the use of authority and power. Among these are the destructive effects on the social contract between the leader and followers. Being a leader allows more influence and power over others' outcomes and events more broadly. The leader also has many benefits and privileges, including higher financial rewards and the freedom to keep at a distance, if desired. But these benefits come at the price of responsibility and accountability to followers (see Hollander 1978b). Where the leader is seen to be power-oriented, exploitative, and self-serving, especially in the face of failures, the goal of mutual identification is hardly attainable. Instead, followers may feel alienated and ultimately take their allegiance elsewhere. That prospect poses an essential challenge today.

NOTES

This chapter is based upon a presentation made on July 8, 1993, in the Ethics Symposium at the Sixteenth Annual Scientific Meeting of the International Society of Political Psychology, Cambridge, Massachusetts. It was originally published in *Business Ethics Quarterly* (Vol. 5, No. 1).

The assistance of Elisa H. Schwager and Ketty Russeva in the preparation of this chapter is gratefully acknowledged.

REFERENCES

Allport, F. H. 1924. *Social Psychology*. Boston: Houghton-Mifflin.
Barnard, C. I. 1938. *The Functions of the Executive*. Cambridge, Mass.: Harvard University Press.

Bass, B. M. 1985. *Leadership and Performance beyond Expectations*. New York: Free Press.

Bok, D. 1993. *The Cost of Talent*. New York: Free Press.

Burns, J. M. 1978. *Leadership*. New York: Harper & Row.

Byrne, J. A., W. C. Symonds, and J. F. Siler. 1991. "CEO Disease." *Business Week*, April 1, 52–60.

Cantril, H. 1958. "Effective Democratic Leadership: A Psychological Interpretation." *Journal of Individual Psychology* 14: 128–38.

Crystal, G. 1991. *In Search of Excess: The Overcompensation of American Executives*. New York: W. W. Norton.

Deming, W. E. 1992. Quoted in *The Economist*, February 1, 19.

DePree, M. 1989. *Leadership Is an Art*. New York: Doubleday Dell.

DeVries, D. L. 1992. "Executive Selection: Advances but No Progress." *Issues & Observations* 12: 1–5.

Deutsch, M. 1975. "Equity, Equality, and Need: What Determines Which Value Will Be Used as the Basis of Distributive Justice?" *Journal of Social Issues* 31: 137–49.

Drucker, P. F. 1988. "Leadership: More Doing Than Dash." *Wall Street Journal*, January 6, p. 14.

Emerson, R. M. 1962. "Power-Dependence Relations." *American Sociological Review* 27: 31–41.

Emler, N., and R. Hogan. 1991. "Moral Psychology and Public Policy." In W. M. Kurtines and J. L. Gewirtz, eds. *Handbook of Moral Behavior and Development*. Volume 3: *Applications*, pp. 69–93. Hillsdale, N.J.: Lawrence Erlbaum.

Erikson, E. H. 1975. *Life History and the Historical Moment*. New York: W. W. Norton.

Freud, S. 1921/1960. *Group Psychology and the Analysis of the Ego*. New York: Bantam. (Originally published in German in 1921.)

Fromm, E. 1941. *Escape from Freedom*. New York: Rinehart.

Gabriel, R., and P. Savage. 1978. *Crisis in Command*. New York: Hill and Wang.

Gardner, J. W. 1990. *On Leadership*. New York: Free Press/Macmillan.

Greenwald, A. 1985. "Totalitarian Egos in the Personalities of Democratic Leaders." Symposium Paper, International Society of Political Psychology Annual Meeting, Washington, D.C., June 20.

Hackman, J. R. 1989. *Groups That Work (and Those That Don't)*. San Francisco: Jossey-Bass.

Heider, J. 1995. *The Tao of Leadership*. Atlanta: Humanics New Age.

Hevesi, D. 1992. "United Ways Challenge Method Used to Divide Their Donations." *New York Times*, March 20, B4.

Hicks, J. P. 1992. "The Steel Man with Kid Gloves." *New York Times*, April 3, D-1.

Hodgkinson, C. 1983. *The Philosophy of Leadership*. Oxford, England: Basil Blackwell.

Hogan, R., R. Raskin, and D. Fazzini. 1990. "The Dark Side of Charisma." In K. E. Clark and M. B. Clark, eds. *Measures of Leadership*. West Orange, N.J.: Leadership Library of America, pp. 343–54.

Hollander, E. P. 1978a. *Leadership Dynamics: A Practical Guide to Effective Relationships*. New York: Free Press/Macmillan.

————. 1978b. "What Is the Crisis of Leadership?" *Humanitas* 14: 285–96.

————. 1992a. "The Essential Interdependence of Leadership and Followership." *Current Directions in Psychological Science* 1: 71–75.

————. 1992b. "Leadership, Followership, Self, and Others." *Leadership Quarterly* 3: 43–54.

————. 1993. "Legitimacy, Power, and Influence: A Perspective on Relational Features of Leadership." In M. Chemers and R. Ayman, eds. *Leadership Theory and Research: Perspectives and Directions.* San Diego, Calif.: Academic Press, pp. 29–47.

Hollander, E. P., and D. R. Kelly. 1990. "Rewards from Leaders as Perceived by Followers." Paper presented at the meeting of the Eastern Psychological Association, Philadelphia, March 30.

————. 1992. "Appraising Relational Qualities of Leadership and Followership." Paper presented at the 25th International Congress of Psychology, Brussels, July 24.

Hollander, E. P., and L. R. Offermann. 1990. "Power and Leadership in Organizations: Relationships in Transition." *American Psychologist* 45: 179–89.

House, R., and B. Shamir. 1993. "Toward the Integration of Transformational, Charismatic and Visionary Theories." In M. M. Chemers and R. Ayman, eds. *Leadership Theory and Research: Perspectives and Directions.* San Diego, Calif.: Academic Press, pp. 81–107.

Howell, J. M., and B. J. Avolio. 1992. "The Ethics of Charismatic Leadership: Submission or Liberation?" *Academy of Management Executive* 6: 43–54.

Katzenbach, J. R., and O. K. Smith. (1993). *The Wisdom of Teams: Creating the High-Performance Organization.* Cambridge, Mass.: Harvard Business School Press.

Kelley, R. E. 1988. "In Praise of Followers." *Harvard Business Review* 88: 142–48.

Kipnis, D. 1976. *The Powerholders.* Chicago: University of Chicago Press.

Kouzes, J. M., and B. Z. Posner. 1987. *The Leadership Challenge: How to Get Extraordinary Things Done in Organizations.* San Francisco: Jossey-Bass.

LeBon, G. 1896/1922. *The Crowd: A Study of the Popular Mind,* 2nd ed. London: T. F. Unwin.

Lord, R. G., and K. J. Maher. 1990. "Leadership Perceptions and Leadership Performance: Two Distinct but Interdependent Processes." In J. Carroll, ed. *Advances in Applied Social Psychology: Business Settings* 4: 129–54. Hillsdale, N.J.: Erlbaum.

Manz, C. C., and H. P. Sims. 1989. *Super-Leadership: Leading Others to Lead Themselves.* New York: Prentice Hall Press.

McCall, M. W., M. M. Lombardo, and A. M. Morrison. 1988. *The Lessons of Experience.* Lexington, Mass.: Lexington Books.

Menzies, H. D. 1980. "The Ten Toughest Bosses." *Fortune* 101: 62–69.

Mulder, M. 1981. "On the Quantity and Quality of Power and the Q. W. L." Paper presented at the International Conference on the Quality of Work Life Toronto.

Pfeffer, J. 1977. "The Ambiguity of Leadership." In M. W. McCall, Jr., and M. M. Lombardo, eds. *Leadership: Where Else Can We Go?* Durham, N.C.: Duke University Press.

Post, J. M. 1986. "Narcissism and the Charismatic Leader-Follower Relationship." *Political Psychology* 7: 675–88.

Rost, J. C. 1991. *Leadership for the Twenty-First Century*. New York: Praeger.

Reeves, F. 1991. "Pitt Misled Us, Lawmaker Asserts." *Pittsburgh Post-Gazette*, April 25, p. 1.

Samuelson, R. 1993. "The Death of Management." *Newsweek* (May 10): 55.

Schmidt, K. O. 1975. *Tao Te Ching*. Lakemont, Ga.: CSA Press.

Tarde, G. 1903. *The Laws of Imitation* (translated from 2nd French edition by E. C. Parsons; original, 1890). New York: Holt.

Vanderslice, V. J. 1988. "Separating Leadership from Leaders: An Assessment of the Effect of Leader and Follower Roles in Organizations." *Human Relations* 41: 677–96.

Weber, M. 1921. "The Sociology of Charismatic Authority." Republished in translation (1946) in H. H. Gerth and C. W. Mills (eds. and trans.), *From Max Weber: Essays in Sociology*. New York: Oxford University Press, pp. 245–52.

Will, G. 1991. "Corporate Raiders." *Boston Globe*, September 2, p. 15.

4

Leadership and the Problem of Bogus Empowerment

Joanne B. Ciulla

Empowerment conjures up pictures of inspired and confident people or groups of people who are ready and able to take control of their lives and better their world. The empowered are the neighbors in a community who band together and take action to drive out drug dealers; the longtime welfare mother who gets a job and goes on to start a business; the child who learns to read and to ride a bike. Power is a relationship between people with mutual intentions or purposes.[1] Empowerment is about giving people the confidence, competence, freedom, and resources to act on their own judgments. Hence, when a person or group of people are empowered, they undergo a change in their relationship to other people who hold power and with whom they share mutual goals. In a community, empowering citizens changes their relationship to each other and to other holders of power such as business and government. In a business, empowering employees changes their relationship to each other, management, and the work process.

You can hardly pick up a business book today without seeing the words *leadership, empowerment, trust,* or *commitment* either on the cover or in the text. Gone are the bosses of the industrial era. Organizations have entered a new age where employees are partners and part of the team. Not only are managers supposed to be leaders, but all employees are leaders in their own way. This is good. It's democratic. It shows respect for persons, and it sounds very ethical. So why isn't everyone happy? Why do business leaders worry about trust and loyalty? Why are employees cynical? One reason is that people are less secure in their jobs because of downsizing, technology, and competition from the global labor market. The other reason, and focus of this chapter, is that in many organizations, promises of empowerment are bogus. The word *bogus* is often used by young people to express their anger, disappointment, and disgust over hypocrisy, lies, and misrepresentations. This is how people feel when they are told that they are being empowered, but they know that they are not. When leaders promise empowerment, they raise the moral stakes in their relationship to followers. Failure to deliver can lead to even greater cynicism about leadership, alienation, and abdication of moral responsibility by employees and/or citizens.

When you empower others, you do at least one of the following: you help them recognize the power that they already have; you recover power that they once had and lost; or you give them power that they never had before. In his study of grass-roots empowerment, Richard Couto says there are two main kinds of empowerment. The first kind he calls psycho-political empowerment. It increases people's self-esteem and results in a change in the distribution of resources and/or the actions of others. In other words, empowerment entails the confidence, desire, and—most important—the ability of people to bring about real change. This is probably what most people think of when they think of empowerment. Couto calls the second form of empowerment psycho-symbolic empowerment. It raises people's self-esteem or ability to cope with what is basically an unchanged set of circumstances.[2] More often than not, leaders promise or appear to promise the first kind of empowerment but actually deliver the second.

In this chapter I argue that authentic empowerment entails a distinct set of moral understandings and commitments between leaders and followers, all based on honesty. I begin by looking at the cultural values behind the idea of empowerment, particularly as it applies in the workplace. My primary focus is on business organizations, but much of what I have to say about the moral aspects of empowerment applies to leaders and followers in community, nonprofit, and political contexts as well. I briefly outline how the idea of empowerment has evolved over the past fifty years of management theory and practice. Critical analysis of this history and the ways in which empowerment is manipulative and unauthentic then helps me talk about the moral aspects of empowerment and their implications for leadership.

PART I. THE SOCIAL VALUES BEHIND EMPOWERMENT

The idea of empowerment has its charm. Americans treasure democracy and its accompanying values of liberty and equality. If democracy were the only goal of empowerment, Americans would have the most democratic workplaces in the world, but they don't. As Tom Wren points out, ever since American independence, there has been a conflict between the values of equality and authority.[3] This tension is clearly evident in all organizational life. However, there are other values in our culture that shape the leadership and values of the workplace. Charles Taylor identifies three values of the modern age that he says cause tremendous personal anxiety and social malaise: individualism, instrumental reason (which causes disenchantment with the world), and freedom (which people seem to be losing because of individualism and instrumentalism).[4] Ideally empowerment is what makes humans triumph over the anxiety they have over these values and provides the antidotes to the social malaise.

In the workplace are constant tensions among individualism, freedom, and instrumental value and/or economic efficiency (I count these as two aspects of the same value). In a society where people value individualism and freedom, the challenge of leadership in organizations is the challenge of leading a flock of cats, not sheep.[5] This means that leaders have to use more powerful means of control than they would in a culture where people live in accepted hierarchies. For example, Americans were first smitten with Japanese management because it was effective and seemed so democratic. What they failed to realize was that the Japanese could afford to be democratic because the social controls imposed by hierarchy and community were internalized in workers, hence requiring less overt control by managers. American business leaders face the challenge of maintaining control without overtly chipping away at individualism and democratic ideals. This is why the language of empowerment is so attractive.

Economic efficiency and instrumentalism are the most powerful and most divisive values in the workplace. They trump all other values, and our current faith in the market makes it difficult to sustain plausibly any other ethical values in an organization. The market is a mean, ruthless boss. Instrumentalism or the value of getting the job done is more important than the means and people used to get it done. Business leadership is effective if it gets results. Leaders and their organizations are successful if they make the most amount of money or do the most amount of work in the least amount of time. Not only are the ends more important than the means, but there is little if any room for things that have intrinsic but noninstrumental value in business. The greatest of all impediments to empowerment in business, and increasingly in all areas of life, is economic efficiency. It acts on rules that refuse to take into account special circumstances.

In addition to the values of instrumentalism, individualism, and freedom, I add a fourth social value that I call "niceness." It might sound strange to say that our culture values niceness at a time when there seems to be little civility. Niceness is not civility. Historian Norbert Elias traces the origin of civility to the sixteenth-century Dutch philosopher Erasmus. His book *De Civilitate Morum Puerilium* (*On Civility in Children*) is dedicated to a prince's son. It chronicles the proper behavior of people in society with a special emphasis on outward physical behavior. In short, it is an etiquette book about properly blowing one's nose, eating at the table, and relieving oneself. Published in 130 editions and translated into English, French, Czech, and German, Erasmus's book established the concept of civility as behavior that was considerate of other people in a society.[6] Kant later points out that civility is not morality (because it doesn't require a good will), but the similitude of morality—an outward decency.[7] Civility is the behavior that citizens should have toward their fellow citizens. It includes an obligation of citizens to be polite and respectful of the private rights of others.

Whereas the concept of civility develops as a form of outward consideration for others (for example, not picking your nose in public), niceness is used as a means of gaining the favor and trust of others by showing a willingness to serve. Niceness fits the description of courtly behavior, from which we get the term *courtesy*. This selection from the *Zeldler Universal Lexicon of 1736* captures the basic elements of commercial niceness:

The courts of great lords are a theater where everyone wants to make his fortune. This can only be done by winning favor with the prince and the most important people of his court. One therefore takes all conceivable pains to make oneself agreeable to them. Nothing does this better than making the other believe that we are ready to serve him to the utmost capacity under all conditions. Nevertheless we are not always in a position to do this, and may not want to, often for good reasons. Courtesy serves as a substitute for all this. By it we give the other so much reassurance, through our outward show, that he has a favorable anticipation of our readiness to serve him. This wins us the other's trust, from which an affection for us develops imperceptibly, as a result of which he becomes eager to do good to us.[8]

There are other distinctive facets of niceness that are embedded in the observations of social critics since the mid-twentieth century. The first element of niceness is the belief that social harmony means lack of conflict. In *An American Dilemma* Gunnar Myrdal explains one facet of niceness. He argues that American social scientists derived their idea of social harmony from liberalism based on the Enlightenment ideal of *communum bonum* or common good. Radical liberals wanted to reformulate corrupt institutions into places where natural laws could function. The radical liberal, who could be a communist, socialist, or anarchist, wanted to dismantle power structures of privilege, property, and authority. In the utopia of the radical liberal, the concept of empowerment would not be useful. People wouldn't need to be given power or made to feel powerful, because the restraints that institutions had on their lives would in theory be removed. However, the dominant view in the social sciences (and certainly among those who were management theorists) was conservative liberalism. The conservative liberal took society as it was and, under the influence of economics, adopted the idea of social harmony as stable equilibrium.[9] The social scientists studied empirically observable situations and terms such as balance, harmony, equilibrium, function, and social process. They pretended that these terms gave a "do-nothing" valuation of a situation, but behind these words carry a veiled set of value judgments. Myrdal notes: "When we speak of a social situation being in harmony, or having equilibrium, or its forces organized, accommodated, or adjusted to each other, there is almost inevitable implication that some sort of ideal has been attained, whether in terms of 'individual happiness' or 'the common welfare.'"[10]

Traditionally, management theorists have tacitly accepted the valuations behind these terms. Empowerment, like harmony, is assumed to be a good that brings about individual happiness. Social harmony in an organization meant accommodating and adjusting to people. Conflict or disharmony was a sign of failed leadership. Niceness comes out of this one-dimensional picture of stable equilibrium and harmony. If no one complains and yells at work, then there is social harmony. Furthermore, the "do-nothing," value-free stance of social scientists is in part responsible for some of the manipulative theories and practices in management.

David Riesman captured another root of niceness in his 1950 description of the emerging American character. In *The Lonely Crowd* Riesman described inner-directed people who can cope with society because they are directed by internal, general goals implanted in them by their elders. Riesman observed that these people are becoming few and far between. Inner-directed people have less need for empowerment because they have what they need built in. The more prevalent character type identified by Riesman is the other-directed person. These people are shallower, friendlier, and more uncertain of themselves.[11] Other-directed people take more of their clues on values and goals from the outside: They want to be liked and have a strong need to belong.

In his book, Riesman described a society dominated by other-directed people, in which manipulative skill overshadows craft skill and expense accounts overshadow bank accounts. Business is supposed to be fun, and managers are supposed to be glad-handers who joke with secretaries and charm their bosses and clients. Most important, Riesman noted the trend that continues today of rewarding highly skilled people with management positions and power over other people. Hence the skilled engineer who gets promoted has to become a skilled glad-hander. The growth of the service industry shaped this character type into the model leader-manager and employee. To be successful in a service, one has to be friendly, likable, and nice. Since Riesman's day, bank accounts matter more and expense accounts are smaller. What remains the same is the powerful value of the glad hand. Our society may be less civil, and perhaps because of it niceness has been commercialized into the courtly norm of friendly bosses, bankers, and waiters all intent on gaining favor with customers and superiors in order to facilitate a smooth transaction.

As practiced in business, niceness consists of not getting into conflict and behaving in a commercially friendly fashion. Because people don't seem to behave this way naturally, we need the help of the therapist to attain niceness. In *The Triumph of the Therapeutic* Philip Rieff says that truth has become a highly personal matter he calls "psychic truth."[12] He thinks that therapeutic effectiveness has replaced the value of truth in our culture. Truths that make people feel better and help them adjust and fit in are far more desirable than truths that rock the boat. If our culture places more importance on psychic truths than on real truths, and if some "truths" or therapeutic fictions are effective because they make people happier, then leaders only have an obligation to make people feel empowered. They don't have to give them actual power.

It is obvious why niceness, as based on therapeutic lies, conflict-free environments, and the kind of bland friendliness that we experience when we go the store or a bank, is one of the values that lurk behind the history of empowerment in business. Leaders often prefer the nice kind of empowerment over the kind that leads to chaos and loss of control. As I have said, there is empowerment and bogus empowerment. I describe bogus empowerment as the use of therapeutic fictions to make people feel better about themselves, eliminate conflict, and satisfy their desire to belong (niceness); so that they will freely choose to work towards the goals of the organization (control of individualism), and be productive (instrumentalism). Leaders who offer bogus empowerment are unauthentic, insincere, and disrespectful of others. They believe that they can change others without changing themselves.

PART II. EMPOWERMENT AND THE ORGANIZATION MAN

C. Wright Mills offers one of the clearest articulations of bogus empowerment: "The moral problem of social control in America today is less the explicit domination of men than their manipulation into self-coordinated and altogether cheerful subordinates."[13]

Mills believed that management's real goal was to "conquer the problem of alienation within the bounds of work alienation."[14] By this he meant that the problems of the workplace had to be defined and solved in terms of the values and goals of the workplace itself. By controlling the meanings and the terms under which alienation was conquered and satisfaction found, employers could maintain control without alienating workers. William H. Whyte echoed Mills's concern about psychological manipulation in *The Organization Man*, only Whyte zeroed in on people's need to belong. The workplace of the late 1950s is both radically different from and strikingly the same as today's workplace. Whyte criticized the social ethic that makes morally legitimate the pressure of society against the individual. The social ethic rationalizes the organization's demand for loyalty and gives employees who offer themselves wholeheartedly a sense of dedication and satisfaction. The social ethic includes a belief that the group is a source of creativity. A sense of belonging is the ultimate need of the individual, and social science can create ways to achieve this sense of belonging.[15]

Whyte feared that psychologists and social engineers would strip people of their creativity and identity. He attacked the use of personality tests to weed out people who don't fit in. He also challenged the notion that organizations should be free from conflict. The critique of the workplace in Whyte's book is similar to the critiques that liberals have of communitarianism. Community-oriented life looks good, but it is ultimately oppressive and authoritarian. In the 1950s social critics worried about the conformity of people to institutions and the values of suburban life. Today we worry about lack of consensus about values and the breakdown of urban and suburban communities. There is an increasing effort in the workplace to build teams and emphasize the value of groups. No one seems worried about loss of creativity and submission of individual identity to group identity. Managers care more about the problem of the individual who isn't a team player, and a majority of management theorists today believe that groups and teams are the foundation of all that is good and productive.

Whyte says, "The most misguided attempt at false collectivization is the attempt to see the group as a creative vehicle."[16] Contrary to popular management thinking today, Whyte does not believe that people think or create in groups. Groups, he says, just give order to the administration of work. Whyte describes an experiment done at the National Training Lab on leaderless groups. Theoretically, when the group "jelled," the leader would fade into the background, to be consulted for his expertise only. These groups resulted in chaos, but as Whyte puts it, the trainers hoped that the resulting "feeling draining" of the group would be a valuable catharsis and a prelude to agreement.[17] According to Whyte, the individual has to enter into the process somewhere. If everyone wants to do what the group wants to do, and nothing gets done, then the individual has to play a role in the process. However, Whyte wonders if we should openly bring individuals into the process or "bootleg" it in an expression of group sentiment. Basically, he sees the leaderless group as intellectual hypocrisy. The power and authority of groups simply mask the real power and authority of leaders.

Whyte urges people to cheat on all psychological tests given during job interviews and at the workplace. He takes a strong stance against the organization and what he sees as the social scientist's coercive idea of belongingness. Another famous illustration of the struggle against the organization is in Sloan Wilson's novel *The Man in the Gray Flannel Suit*, published a year before Whyte's book. In the novel a personnel manager asks the main character, Tom Rath, to write an autobiography in which the last line reads, "The most significant thing about me is . . . ." Rath, revolted by the exercise, debates whether to say what the company wants to hear (the therapeutic lie) or write about his most significant memory, concerning a woman he met during the war. Caught between truth and fiction, Rath holds on to his dignity by stating the facts—his place of birth, his schooling, and the number of children in his family. He writes that the most significant thing about him is the fact that he is applying for the job. He also says that he does not want to write an autobiography as part of his application.[18]

Rath draws a fine line between himself and the organization. Whyte misses the moral in the first scene of Wilson's book: Telling the truth strikes a much stronger blow for individual dignity than beating the organization at its own game. Wilson's novel resonates with students today because all of them at some time will have to decide how truthful they have to be in a job interview or with an employer and how much of themselves they are willing to give to an organization. It is sometimes hard to tell the truth when you want someone to like you. The thin line is not about the amount of hours or work one does. It is the boundary that people draw between their inner self and the parts of them needed to do their job. It is the line that allows a person to be both an individual and part of a group. In the modern workplace it isn't always easy to draw this line; some workplaces use programs with the language of leadership and empowerment in them to erase the line between the two parts.

The Race for the Worker's Soul

In the 1960s the centralized bureaucratic organization of the 1950s gave way to the sensitive approach to management. The National Training Labs developed sensitivity training and T-Groups to transform bossy managers into participative ones. After much crawling around on the floor together and getting in touch with their inner feelings, few managers were transformed. During the 1970s and 1980s, management fads designed to capture the souls of workers bombarded the workplace. Fueled by global competitive pressures, managers were ready to try anything to get people to work hard and be productive. In 1981, William Ouchi's *Theory Z* and Richard Pascal and Anthony Athos's *The Art of Japanese Management* were best-sellers. The "new" idea from Japan was job enrichment and quality circles—after all, it worked for the Japanese. In 1982, the mystical Eastern touch of these two books gave way to Thomas J. Peters and Robert H. Waterman's blatantly evangelical *In Search of Excellence*. Peters and Waterman realized outright that the role of a manager is to make meaning for employees and create excitement. They argued that excellent organizations do not produce the conformist described by Whyte. They assure us that "In the very same institutions in which culture is so dominant, the highest levels of true autonomy occur. The culture regulates rigorously the few variables that do count, and it provides meaning." Nonetheless, in these organizations "people are encouraged to stick out, to innovate."[19] If a strong culture provided meaning, it could reach to the very souls of employees, hence allowing for great freedom and creativity within the boundaries of the culture and the meanings provided by the culture. This kind of organization is designed to foster Mills's cheerful subordinates.

Popular books on management and leadership exert more influence on the way organizations are run than do most studies done by scholars in the fields. Another 1982 best-seller was Kenneth Blanchard's *The One-Minute Manager*. Blanchard's adult fairy tale portrayed a kindly and therapeutic manager who inspired fealty and commitment. It makes the manager into a combination Mr. Rogers–Captain Kangaroo. Some companies required all of their managers to read it; it sold over three million copies. In the 1990s, real softies can regress and read what Winnie the Pooh has to say about management.[20] The fairy-tale format continues to be popular. Books such as *Zapp! The Lightning of Empowerment* and *Heroz: Empower Yourself, Your Coworkers, Your Company* by William C. Byham and Jeff Cox take the form of heroic and inspiring fables.[21] The fables include knights and dragons and demonstrate how sharing power with workers can revitalize a company. Stephen Covey is the top evangelical crusader of leadership literature in the 1990s. A recent article described "Coveyism" as "total quality management for the character, re-engineering for the soul."[22] Covey preaches that businesses have to focus on making employees "feel good" about the organizational structures in which they work.

In the 1980s and 1990s the word *leadership* began taking the place of the word *management* in business books. The semantic change is also a conceptual change from the idea of a manager as a boss who commanded and controlled the process of production to the leader who inspires people to work towards mutual goals. Joe Rost says that in the old industrial paradigm, leadership was nothing more than good management.[23] Empowerment is at least implied in most recent articulations of leadership in business books today. What is confusing about this literature is that it continues to be written for people who usually hold the position of manager. In ordinary discourse people talk about managers who lead and managers who manage. The carefully crafted distinctions made in the scholarly leadership literature are not always present in popular discourse. What we do see in ordinary discourse is that leadership has positive connotations and is sometimes used as an honorific, whereas management is either neutral or slightly negative.

The management fads of the 1980s and 1990s have appealed to business leaders (and those who aspire to be business leaders) because they make them feel powerful, inspiring, adventuresome, and lovable all at the same time. The lovable leader is an attractive image, especially given the lack of respect and trust for authority figures in our society. Lovable leaders are nice because they are democratic and they do not openly exert power over others. Practicing lovable leadership requires some therapeutic fictions. CEOs of large corporations have spent fortunes on consultants and training programs. The goal of most of the programs has been to make work more enjoyable and participatory and to push power relationships between employees and management into the background. All of this is done in hope of creating a more competitive business. Sometimes these programs have backfired.

In 1987, the California Public Utilities Commission asked Pacific Bell to stop its leadership-development program. The program intended to move away from the old AT&T culture, empower low-level managers and give them more responsibilities, cut middle managers, and become more customer-focused. At Pacific Bell twenty-three thousand of sixty-seven thousand employees took the two-day training.[24] Charles Krone created the Leadership Development program that came to be called "Kroning." This New Age program aimed at getting all employees to use the same language and think at all times about the six essentials of organization health: expansion, freedom, identity, concentration, order, and interaction. The program was based vaguely on the Armenian mystic Gurdjieff's Law of Three, which teaches that there are no constraints that can't be reconciled.[25]

After a two-month investigation of this $40 million training program, the commission reported that employees complained of brainwashing. An employee survey turned up repeated descriptions of the program as Big Brother, thought control, and mind restructuring. Employees also claimed that the Krone program used obtuse language and unnecessary concepts that made some people feel stupid. The irony was that the investigation discovered that a large majority of employees expressed a love of and commitment to Pacific Bell and mistrust of its management.[26] A Meridian survey of two thousand Pacific Bell employees concluded that top managers at Bell "blame the employees for the lack of productivity and are trying to make them think better. However, the Pacific Bell workforce already knows how to think."[27]

Thirty years after *The Organization Man*, corporations spent $30 billion dollars on training. Most of the training was in skills, but in 1986 about $4 billion went to programs such as Krone's and Werner Erhard's rehashed EST franchise called Transformation Technologies Inc. In 1987, *California Business* surveyed five hundred corporate owners and presidents and found that half their companies used some form of consciousness-raising.[28] These programs focused on the same themes espoused today: empowerment, leadership, and positive thinking. They are distinctive because they used such unorthodox training techniques as meditation, biofeedback, and hypnosis. For example, a company called Energy Unlimited escorted executives across hot coals as a means of empowering people. Although many of these programs now look silly to the outsider, they gained serious followers among corporate managers. Their impact on other employees is unclear. We rarely hear about cases in which employees complain about a company motivational program. That's why the Kroning scandal is so interesting. Most employees are a captive audience: Their success in the organization is contingent on buying into these programs. Motivational human potential courses often create a short-lived sense of euphoria among employees and/or a Hawthorn effect. They raise the expectation that employees will be enriched and empowered. However, after the dust settles, everything seems the same until the next initiative.

Did these attempts to redistribute power and responsibility in the organization succeed? On the one hand, employees were being promised more power and control over their work; on the other hand, some felt that they were being manipulated by the training programs. The standard answer given today is that programs to empower employees often failed because supervisors and line managers did not want to give up power.

Empowerment and Participation

Discussions of worker participation, including such issues as empowerment and the team approach, derived from two sources: industrial relations research and management research (largely based on organizational behavior). On the industrial relations side, discussion in the 1970s focused on workplace democracy. Admirable models of workplace democracy included democratic worker councils employed at the time in Yugoslavian industries. These councils allowed workers to play an active part in all facets of the business. Employees even elected their own managers. Other researchers in the 1960s and 1970s studied worker cooperatives in hopes of finding clues to constructing new forms of truly democratic organizations.[29] The workplace-democracy advocates wanted employees to have control of the organization as a whole and to discover new possibilities for organizing work.[30] Behind their thinking was the idea that participation was central to democracy, where citizens had a say in all significant institutions, including family, school, and work.[31] Worker participation fit Couto's model of psycho-political empowerment. However, back in the Cold War era, real democracy in the workplace was considered un-American.

Researchers on the management side focused on quality of worklife and job enrichment and motivation. They were interested in giving employees more discretion over the actual task that they performed, not over the organization itself. A major emphasis was on making the employee feel good about work. This approach, which is the one usually emphasized in business schools, aimed towards therapeutic effectiveness and tended to fall into Couto's category of psycho-symbolic empowerment. One of the biggest problems with empowerment schemes is that the language used often raises unrealistic expectations about how much power and control employees actually gain over their work. They also fail to see any change in their relationship to other power holders. When employees discover the limits of their participation, they are disappointed. (One also wonders if people have addictive and/or insatiable desires for power.) For example, people in a quality circle could suggest changes on the production line, but not changes in their work hours. Many managers were ambivalent about giving away their own supervisory power. The Japanese never had these problems, because supervisors usually headed up quality circles.[32]

It is useful to compare the impetus for and terms of participatory schemes in other countries with those in the United States. In his study of the macropolitics of organizational change, Robert E. Cole tells us that in the 1960s Japan, Sweden, and the United States gave small groups more discretion to make work more interesting, attract employees looking for satisfying work, and motivate employees. The Japanese called innovations such as quality circles *decentralization of responsibility*. These small-group structures did not challenge the hierarchical structure of the organization. Sweden, in contrast to Japan, challenged the hierarchy of managerial authority and cast the early debate over these innovations in the political terms of *joint influence* and *democratization*. In the United States, while there were some union supporters of industrial democracy, discussion of empowerment was categorized in terms of *participation, quality of worklife, leadership,* and *employee involvement*.

Cole's study compares the amount of control given the workers and the success of the programs in different countries. The study concludes, "The Swedish tried more and accomplished less, while the Japanese tried less and accomplished more. By contrast, the Americans tried still less and accomplished very little."[33] The Japanese and the Swedes were clear about the boundaries of employee involvement. In Japan the aims were aesthetic: to give workers autonomy to make their work more challenging and enjoyable. The Swedes wanted to bring real democracy into the workplace. The Americans had goals similar to those of the Japanese. However, the language used by Americans, their adversarial labor climate, and cultural values of individualism and freedom made the scope of these programs appear to reach beyond the aesthetic aspects of work and hint at a greater say in the organization. Most participatory schemes were really benevolent ways of motivating people by making work more satisfying. What wasn't clear was whether a boring job in a democratic workplace was better than an interesting job in an undemocratic one. Americans tended to assume that the latter was the case.

The 1935 Labor Relations Act recognized the need to protect workers from bogus empowerment of participatory programs. Under it, quality circles and other similar participatory schemes are illegal unless employees have the right to choose their representatives and have a genuine voice in decisions. The act prohibited "sham unions" or in-house unions formed by employers attempting to keep out real unions. Because it is obvious to most people today that employers have to forge a cooperative partnership with employees to be competitive, the 1935 act looks like an atavism that ought to be eliminated. However, the law recognized that companies prefer cooperation and participation of their employees on their own terms. Most important, companies fear the loss of control that would come with unionization. In most businesses, empowering employees does not change the balance of power within the organization. Unions are still the only institution in history that ever addressed the asymmetry of power between employers and employees. Unions can be a strong form of empowerment because they give employees an independent voice that terrifies most employers. Businesses have always had such an intense fear of unions that one has to question what they mean when they talk about empowerment.

Teams and Quality

Management language in the 1990s is a continuation of terms that started in the 1960s. *Empowerment* replaces terms such as *worker involvement*. The emphasis on power gets at what managers failed to deliver despite their claims over the past thirty years. What has become abundantly clear in research done on productivity is that workers do a better job when they have a say in the way they do their work, the redesign of their jobs, and the introduction of technology into the workplace. Yet, over the past twenty years managers have been constantly amazed by this phenomenon, which tells us something about the respect they have had for their employees.

The twentieth century began with scientific management with its physical control over production. It will end with Total Quality Management (TQM) and its social control over production. They are two sides to the same coin. Scientific management separated the mind from the body of the worker to mass-produce goods. TQM puts workers together in teams to produce quality goods and services. Both systems assert a high level of control at all phases of production (albeit using different means of control), and both systems have been extremely successful at improving production of goods and services.

Teams are a powerful form of social control. Peer pressure from the group keeps everyone in line and pulling his or her weight. Teams affect the individual more directly than does the larger culture of the organization. If the group puts out a measurable product, it can "keep score," which makes it accountable and allows for direct feedback and reinforcement. Hence, it is not surprising that along with excitement over teams some businesses engender a religious fervor for Total Quality Management. Originating from statistical quality control, TQM pieced together quality circles, team approaches, and leadership into a new philosophy that required leaders "to accept TQM as a way of life."[34]

In his book on leadership and TQM, Richard Pierce advises front-line supervisors to act like leaders and become "more participatory and less authoritarian." According to Pierce, participatory means listening to employees' ideas and, when appropriate, implementing their ideas. The author goes on to say that employees, too, have to change. They need to know "that improved quality performance on their part, while vital, may bring no added compensation ('What's in it for me?'), but in the long run, productivity and quality improvement are necessary for survival."[35] Behind TQM is the idea of reinstating a craft ethic in workers, which includes pride in workmanship and the intrinsic value of a job well done. Though this is a positive and rewarding model of work, it cannot be isolated from the context in which a job is done and the kind of work that is done. In this setting the manager does not want employees to behave as if they are engaged in an economic transaction. Yet the employer bases most of his or her decisions regarding the employee on economic considerations. This is a good example of a therapeutic fiction: Everyone pretends that work is not guided by the values of instrumentalism and economic efficiency.

A great attraction of TQM for business leaders is that it gives the impression that they are giving up control and being democratic (and nice), but they end up with more control. Furthermore, TQM has been very effective in improving the quality of goods and services. However, TQM theorists are not satisfied at stopping with improved quality. They assert that quality is a matter of ethics and that quality requires ethical leaders at the top giving customers what they want. One writer concludes that "companies have a moral obligation to live up to the promises they have made in advertisements, product brochures, and annual reports."[36] Ethical commitment in TQM focuses largely on a company's obligations to customers. True believers assume that TQM is intrinsically ethical because employees are empowered to participate in decisions and management listens to their employees. This is a fairly thin description of an ethical arrangement. The key issue here is the relationship of employees to management. Listening to employees and allowing them to participate in decisions does not mean that their relationship to management or each other has changed, especially if the listening and participation takes place between parties of unequal power. Furthermore, TQM says that managers should treat employees like customers. This is a therapeutic fiction. Can a business really treat employees like customers? It's a nice idea, but it breaks down in practice.

In a recent book documenting the wonders of teamwork in various organizations, Kimball Fisher emphasizes the importance of authenticity. He says that the key values of a team leader are belief in the importance of work, a belief that work is life, a belief in the "aggressive" development of team members, and a conviction to "eliminate barriers to team performance." Team leaders have to be themselves, or authentic, Fisher quotes a manager as saying. "The distinction between the work person and the family person is unhealthy and artificial."[37] In today's volatile economic environment, rhetoric like this rings false because, as Robert Frost said, "Home is the place where, when you have to go there, / They have to take you in."[38] We don't have many workplaces that do that. Team leaders also know that no matter how hard they or their team work, it may still not be enough. Kimball is right that authenticity is a fundamental part of leadership, but unauthentic in his denial of the distinction between work and the family. People may choose to lead lives with no distinction between work and home, but this choice is up to the individual and often rests on the nature of his or her work.

PART III. WHAT MAKES IT ALL WORK

Sincerity and Authenticity

At this point, some readers may be irritated by the unkind portrayal of management practices that most people consider a vast improvement over scientific management and traditional bureaucratic forms of work. Clearly there are sincere and committed business leaders all over America who really care and do their best to make work more rewarding for employees. I am not claiming that all the management theories and programs of the past fifty years have been designed to fool the American worker, nor am I saying that all of the social scientists behind these theories and the consultants who develop these programs are evil manipulators. Yet I do ask the irritated reader to consider the irony of the effort put into empowerment programs in an era of downsizing, when the ultimate fate of workers is not decided by business leaders but by the invisible hand. I have painted this dark picture to underscore the bankruptcy of empowerment without the honesty necessary for authentic empowerment. Clearly not all empowerment programs are intended to manipulate people, and some leaders really do want to empower their followers. However, to do so, they must be sincere and authentic.

In his book *Sincerity and Authenticity*, Lionel Trilling tells us that the public value of sincerity, like the concept of civility, emerged during the sixteenth century, a period of increasing social mobility in England and France. The art of acting with guile and expressing certain false emotions publicly became a tool for taking advantage of new social opportunities. Trilling says that sincerity was devalued when mobility and acting became accepted behaviors in a mobile society. People considered the sincere person stupid and unsophisticated. Audiences were no longer interested in seeing plays about "hypocrite-villains and conscious dissemblers."[39] It was more interesting to read or watch plays about people who deceived themselves. Authenticity replaced the notion of sincerity as a subject of dramatic interest.

The question of authenticity takes us back to Mills, Whyte, and Wilson's *Man in the Gray Flannel Suit*. Mills believed that people had to sell their personalities to work in bureaucratic organizations; Whyte was concerned with the toll of conformity on the individual; and in the opening scene of Wilson's novel, Tom Rath is both sincere, in that he tells the truth, and authentic, in that he tries to come to grips with who he is. Nevertheless, the remainder of the novel is really about his struggle to be truthful to himself. It's ironic that the phrase "man in the gray flannel suit" has come to characterize a boring conformist organization man. Tom Rath is anything but that. He is a man wrestling with the organization and struggling to be honest with himself and others.

According to Trilling, we have deprecated the value of sincerity by treating it as such a common commodity in society and the market place. If this is true, then the really valuable emotional commodities are authenticity and "true" emotions. Thus, either people who serve customers will require even better acting skills, or training will have to dig even deeper into the employee to evoke the appropriate real emotions. If training programs could get at people's real feelings, find the "hot buttons," employees would either no longer have to act, or they could engage in "deep acting." This may be the real reason for the use of intrusive motivational programs like EST and the Krone program. It also lurks in the background of the ideology of strong cultures. Make the workplace your family and carry to it all the sense of caring and responsibility that you feel naturally for family members. Although this sounds sinister, it is true that most organizations want their employees to have a certain "genuine" feeling about their work, the people whom they work with, and the organization. At Pacific Bell, employees really cared and were concerned about the company. Perhaps one thing that we learn from the Krone case is that attempts at engineering appropriate attitudes and emotions can actually undercut genuine feelings for a company. If a workplace is run honestly, people do care and are friendly; however, their emotions have to be free to be real. Nonetheless, the broader issues at stake remain the line between motivation and manipulation of emotions, and the claims that an organization can make on the inner self and emotions of an employee.

The principle of authenticity applies to organizations as well as individuals. Often motivational programs and leadership programs are just polite lies within a company. Quality of worklife and employee

involvement programs and redesigned jobs benefit employees by making their work more interesting. They intend to make employees feel
empowered and feel that the organization cares about their development. Nonetheless, there is a difference between feeling empowered
and really being empowered. One wonders if employees willingly buy
into the fiction of empowerment because of their own need to believe
that they have power and control. If so, symbolic empowerment works
because employees are unauthentic.

Reality and Truth

The obvious difference between authentic and bogus empowerment
rests on the honesty of the relationship between leaders and followers.
Honesty entails a set of specific practical and moral obligations and is
a necessary condition for empowerment. In the beginning I outlined
three social values behind empowerment: individualism; freedom; and
instrumentalism and economic efficiency. The fourth value, which encompasses the first three, I have called niceness. I characterized the
value of niceness as a kind of self-interested social harmony, commercial friendliness, and therapeutic truth. All the values color the way that
people view the context of their work. To empower people, leaders must
take into account the social and economic conditions under which they
operate.

The issue for most businesses is not democracy in the workplace or
the workers' need for self-esteem or self-fulfillment. Plainly and simply,
it is competitiveness. According to today's conventional wisdom, businesses of the twenty-first century have to be lean, mean, and flexible.
This condition requires a flatter organization structure and employees
willing to learn and change with the changing demands of their job, the
market, and technology. Companies must innovate constantly, which
means workers need the flexibility and work ethic of the old craft
guilds.[40] This is what TQM tries to do and why there is so much
discussion about commitment.

In this new business environment, in a sense employees already have
more power than they had in the past and employers have less. Information is a source of power. On the one hand, the use of and access to
information technologies in the workplace give employees far more
power than they had in the past. On the other hand, computerized
control systems can impose even stricter discipline on workers and
replace layers of management. Competition is the reality of company
life, and the market rules the lives of business leaders. Business leaders,
especially those who are responsible to stockholders, have significantly
less power and control over their firms than in the past. The decisions

of even those with the best of intentions are dominated by the demands of the market.[41] Internal power shifts occur not necessarily because one group intentionally gave up power, but because the demands of technology and economic efficiency required a new distribution of power. Power also decreases in organizations because of flattened organizational structure. Why does this matter? It matters because empowerment requires good faith. It is a kind of giving. You don't tell people that you are giving them power that they have already gotten through structural and technological changes.

Perhaps the greatest obstacle to empowerment today is downsizing, despite low unemployment figures. Although most workers remain unaffected by it, downsizing strikes fear into the hearts of all workers because it reminds them of the fundamental way in which they are totally powerless over their lives when business leaders act as if they are powerless to do anything but downsize. It would seem virtually impossible to empower people in organizations that do not make a strong commitment to keeping their workers employed through good times and bad. In their enthusiasm for downsizing, some companies may discover that they have demoralized workers who lack the security necessary to produce the creative and innovative products needed to be competitive in the world market.

The second requirement for empowerment in the workplace is a commitment by employers to go to great lengths to protect employees' jobs. For example, consider the case of Malden Mills. On December 11, 1995, the factory burnt down. Owner Aaron Feuerstein distributed Christmas bonuses. Furthermore, for the next three months he continued to pay his employees their full salaries while the factory was being repaired. If job security is related to empowerment, there is a sense in which Feuerstein's workers felt more empowered than those who took part in the AT&T and Xerox leadership programs that same year. One can write this off as old-fashioned paternalism, but I doubt that any company initiative could produce in employees the trust, commitment, and self-esteem of the employees at Malden Mills. Many companies try smoke and mirrors, but moral action is stronger and longer lasting than any therapeutic intervention. The great moral leaders of business choose moral commitment to people and society over economic efficiency. When they come out ahead, they demonstrate to other business leaders that when employees really are the most important resource, ethics really pays.

Empowerment as a Reciprocal Moral Relationship

When leaders really empower people, they give them the responsibility that comes with that power. But this does not mean that with less power, leaders have less responsibility. This point is often misunderstood. Perhaps one of the most ethically distinctive features of being a leader is responsibility for the actions of one's followers. For example, transformational leaders don't have less responsibility for their followers when they transform them; the followers have chosen to take on more. Couto offers a good example of a bogus empowerment relationship. Couto says he listened in amazement as a hospital administrator "told federal health-policy makers about her hospital's patient advocacy program that empowered low-income patients to find means to pay their hospital bills."[42] Is the administrator really giving people power, or is she simply unloading the hospital's moral responsibility on them? In the workplace, employees can only take full responsibility if they have the power and access to resources to influence outcomes. Empowerment programs that give employees responsibility without control are cruel and stressful. Authentic empowerment gives employees control over outcomes so that they can be responsible for their work.

When empowering employees, leaders must keep their promises. The best way to do this is to make promises that they can keep. When leaders empower employees, they need to be clear about the extent of that power and avoid the temptation of engaging in hyperbole about the democratic nature of the organization. An organization can always give employees more responsibility, but employees feel betrayed when they discover that they have been given less than the leadership's rhetoric implied. A leader who keeps his or her promises establishes the dependability necessary for trust.

Modern leadership consists of two ideals, trust and power, that often conflict with each other.[43] Trust has taken over from authority as the modern foundation of leadership. The moral concepts behind empowerment—responsibility, trust, respect, and loyalty—are reciprocal moral concepts: that is, they only exist if they are part of the relationship between followers and leaders. Like all the other moral principles that I have been examining in relationship to leadership and empowerment, they are related to truth and honesty. Honesty is one way to resolve the tension between power and trust. It is morally wrong to lie because lying shows lack of respect for the dignity of a person. This is why bogus empowerment is so devastating. Employees are made to feel foolish about falling for inflated claims and undelivered promises. Leaders lose credibility and respect because they have blatantly failed to respect their employees. Business leaders often overlook the reciprocal nature of these moral concepts, particularly the notion of loyalty or commitment. If leaders don't demonstrate in substantive ways that they are loyal and committed to their employees through good times and bad, they simply cannot expect employees to be loyal to them; and therapeutic interventions will be short-lived at best.

Last, if leaders are to establish a moral relationship with employees that allows for authentic empowerment, they need to think about reapplying constructively the traditional values behind empowerment. They must consider how to protect individualism even in team settings. Individualism has taken a beating by the communitarians in recent years, but there are some ethically important aspects to individualism, such as recognition and tolerance of difference and diversity.[44] Teamwork without tolerance of difference in opinion, gender, racial, or cultural background is unacceptable. Morally imaginative business leaders will challenge the dogma of instrumentalism and economic efficiency that sometimes mindlessly dominates all business decisions. It is difficult to say whether employees are more or less free on the job today then they were in the past. Though many are liberated from harsh physical toil and a dictatorial boss, others are caged in by competition, insecurity, and peer pressure. Empowerment means more than discretion on the job. It also requires freedom to choose and freedom from emotional manipulation.

To empower people authentically, business leaders have to be ready to overthrow some of the aspects of niceness. The truth is not always pleasant. It can disrupt the harmony of an organization and introduce conflict. When you really empower people, you don't just empower them to agree with you. Employees don't always feel good when they hear the truth, and leaders don't like to deliver bad news. As a result of the therapeutic fictions that are part of niceness, managers aren't forthright in their assessment of employees' work and teachers aren't forthright about the quality of their students' work. Assessment inflation makes people feel good in the short run, but it does not build the self-esteem necessary for empowerment in the long run.

I close with the notion of authenticity. Leaders cannot empower people unless they have the moral courage to be honest and sincere in their intention to change the power relationship that they have with their followers. If leaders want to be authentic about empowering people, they must first be honest with themselves. Too many leaders are not authentic. They talk about empowerment and participation and even believe that they are participatory, but in practice they lead in autocratic ways. Employees are "empowered" to organize their work, but when they do, management steps in and tells them how to do it their way.

James MacGregor Burns points to Franklin Roosevelt's decision to support the Wagner Act as an example of authentic empowerment. According to Burns, Roosevelt knew that the act gave a substantial amount of power to the people. He didn't necessarily like this fact;

84 Ethics, the Heart of Leadership

nevertheless, he supported the act.[45] Authentic empowerment requires leaders to know what they are giving away and how they are changing the relationship between themselves and their followers. This is the only way that they can commit to keeping their part of the empowerment relationship. It is difficult for leaders to give away their own power and even more difficult for them to take away power from others.

Leadership is a distinct kind of moral relationship between people. Power is a defining aspect of this relationship. Whenever there is a change in the distribution of power between leaders and followers, there is a change in the specific rights, responsibilities, and duties in the relationship. Both sides have to be honest when they make these changes and have to understand fully what they mean. Bogus empowerment attempts to give employees or followers power without changing the moral relationship between leaders and followers. Empowerment changes the rights, responsibilities, and duties of leaders as well as followers. It is not something one does to be nice in order to gain favor with people. Over the past fifty years business leaders have tried to harness the insights of psychology to make people feel empowered. These attempts have often failed and led to cynicism among employees because business leaders have ignored the moral commitments of empowerment. Without honesty, sincerity, and authenticity, empowerment is bogus and makes a mockery of one of America's most cherished values, the freedom to choose.

NOTES

1. James MacGregor Burns, *Leadership* (New York: Harper and Row, 1978), 13.

2. Richard Couto, "Grassroots Policies of Empowerment," paper given at the annual meeting of the American Political Science Association, Sept. 1992, 13.

3. J. Thomas Wren, "Historical Background of Values in Leadership," Kellogg Working Papers, 1996.

4. Charles Taylor, *The Ethics of Authenticity* (Cambridge, Mass.: Harvard University Press, 1991), 2–9.

5. James O'Toole, *Leading Change* (San Francisco: Jossey-Bass, 1994).

6. Norbert Elias, *The History of Manners* (New York: Pantheon Books, 1978), 53–55.

7. Immanuel Kant, "Idea for a Universal History with a Cosmopolitan Intent," *Perpetual Peace and Other Essays,* translated by Ted Humphrey (Indianapolis: Hackett Publishing, 1983), 31–32.

8. Elias, 9.

9. Gunnar Myrdal, *An American Dilemma,* vol. 2 (New York: Harper and Row, 1962), 1046–47.

10. Ibid., 1055.

11. David Riesman, *The Lonely Crowd* (New Haven: Yale University Press, 1950), 14–21.

12. Philip Rieff, *The Triumph of the Therapeutic* (New York: Harper and Row, 1966), 137. A similar point is made in Robert Bellah et al., *Habits of the Heart* (Berkeley, Calif.: University of California Press, 1985), chapter 2.

13. C. Wright Mills, "Crawling to the Top," *New York Times Book Review,* Dec. 9, 1956.

14. C. Wright Mills, *White Collar* (New York: Oxford University Press, 1951), 232–37.

15. William H. Whyte, Jr., *The Organization Man* (New York: Simon and Schuster, 1956), 6–7.

16. Ibid., 51.

17. Ibid., 54.

18. Sloan Wilson, *The Man in the Gray Flannel Suit* (New York: Arbor House, 1955), 14.

19. Thomas J. Peters and Robert H. Waterman, Jr., *In Search of Excellence* (New York: Warner Books, 1982), 105.

20. Roger E. Allen, *Pooh on Management* (New York: Dutton, 1994).

21. William C. Byham and Jeff Cox, *Zapp! The Lightning of Empowerment* (New York: Harmony Books, 1990); *Heroz: Empower Yourself. Your Coworkers. Your Company* (New York: Harmony Books, 1994).

22. "Confessor to the Board Room," *The Economist,* February 24, 1996.

23. Joseph C. Rost, *Leadership for the Twenty-First Century* (New York: Praeger, 1991).

24. *Telephony,* June 22, 1987, p. 15.

25. Annetta Miller and Pamela Abramson, "Corporate Mind Control," *Newsweek,* May 4, 1987.

26. Ibid., 6.

27. Ibid., 70.

28. *Venture,* March 1987, p. 54.

29. Two good studies of cooperatives are Joyce Rothschild and Allen Whitt, *The Cooperative Workplace* (New York: Cambridge University Press, 1986); and Edward S. Greenberg, *Workplace Democracy* (Ithaca: Cornell University Press, 1986).

30. For example, see Martin Carnoy and Derek Shearer, *Economic Democracy: The Challenge of the 1980s* (Armonk, N.Y.: Sharpe, Inc., 1980); and Gerry Hunnius, G. David Garson, and John Case, eds., *Workers' Control* (New York: Vintage Books, 1973).

31. See Carol Pateman, *Participation and Democratic Theory* (London: Cambridge University Press, 1970).

32. Robert E. Cole, "The Macropolitics of Organizational Change: A Comparative Analysis of the Spread of Small-Group Activities," in Carmen Sirianni, ed., *Worker Participation and the Politics of Reform* (Philadelphia: Temple University Press, 1987), 39–40.

33. Ibid., 40.

34. See Richard S. Johnson, *TQM: Leadership for the Quality Transformation* (Milwaukee: ASQC Quality Press, 1993).

35. Richard J. Pierce, *Leadership. Perspective and Restructuring for Total Quality* (Milwaukee: ASQC Quality Press, 1991), 11.

36. Ibid., 13.

37. Kimball Fisher, *Leading Self-Directed Work Teams* (New York: McGraw-Hill, 1993), 105–9.

38. "The Death of the Hired Man," in *The Poetry of Robert Frost*, ed. Edward C. Lathem (New York: Holt, Rinehart and Winston, 1979), 38.

39. Lionel Trilling, *Sincerity and Authenticity* (Cambridge, Mass.: Harvard University Press, 1972), 13.

40. This description comes from Michael J. Piore and Charles F. Sable, *The Second Industrial Divide* (New York: Basic Books, 1984), 282–307.

41. Anthony Sampson, *Company Man* (New York: Times/Random House, 1995), 260.

42. Couto, 2.

43. See Francis Sejersted, "Managers as Consultants and Manipulators: Reflections on the Suspension of Ethics," *Business Ethics Quarterly* 6, no. 1 (January 1996): 77.

44. Taylor, 37.

45. My thanks to James MacGregor Burns for this example and for his other helpful comments on this chapter.

5

Ethical Leadership, Emotions, and Trust: Beyond "Charisma"

Robert C. Solomon

I should begin by saying that I am a novice on the subject of leadership, but after fifteen years of research and consulting in business ethics, I have become convinced that morally sensitive leaders are the essential feature of any good organization. I have never been a leader—although one hopes that teachers and especially philosophy teachers might share a few of the attributes of leaders in terms of inspiration and impact—and I confess that even though I pride myself on my trustworthiness and loyalty, I have never been much of a follower, either. Too many leaders, as Voltaire complained of heroes, "are so noisy." Perhaps that is why I have never before delved into the subject as I should, for so much of what I have noticed about leadership is the noise.

Much of the noise has to do with the well-known but little understood phenomenon of Weberian charisma, the excited appeal supposedly generated and accordingly cultivated by leaders. Charisma, in other words, has much to do with emotion, but not just the emotion generated by leaders. It is also, first and foremost, the passion of the leader. It is strange, then, that the nature of emotion, the very heart of charisma, should have been so long neglected by leadership scholars. What has also been neglected, along with emotion, is the intimate relationship between emotion and ethics. This relationship speaks to several of the more controversial debates about leadership: the role and desirability of charisma; the nature of leadership itself; the dangers of evil leaders (the "Hitler problem"[1]); the nature of ethical leadership; and the nature of the relationship between leaders and the led. (I prefer the word "led" mainly by virtue of its length. I do not deny that following may be as active and autonomous a choice as leading, and in a sense, perhaps more so.)[2] In this chapter, therefore, I want to approach the topic of leadership by way of an often exciting but rarely analyzed set of connections: the connection between emotions and leadership; the connection between emotions and ethics; and, consequently, the connections among emotions, leadership, and ethics. To summarize, I would like to suggest that ethical leadership is essentially based on an emotional relationship, with the emphasis on charisma replaced by the much more mundane (but no less evasive) notion of trust. Whereas charisma is celebrated as a mysterious attribute of a leader, trust, obviously, is a relationship between a leader and his or her followers. The practical applications will, I hope, be obvious. The focus on leadership will bear fruit only if, unlike some lovelorn cowboys, we don't go looking for leaders in all the wrong places.[3]

THE ROLE OF EMOTIONS IN LEADERSHIP

Emotions are rarely the focus of discussions on leadership. When they are discussed, it is usually in terms of their arousal.[4] Emotions tend to be dismissed or ignored in almost every realm of "hard-headed" business, political, philosophical, and scientific discussion. Emotions, after all, are "subjective." They are, according to the popular prejudice, "squishy," "ineffable," "hard to get hold of." They are—because they are "inner" and "private"—unmeasurable. Answers to survey questions, by contrast, are readily quantifiable, easily subject to statistical analysis, and need deal with emotions only in an indirect way. ("Do you have confidence in the leaders of your organization?" "Do you approve of the direction in which the country is going?") By contrast, I would like to explore the role of emotions in a direct manner, in part through what one might call "phenomenology," an appeal to our shared experience. This does not mean that I am describing only my own emotions, nor does it mean that I think it worth placing too much faith on the much-touted "method" of "empathy" or *Verstehen* that has played such an enormous role in the history of anthropology and sociology. But what have emerged from my research on emotions over the years are the conclusions that many, if not most, emotions are cognitively and evaluatively rich and insightful, not the brute forces or mere "arousal" discussed by many theorists. In short, emotions are essential to ethics, and emotional sensitivity, rather than only rationality and obeying the rules, is what ethics is all about. Furthermore, emotions are largely socially constituted; not in their biological origins, perhaps, but in their aims, expressions, and nuances.[5] In terms of the present discussion, this means that emotions should be understood in terms of emotional relationships.

There are ordinary and extraordinary leaders, who often but not always correspond or fail to respond to ordinary and extraordinary situations. It is not surprising that much of the literature on leadership focuses on extraordinary leaders in extraordinary times: for example, Lincoln, Churchill, and Truman, to limit ourselves to three relatively recent Anglo-American examples. At such times (in the course of a civil war, a world war, the use of the first thermonuclear bomb), the emotions of all the world are extraordinary as well. Extraordinary emotions motivate and provoke extraordinary behavior, which in turn produces and provokes even more extraordinary emotions. In extraordinary situations, predictions are extraordinarily difficult to make, if only because the extraordinary is by its very nature also relatively rare. How people will behave in war, under fire, in circumstances in which their everyday bearings and sources of security and routine have been destroyed or rendered irrelevant continues to be a matter for extensive study, but the behavior of supposedly ordinary people is no less fascinating than the behavior of the most distinguished and extraordinary leaders.

But what do I know of the emotions of a Martin Luther King Jr., facing down the dogs and bullhorns of a well-armed and hostile Alabama police force? For that matter, what do I know of the emotions of those who stood with him, trusted him, confident in the face of their own fear that what they were doing was both important and effective? What can I imagine of the emotions of a Roosevelt or Churchill, a Stalin or a Mao, or, for that matter, a Reverend Moon or a David Koresh or their benighted followers? Accordingly, I want to approach the subject of emotion in leadership in rather ordinary situations. But by understanding such ordinary feelings and emotions, we need not pretend that we are easily capable of imagining or projecting ourselves into dramatic, tragic, or heroic situations that in fact lie quite beyond most of our experiences. That, I think, is part of the difficulty of understanding the greatest as well as the most evil leaders. What we tend to understand is just those aspects of their personalities that are most common, most like ourselves, most "human-all-too-human," as Nietzsche called it. The extraordinariness escapes our study. On the other hand, by examining ordinary situations, we can bypass such captivating but perhaps impossible questions as, Why can we not now find or produce an extraordinary leader of the ilk of a Lincoln, Churchill, or a Truman? One probable answer, of course, is that we do not want and will not allow for one.

But our society is filled with leaders—heads of departments, agencies, associations, corporations. It would be a mistake to dismiss them all as something less than real leaders, as mere "managers," because they do not have that sparkle and celebrity usually identified as "charisma." And so my focus will be on corporate executives and institutional administrators, university presidents and deans, cabinet ministers and trade union leaders rather than on heroes. What sorts of emotions enter into their success and failure? The too familiar reply is couched in terms of "cool": the lack of emotion, an imperviousness or immunity to emotions. In other words, the less prone to "emotional" behavior, the more effective the leader. (In Taoism, one is taught that lessened emotional involvement results in a more intuitive response, but, then, the Taoists did not believe in leaders.) First, I would like to undermine and utterly reject that viewpoint. Second, I would like to insist that a rich and energetic emotional life is very different from the rather unflattering notion of behaving "emotionally," that is, "out of control." Leadership intimately involves the former, not the latter.[6]

A dominant theme in the current literature is the search for an all-encompassing definition (paradigm, model) of leadership.[7] I am not interested in joining the search here, nor am I impressed with the use of singular "definitions" to analyze complex and ambiguous social phenomena.[8] But I would like to make a point or two about the underlying emotional themes that are to be found in virtually all of such attempts to define "leadership." I have highlighted certain terms that keep recurring. I have also retained the distinctively male references in brackets to remind us of how embarrassingly sexist the field has been. This is not incidental to my point, of course. The assumption that leaders are men (with distinctively "masculine" virtues) as opposed to women (whose "feminine" features almost inevitably include some form of sentimentality or supposedly excessive emotionality) explains, in part, why the emotions have been ignored in favor of such dispassionate notions as "influence" and bureaucratic "management skills." This also goes some distance in explaining, I would suggest, why the distinction between "leader" and "manager" has been so problematic in the recent literature. So long as leadership is defined instrumentally or simply in terms of change versus status, without explicit reference to and analysis of the emotions involved both in leading and in being led, the distinction is a negligible one, and leadership might be just as well reduced to the role of a mere "organizer."[9] I will come back to this point in a moment.

Consider the following definitions of leadership:[10]

1. "the ability to **impress** the will of the leader on those led and **induce** obedience, **respect, loyalty,** and cooperation" (B.V. Moore, 1927)

2. "an ability to **persuade** or direct [men]" (Reuter, 1941)

3. "authority **spontaneously** accorded [him] by [his] [fellow] group members" (C. A. Gibb, 1954)

4. "acts by a person which **influence** other persons in a shared direction" (M. Seeman, 1960)

5. "discretionary **influence**" (R. N. Osborn, J. G. Hunt, 1975)

6. "a [man] who has the ability to get other people to do what they don't want to do, and **like** it" (Harry Truman)

I have highlighted the terms "impress," "induce," "respect," "loyalty," "persuade," "spontaneously," "influence," and "like" because they all strongly suggest (though obviously do not entail) emotional evocation. To be sure, there are skills and techniques of leadership (whether learned or "natural"), but leadership is not just instrumentality, not just "getting things done." It is also *moving* people, in both senses of that term. It involves stimulating their emotions, and it involves motivating them. Burns is perhaps most explicit about this, and his terms "exploiting tensions," "raising consciousness," and "strong values" all suggest strong emotion. What are "strong values," for example? They are values deeply held, values that are deemed important, but also, therefore, values with enormous emotional significance. "Transactional" leadership is, for him, a highly emotionally charged and infectious process. So, too, even when Joseph Rost employs the much more modest terminology of "an influence relationship," we immediately want to know "what kind of influence," and some reference to emotions and affections is unavoidable.[11]

According to much of the recent literature, a leader is one who inspires and motivates, not just resolves or "manages." (The disdain heaped on the concept of "management" as a result of the search for "leadership" is a phenomenon that requires a detailed investigation of its own.) I think we might well distinguish between moral leadership and *moral leadership*, where the latter is truly inspirational and deeply emotional and the former is routine moral sensitivity. The latter may be what fascinates us, but the former, I would argue, is much more important for maintaining ethical organizations, institutions, and communities. To limit the honorific phrase "ethical leadership" to moral heroes is, again, to deny or demean what is perhaps most substantial to ethics and leadership, and no less based on emotion. More to the point of this chapter, however, one might notice that in terms of the above definitions, most of the emotions of leadership tend to fall on the side of the led, the "followers," rather than the leader. This suggests an unfortunate paradigm, one unhappily much in evidence in the behavior of any number of demagogues. They certainly provoke emotions, often violent and extremely effective and well-directed emotions, but they often evidence very little of those same passions themselves. Thus we should avoid the temptation to suggest that leadership does not so much involve emotions (that is, the emotions of the leader) as it does the emotional impact or effect of the leader on the led. This would reduce leadership to manipulation, perhaps even to creating appearances that affect followers, perhaps to mere "acting," and raise the question of authenticity. The emotions of leadership must, in part, be the emotions of the leader. He or she is not a puppeteer, a strategic manipulator of other people's feelings. He or she is, first of all, the subject of passions.

Leadership is the very opposite of "control," and to say that leadership is a matter of emotions is not to say that it is a matter of emotional control or, for that matter, manipulation either. Control is a quasi-mechanical term and, in human relationships, implies at the very least some sort of coercion, which virtually every leadership theorist has rightly distinguished from leadership. For example, leadership through naked terror—imperatives backed up by threats—is hardly leadership. Thus we do not think of those military commanders who threaten to shoot their own troops if they retreat as "leaders." So, too, "manipulating" emotions, as if they were circuits simply to be stimulated, is not leadership either. If Hitler had wholly relied on the Gestapo and threats of violence against his own people, or if he had only pressed the red buttons of prejudice against gypsies and Jews, his "leadership" would not be so problematic. He would not be considered a leader at all. But instead, he evidently did inspire real devotion and action, although the values he represented and the horrible results of his leadership haunt our use of this term.[12] Because emotions are often (mis)conceived as involuntary, appealing to people's emotions is too easily (mis)conceived as trying to control or manipulate them; thus our highly negative reactions to mawkish leadership pleas and overt appeals to our baser passions. But emotions occupy an intermediate and problematic position between straightforward, voluntary, rational decision making and the merely mechanical. For example, zombies and robots may be commanded to behave without reference to their "will," but we do not think of someone as a "loyal follower" if he or she is merely a zombie or a robot.

Thus we talk in politics as well as romance about "winning hearts." When Harry Truman defines leadership as getting people to do something they did not want to do initially and "liking" it, he is not conferring retrospective approval or necessarily any kind of enjoyment. Rather, he captures in the simplest language the idea that emotional behavior is voluntary behavior, and what leaders do with their followers is to "move" their emotions in the direction already passionately chosen by the leader. This choice, however, need not be thought out or fully understood (although one might argue, not always convincingly, that the more thought and understanding, the better the leader). This brings to the surface a rather difficult point about knowledge in leadership. It is often said that leadership is a skill or set of skills (which it certainly is) and that skills by their very nature require knowledge. This is so, but such "know-how" is not always articulated or propositional knowledge. Just as people need not know the direction in which they are being led, it does not follow that the leaders themselves know the direction in which they are leading. Hegel captured that lack of clarity in his stunning phrase "the cunning of reason." Tolstoy illustrated the thesis in detail in his unflattering treatment of the principals in the 1812 Napoleonic invasion of Russia and the battle of Borodino in particular. But "not knowing the direction" does not mean "in complete ignorance." The leader may well be "feeling his way along" or "following his intuitions," and his followers may know only that they trust him and are faithfully following. To be a bit polemical, we might say that too much is made of the role of knowledge in leadership and not enough of such emotional features as trust and loyalty. More plainly, knowledge (for example, managerial knowledge) is effective in leadership only insofar as that knowledge is in the service of the appropriate emotions.

That demand, that "knowledge be in the service of the appropriate emotions," is the beginning of an all-important answer to the most devastating challenge to the role of emotions in leadership. It is often noted that Hitler inspired at least as great devotion as Roosevelt and considerably more than Lincoln, and so the question is raised how one set of emotions can be judged superior to another. In ethics in general, this is often referred to as the problem of "relativism," that is, whether a set of values held sacred by a community is thereby right and proper for them, and beyond criticism from anyone else. This assumes that there are no common "non-relative" values, or, in the case of emotions, that there are no standards for emotion apart from those already contained within the emotion. But there are such common values, and there are such standards: social harmony and well-being, to begin with. Thus we might suggest a criterion to distinguish between effective but evil leadership and ethical leadership: the promotion of harmony and the public good. But these are not self-contained within a society, nor can they apply to one part of a society without including consideration of all other parts as well. "Us versus them" leadership, I would argue, always contains at least the potential for evil (although when an oppressed group is struggling against an oppressor group, this danger may remain invisible for some time). The "appropriate emotions," therefore, will be those that are conducive to these larger concerns as well as sensitive to the nuances of the current situation. An ethical leader, in short, is one who shares with his or her followers the emotions of fairness, mutual well-being, and harmony. In corporations, all of this might well be stated in terms of real concerns for "stakeholders" rather than the tempting but ultimately divisive focus on "the bottom line." In politics, it would be stated in terms of the urgency of winning elections. The "appropriate emotions" in ethical leadership motivate not the grudging decision to sacrifice profits or lose an election but rather the overriding passion to do the right thing.

FALSE LEADS: THE MYTH OF CHARISMA

"Charisma" is shorthand for the emotional power of certain (rare) leaders, but it is, unfortunately, without ethical value and, I argue, without much explanatory value either. It is one of the most frequently recurrent terms in discussions of leadership. Derived in its current usage from the German sociologist Max Weber, it is, perhaps, the only such term that so explicitly refers to the emotional quality of leadership, albeit at considerable cost to clarity, imbued as the term is with mystery and magic. It is also used at great cost to an adequate understanding of emotions, because the very notion of charisma connotes an irrational as opposed to a rational influence. Although Weber is noted for his analysis of institutions and bureaucracy in terms of "rationality," he himself was an ethical noncognitivist and viewed rationality and rationalization as a costly "disenchantment" with the world. At the end of his famous book, *The Protestant Ethic and the Spirit of Capitalism*,[13] he argued that rationalism is destructive of value, an "iron cage" in which both freedom and meaning are sacrificed to efficiency. One should not be surprised, therefore, that for him charisma offered a significantly religious promise.[14]

The Weberian term is defined by the *American Heritage Dictionary* as follows: "1.a. A rare personal quality attributed to leaders who arouse fervent popular devotion and enthusiasm. b. Personal magnetism or charm. 2. Theology. An extraordinary power, such as the ability to perform miracles, granted to a Christian by the Holy Spirit."

The theological dimension of the term is to be noted, especially in Weber's classic use of the concept, as is the idea that charisma is by its very nature "rare." Its nature does not invite analysis; in fact, it discourages it. Even careful analytic writers like Robert Nozick are reduced to such impoverished New Age metaphors as an "aura."[15] It will not do to take the nature of charisma as given, trying only to understand its use and effects.[16] The fact that it is rare (and "blessed") encourages gratitude and reverence rather than critical analysis, and its kinship to "magnetism and charm" tends to foreclose any meaningful investigation. Indeed, James MacGregor Burns warns that the "term is so overused it threatens to collapse under close analysis."[17]

Bernard Bass describes charisma as displayed by leaders "to whom followers form deep emotional attachments and who in turn inspire their followers to transcend their own interests for superordinate goals."[18] This is true, perhaps, but what are these emotional attachments? How do they work? What are their vicissitudes? The mysterious origins of charisma also invite a serious worry: What happens when this "blessing" turns into a curse and serves evil rather than good (the "Hitler Problem" again)? How do we know that the gift is from God rather than from Satan, except by the results?[19] Thus C. Hodgkinson warns, "Beware charisma,"[20] and Michael Keeley, in a powerful essay, attacks "transformational leadership" precisely on the grounds that it gives too much credence to charisma and too little to the Madisonian "checks and balances" that control or contain charisma.[21] Charisma, according to such authors, is a dangerous genie to let out of the bottle. But few of them pay much if any attention to what charisma actually is, leaving unanalyzed charisma's enviable status as "an extraordinary power" (if not exactly "the ability to perform miracles"), "a rare personal quality" of leaders "who arouse fervent popular devotion and enthusiasm."

I want to argue that charisma is not anything in particular. It is not a distinctive quality of personality or character, and it is not an essential implement of leadership. Rather, it is a misleading even if exciting concept that deflects us from the emotional complexity of leadership, which might better occupy our attention. Charisma is not a single quality, nor is it a single emotion or set of emotions. It is a generalized way of pointing to and emptily explaining an emotional relationship that is too readily characterized as fascination but should more fundamentally be analyzed in terms of trust. Within the range of what is usually identified as "charisma," I would want to make some distinctions.[22]

What the leader is saying. Is it the message itself that is fascinating? Steve Forbes smartly suggested a simplified "flat tax" at precisely the time that most American taxpayers were brooding over, struggling with, and hating the brain-twisting annual exercise called "filling out your 1040." It is not surprising that people were fascinated, and other candidates quickly adopted the idea. The attention Forbes received had nothing to do with charisma. Often a good idea—even sound common sense—will evoke sufficient emotion that the praise goes to the speaker when it is the idea that is really being endorsed. (Ross Perot's appearance in 1992 is probably a case in point.)

The rhetorical persuasiveness of how he or she says it. Martin Luther King Jr. was a brilliant orator, although that by itself is not what made him a great leader. More recently, Pat Buchanan, though more of a curmudgeonly televangelical than a voice of hope, has obviously found the "hot buttons" of a substantial portion of the American public. Rhetorical skills alone do not count as charisma, or many English professors would be leaders. Nevertheless, rhetorical skills certainly play a considerable role in what is called charisma. Such skills may make a mediocre message—and the speaker—much more memorable than the ideas themselves deserve.

The hopes, wishes, fears of the audience. Obviously, what gets said is fascinating not just for its own sake; it speaks to powerful emotions on the part of the audience. But this by itself says more about the receptivity of the audience than the character of the speaker—riling people up is not yet leading them. Yet, insofar as leadership is an emotional relationship that concerns the future, responding to hopes, wishes, and fears may well be interpreted as charisma by an appreciative audience. Paranoia, notably, produces some of the most "charismatic" leaders.

His or her degree of enthusiasm, "infectiousness." What is obviously an aspect of the personality of a leader is his or her ability to excite and transmit emotion, even against the initial resistance or opposition of others. A recent analysis of Franklin Roosevelt suggests "his remarkable capacity to transmit his internal strength to others."[23] Enthusiasm is certainly high up on the list of ingredients of charisma, and enthusiasm plus infectiousness takes us a long way to understanding what is meant by the term. Motivational speakers are often called "charismatic," but we should note again that this does not imply leadership.

Such personality traits as charm, intelligence, sincerity. Much of what passes for charisma is in fact some combination of much more easily understood character traits. "Charm" may be difficult to define (although literature abounds with some excellent witticisms, such as "charm is getting what you want without asking"). Much of John Kennedy's famous charisma was, no doubt, a combination of his straightforward charm and his good looks. Inevitably, a fascinating or comforting leader is characterized as "attractive," "sexy," "fatherly," or "motherly." (A concept that deserves some rigorous analysis is "presence." Although this term shares many of the problems of "charisma," at least it is rarely confused with magic. It is, for example, highly correlated with such mundane features as height.)

"Celebrity." These days celebrity is often confused with leadership, and it is celebrity, not leadership, that attracts the attribution of "charisma." But celebrity clearly requires no particular virtues or characteristics other than merely being much in the news, often on television, the butt of popular jokes and late-night humor, or being readily recognized. (Indeed, the talking heads who do nothing but read the news headlines on television are typically viewed as celebrities.) This is what Jay Conger calls "attribution." What does this have to do with leadership?

The nature of the situation or "context." Sometimes an individual who stands up or comes through in terrifying, dangerous, promising, or hate-filled circumstances may thereby get accepted as a leader (Boris Yeltsin facing the tanks is an apt example). This is not charisma; the circumstances, rather than any particular quality of the character in question, supply the aura of seeming greatness, at least for a while.

Change. Many leadership theorists (for example, Burns, Rost) note presiding over change as an essential ingredient in leadership. Whether this is so, being visibly "in charge" of change is itself often conflated with the dynamism of charisma. But, as in Tolstoy, there is always the question of where the action really is, in the leader or in the change itself. True, there is much to be said about managing change, and much to be debated about the ability of any leader to bring about change without the forces of society already mustered. But my point here is that the dynamics of change itself may be readily confused with the dynamic character of the leader.

Resemblance/continuity. On the other hand, sometimes charisma may be little more than continuity, a carryover, an echo of previous leadership or, perhaps, the result of an enduring myth or faulty memory. George Bush had enough seeming charisma to carry him through one presidential election, but it quickly became apparent that this was merely the fading continuation of the Reagan "magic." Harry Truman, by contrast, suffered from comparison with his great predecessor. Regardless of whether he had his own degree of charisma, he had to establish his reputation for leadership from a decidedly disadvantaged position.

What is called charisma may be some blend or mixture of all these different ingredients, and no doubt more besides, but that is not the point of this crude dissection. I suggest that charisma doesn't refer to any character trait or "quality" in particular, but is rather a general way of referring to a person who seems to be a dynamic and effective leader. And as a term of analysis in leadership studies, I think that it is more of a distraction than a point of understanding.

THE EMOTIONAL CORE OF LEADERSHIP: TRUST

Charisma distracts us from looking at the relationship between the leader and the led, and, in particular, the relationship of trust. The mistake is not so much that charisma is dangerous in the "wrong" leaders, but rather that it is a distorted perspective on leadership. The word "trust" appears in virtually every current book on leadership, and it is taken as a commonplace that without trust, leadership is impossible. This has not always been the case. Machiavelli, for example, suggests that leaders should strive to be feared, not loved. But trust is hard to analyze, and it is hard to say anything very useful about it. Francis Fukuyama has recently published a four-hundred-page book simply entitled *Trust*,[24] but one is hard put to find any discussion of the subject in those many pages. Fukuyama utterly ignores the dynamics of trust, the ways in which trust is created and cultivated, particularly between cultures and rival subcultural groups. Nevertheless, many of the examples of what Fukuyama calls "spontaneous sociability" are revealing.

Several standard definitions of trust (for example, N. Luhmann and B. Barber) characterize it primarily in terms of *expectations*,[25] but this is only half the story. It also involves decisions and the dynamics of a relationship. Trust, in other words, is an emotional relationship, as is leadership. Putting it more succinctly, leadership is an emotional relationship of trust.

Niklas Luhmann distinguishes trust from confidence, noting that we trust (or don't trust) people but have (or do not have) confidence in institutions. This points to an important distinction, but it does not yet reach it. The distinction between persons and organizations is convenient and obvious but often, especially in business and organizational ethics, misleading or counterproductive. Organizations and institutions have many features of persons (not least, that in the eye of the law they are persons, with fiduciary obligations, rights and responsibilities). As such, we trust them (or not) much as we would trust a person who had made us a promise or with whom we had agreed upon a contract. On the other hand, we sometimes have confidence in people we do not or would not trust; for example, bureaucrats who are known for their fairness and efficiency but are personally unknown to us. We may also have confidence in someone precisely because we do not trust him or her; for instance, when we place our confidence in the double-dealing habits of an old enemy, or "have confidence" that our friend M will fail to quit smoking this time as he has failed in every one of the last thirty-one attempts to do so. (This use of "have confidence" is not wholly ironic.)

The distinction that Luhmann is after has been stated by Laurence Thomas, among others, who distinguishes between trust and prediction.[26] We predict that something will happen. We trust that someone will do something. The distinction is between mechanism and agency, nature and persons. Trust, in other words, is not predicting that something will be the case. This, it seems to me, is fairly obvious, yet it has taken up a substantial portion of the literature (perhaps just because it is so seemingly straightforward). Here, I think, is where Luhmann is aiming us as well, although he mislocates the cleavage. Organizations and institutions are not mechanisms, no matter how efficiently (that is, "mechanically") they may be constructed. Organizations and institutions are people, working together. Those people, and consequently the organizations and institutions they create, are agents. Thus they have obligations, rights, and responsibilities. What they will do is not simply a matter of probabilities. It is a matter of trust. This is why the common-sensical notion (advocated by Luhmann and adopted by Barber) that trust is first of all a set of expectations is misleading. It is this, of course, but it is much more than this. Trust, as opposed to prediction or confidence, presupposes a relationship. And relationships by their nature involve much more than a calculation of probabilities and outcomes. They involve values and emotions, responsibilities and the possibility of not only disappointment but betrayal.

Trust is an umbrella term. It is not an emotion as such, although in certain situations it can manifest itself as a very powerful emotion, notably and most dramatically in the case of betrayal, but also in its positive display. One way of describing this feature of trust is to say that, by its very nature, it is part of the "background" of our social activities.[27] To say that trust is not as such an emotion is not, however, to remove it from the realm of emotion. Quite the contrary. Trust is the framework within which emotions appear, their precondition, the structure of the world in which they operate. Without trust, there can be no betrayal, but, more generally, without trust, there can be no cooperation, no community, no commerce, no conversation.[28] And in a context without trust, of course, all sorts of emotions readily surface, starting with suspicion, quickly escalating to contempt, resentment, hatred, and worse. Thus "trust" serves to characterize an entire network of emotions and emotional attitudes, both between individuals and within groups and by way of a psychodynamic profile of entire societies. (This is Fukuyama's theme in *Trust*.) In such large contexts, one might even say that trust is something of an "atmosphere," a shared emotional understanding about who is or who is not to be included, contracted, "trusted."

One reason to argue that trust is not as such an emotion is to get rid of the uncritical picture of trust as a "warm fuzzy feeling" of the sort so disdained by hard-headed ethicists and leaders of all sorts. Thus I would disagree with John Dunn when he argues that trust is a human passion or sentiment.[29] It is not, say, like compassion. It is not even an attitude. Not that I object to warm, fuzzy feelings. On the contrary, sentimentality can be a powerful (although easily exploited) quality of leadership and one that is often neglected in the more "macho" emphasis on charisma. But to think of trust as a particular feeling—not to mention a mawkish feeling—is to demean it and to give a misleading characterization of what trust entails. Trusting does not indicate a "softness," a gullibility, or a weakness. It is a strength, a precondition of any alliance or mutual understanding. It is not a vulnerability, except insofar as, by the very nature of the case, someone who is trusted is thereby in a position to betray that trust. And trust is, I would argue, necessarily a reciprocal relation. This is not to say that Franklin can only trust Benito if Benito trusts Franklin as well, but it is to say that trust is a relationship and not merely an attitude. If Franklin "trusts" Benito but Benito has no relation to Franklin, I am tempted to say that this cannot be a matter of trust at all, but rather predictability or confidence.

One might think of trust in negative terms, as, for example, a suspension of fear or a suspension of certain thoughts. However, although this notion captures an important insight (namely, that trust as such doesn't feel like anything in particular), it fails to capture the important positive dimensions of trust, because it fails to appreciate the nature and character of emotion. Put one way, perhaps too starkly, emotions are not feelings, except in the most generic and, for the most part, vacuous sense of that term (as any felt mental state or experience). Even anger, which would seem to be as profoundly "felt" as any emotion, is not just a feeling or even primarily a feeling. It is an attitude toward the world, specifically directed at a person, action, situation, or state of affairs. More accurately, anger is a systematic set of judgments—judgments of blame, especially—that cast their target in a particular role, put him or her on trial, consider him or her for punishment.[30] Trust, by way of this perspective, is a certain conception of the world and other people. It is a way of seeing, a way of estimating and valuing. Thus it establishes a framework of expectations and agreements (explicit or not) in which actions conform or fail to conform. A leader, one might surmise, is one who succeeds in establishing or sustaining a framework of trust. Indeed, perhaps the increasingly evasive distinction between attentive leaders and actively participating followers has not to do with the recommendation or initiation of actions but rather with the primary responsibility for such a framework.[31]

Trust can also be a decision. To talk about trust as background brings it dangerously close to something that is taken for granted, something that is either there or not there (Fukuyama's general assumption about "high trust" and "low trust" societies). But as we all know from our own experience, trust can be a very conscientious, extremely difficult, and deliberative decision. We meet someone new, or we find ourselves in a new situation with someone we do not know very well. Something comes up. Something must be done. We have to decide: Do we trust this person? In such cases, we establish a framework that was not in place before. Of course, there will be a more general framework within which this relationship and this situation takes place, and that general framework will influence and may well define the boundaries of the decision. One does not want to be too deterministic about this. Some of the most important trust decisions—in particular, decisions to trust a new leader—are made in defiance of an existing trust or distrust situation. But trust is not always in the background. Sometimes, such as when we have to decide whether or not to trust someone, it may be very much in the foreground. Indeed, it may be the definitive aspect of the situation. In leadership, the establishment of trust by a new president just taking office, for example, may be the most important factor in his or her success or failure.

But then, trust is also dynamic.[32] As such, it can clearly be talked about in terms of emotion, but I think upon examination it turns out to be something more than an emotion. It is more of a family of emotions, negotiations, deliberations, and decisions. For example, a woman has all of the evidence imaginable that her husband has been and is still being unfaithful. She refuses to accept that evidence, or, rather, she refuses to accept it as evidence and thus refuses to accept the obvious conclusion. One might glibly say that this is self-deception, a blatant attempt to refuse to recognize what she in fact clearly knows.[33] But I would argue that it can also be a conscious decision and not deception at all. It is not that the woman refuses to acknowledge (if only to herself) what she knows. It is rather that she has decided to trust her husband, regardless of his behavior (which can then be conveniently ignored or pushed to the side). So, too, I want to argue, whereas leaders may be said to earn the trust of their followers, it is the followers who have the capacity to give that trust. Trust thus becomes a part of the dynamics of the relationship between those who would be leaders and their followers, even when the leadership position is independently determined, as it usually is. (CEOs, supervisors, officers, deans, and college presidents—at least in Texas—are placed in their positions by such higher authorities as boards of directors and generals, not by those whom they are to lead.)

One problem in analyzing trust is a certain ambiguity, much of it due to the background-foreground contrast. But because trust covers so many situations, one is tempted to try to sharpen the edges and define trust in terms of its context or content. Thus Benjamin Barber distinguishes three different meanings of "trust" by virtue of the object or content of that trust: first, a general meaning regarding social expectations; second, a "competence" sense of trust, that one has the skills and knowledge to carry out one's responsibilities (for example, a doctor, an explosives expert, a White House economist); and third, a "partnership" or "fiduciary" sense, in which one is trusted to carry out certain duties or obligations, as a result of a certain relationship, usually by virtue of some commitment, contract, or agreement.[34] I find such distinctions troubling, mainly because I think that it is a problem to distinguish kinds of trust on the basis of trust's object or content, but also because one's obligations and one's expected competencies are usually correlated in a logical way ("ought implies can," says Kant in a phrase of admirable brevity). Furthermore, it is not clear in what sense the two "specialized" senses of trust are not just that—not different meanings or senses of trust but only more specific instances of trust in general. And, as if to underscore the problem of multiplying senses needlessly, much of Barber's book is spent criticizing alternative accounts of trust on the grounds that they conflate the latter two senses of "trust," which gets in the way of some of his genuinely interesting observations about trust in practice, in the family, in politics, and (in a less obvious sense) in business.[35] What he does not discuss, unfortunately, is the central role of trust in leadership (as opposed to politics) as such.

What I am suggesting is that different dimensions (not "senses") of trust be distinguished not on the basis of the object or content of trust, but on its social role, its role as an emotion, and its role as background. In many situations, paradigmatically in the primordial situation in which as infants we trust our parents, trust might best be considered part of the "background." It is present and taken for granted throughout in every transaction. It is not "at issue" and not in question. Often, such trust relationships are unrecognized as such, until, that is, the trust is breached. For example, banks have been the target of distrust and abuse by American populists and political activists since the last century. President Andrew Jackson even sought to outlaw them. And yet, the amount of trust taken for granted by anyone who has any business with banking at all is astounding. We trust that the money we deposit will be returned to us as promised. We trust that the bills and most checks we receive are valid and genuine. The fact that we ask for a "bank check" or "cashier's check" for absolute security is further evidence of our trust in banks, however great our distrust may be on some more abstract level.[36] And yet, we all have seen the consequences of even a minor bank scare. Not just that bank, but all banks, are suddenly under scrutiny, under suspicion.[37] Banking depends on trust—not as an issue, but as background. Trust has already been compromised once it has become an issue, once the question has come up, Is my money really safe in that bank? So, too, once a leader comes under suspicion, no matter that the charges against him may be malevolent and/or political, trust in him as a leader is already compromised. Thus the political effectiveness of raising the Whitewater issue, which proclaims itself to be a question of Clinton's character but in fact is intended to be and obviously has succeeded in casting doubt on his trustworthiness as a leader.

The emotional dimension of trust is more explicit, more dynamic. Here trust is an active relationship and transaction rather than the background of relationships and transactions. This is most evident when it is most in question; for example, at the negotiating table between two bitter and mutually distrustful enemies (the Bosnians and the Serbs, the Israelis and the Syrians). Trust here involves decisions. One decides to trust the other, however tentatively. It is here that the dynamic of trust gets really interesting, for even the slightest hint of betrayal can be met by the most awesome response. We can also witness the evolution or growth of trust, typically not in a single all-or-nothing decision but rather in incremental increases, although it may be generations before trust is sufficiently established to blend into the background. Sometimes, miraculously, mutual trust can just become a fact. Indeed, what I find most fascinating about trust is the human tendency to trust, despite all of the cynicism and suspicion to the contrary. Most people, in the absence of any clear warning or traumatic past experience, tend to be trusting. Trust in general is not so much an achievement as an assumption. It is the initial state rather than a result. People would rather trust than not (and, obviously, would rather be trusted than not). If this is so, it lends an interesting twist to all the current questions about a "crisis of trust" in American leadership. In a recent column, Alexander

Cockburn sagely suggests that this "crisis" in fact reflects people's resentment and distrust of pollsters and professors rather than of one another.[38] He also adds that the American people have always distrusted their leaders. Based upon my own reading, I believe this to be false, and so one is moved to ask what particular and obviously effective obstacles to trust are operative in the current political environment. Watergate and Vietnam have obviously worn out their explanatory power.

We talk a great deal about earning trust, but I would suggest that *giving* trust is a more promising avenue of pursuit. Earning trust is, ultimately, encouraging trust to slip into the background. Giving trust is a dynamic decision, the transformation of a relationship of the most basic and sometimes most difficult kind. This, I would suggest, is central to any conception of "transforming" or "transformational leadership," indeed, to any leadership at all. But this places an enormous burden on the led. Their decision to trust or not to trust makes leadership possible, and I believe much of the traditional talk about charisma as "a special quality" might better be viewed as the endowment or the projection of such a quality, by way of the people who then "find" that property worthy of following. When it is not part of the background, trust is something that has to be given. But for most leaders in most situations, certainly today, trust cannot be presumed to be part of the background. Thus they must make considerable effort in the name of earning people's trust, but earning usually entails desert, and the history of politics makes all too clear that life in politics is not fair. Ultimately, perhaps, in politics there is no such thing as deserving the people's trust. One is trustworthy, or one is not. One is trusted, or one is not. But whether or not trust can be earned, it can be wisely or foolishly given. Thus it is those who would follow, not those who would lead, who are the ultimate power in any leadership relationship.

CONCLUSION: WHETHER 'TIS BETTER TO BE LOVED OR FEARED

Whether it is "better to be loved or feared" is, of course, one of the more famous questions raised by Machiavelli in *The Prince*, and his answer was unambiguous. Better to be feared, he said, but what should be obvious, even within that grim framework, is that the emotional choices are woefully incomplete. One need not fear a leader to obey, nor need one love a leader to trust. Indeed, the extremes of emotion all too often tend to provoke the extremes of reaction, which Machiavelli clearly sees, and neither provides a very promising guide to leadership, much less ethical leadership. Charisma is designed to solve the problem by providing an emotional intermediary that salvages the power of fear and love but dispenses with the liabilities of both: the hatred generated by fear; the fickleness invited by love. But charisma serves this purpose only by introducing opacities and misunderstandings of its own. Thus I have suggested, albeit briefly, that trust would be a much better emotional vehicle for the discussion of leadership than charisma.

NOTES

1. Can an evil leader be an effective leader? It is tempting to reject the stipulative definition: that is, define a "leader" or a "good/effective leader" as an "ethical leader," thus stipulating Koresh and Hitler out of consideration. But making ethics a necessary condition for leadership simply begs the question, What distinguishes between good and bad (even evil) leaders? The second temptation to avoid is a pseudo-Weberian religious analysis, such that the quality of charisma, which is deemed essential to true leadership, is by its very nature "blessed." We know (as did Weber) that the voice of God seems to be heard by some very unlikely and unlikable ears. For a good discussion of this, see R. Heifetz, *Leadership without Easy Answers* (Cambridge: Harvard University Press, 1994).

2. One can often choose to be a follower without being chosen, but one cannot be a leader without being chosen, in some sense, to lead (even those who, in Shakespeare's phrase, have leadership "thrust upon them").

3. I have benefited from several excellent books in the field: Heifetz; Jay A. Conger, *The Charismatic Leader* (San Francisco: Jossey-Bass, 1989); and, of course, James MacGregor Burns, *Leadership* (New York: Harper, 1978).

4. For example, Heifetz, who begins *Leadership without Easy Answers* with "Leadership arouses passions," 13. Conger remarks, "They [charismatic leaders] touch our emotions," xi.

5. Robert C. Solomon, *The Passions* (New York: Doubleday, 1976; Indianapolis: Hackett, 1993).

6. The role of emotionality in leadership, as opposed to emotions, is complex. An interesting illustration is crying, an explicit display of becoming emotional. Senator Ed Muskie reputedly lost his bid for the Democratic nomination for the presidency when he cried at a press conference during the primaries. Jimmy Carter cried upon losing the 1980 election to Ronald Reagan; his act was treated with considerable disdain. Congresswoman Pat Schroeder cried in public about the same time, but reactions were more mixed, ranging from "just like a woman" to "crying shows strength."

7. See Joseph C. Rost, *Leadership for the Twenty-First Century* (New York: Praeger, 1991).

8. In fact, I would argue that the misguided search for definitions in the social sciences more often paralyzes than clarifies research. Precipitous attempts at definition distort and falsify both hypotheses and data and provoke debates that, by the very nature of the case, cannot be resolved before the research is well under way. The hidden model here, I believe, is that of Socrates, developed twenty-five hundred years ago. Socrates also searched by definitions, but he believed that a definition

would yield a "numenal" (almost mystical) insight into the true nature of reality. But without the fantastic metaphysics that accompanies this belief, the search for definitions is not much more than the naive, sophomoric demand that we "define our terms." The truth is that a proper definition comes at the end, not at the beginning of an intensive research program. Even then, it should be considered no more than a summary account of "work in progress." This applies to wholly technical, stipulative terms, and certainly to loaded historical terms like "leadership."

9. This language is particularly prominent in the work of James MacGregor Burns, who distinguishes between "transactional" and "transformational" leadership on this basis. There is a political sense in which the term "organizer," however, operates very much like "leader" and connotes the passionate "transformation" of a cause rather than coldly bureaucratic efficiency. Labor organizers, for example, would be a case in point, as opposed to the purely managerial 1934 E. S. Bogardus definition quoted by Rost: "Leadership is a process in which the activities of many are organized to move in a specific direction by one" (Rost, 47). See also Joanne Ciulla, "Leadership Ethics: Mapping the Territory," *Business Ethics Quarterly* 5, no. 1 (January 1995): 11.

10. I have taken the definitions from Ciulla and Rost.

11. At one point, Burns attacks Rost on the supposed need for consensus and comments that consensus erodes leadership. It is worth speculating why this might be so. Consensus is usually the outcome of negotiation and compromise, typically "cool-headed" rather than enthusiastic. Thus, we encounter a somewhat traditional philosophical question: Can such cool-headed reason motivate action, or does consensus, even though it may promote harmony and even efficiency, stifle the passionate urge to do something difficult, even seemingly impossible? In other words, does consensus undermine the emotional appeal of, as well as the need for, leadership?

12. Despite decades of denial, that the German people in general were fully knowledgeable participants in Hitler's vision is now generally believed. See, for example, Daniel Goldhagen, *Hitler's Willing Executioners: Ordinary Germans and the Holocaust* (New York: Knopf, 1996).

13. First published in 1904, it appeared in English in 1930 (New York: Scribner).

14. See Hans Gerth and C. Wright Mills, eds., "The Sociology of Charismatic Authority," in *From Max Weber: Essays in Sociology* (New York: Oxford University Press, 1946), 245 ff.

15. Robert Nozick, *Philosophical Explanations* (New York: Simon and Schuster, 1990).

16. See Conger.

17. Burns, 243.

18. See Ciulla.

19. Jim Jones and David Koresh are examples. If not for the ultimately lethal consequences, would such figures ever have been considered "leaders"?

20. Quoted by Edwin P. Hollander, "Ethical Challenges in the Leader-Follower Relationship," *Business Ethics Quarterly* 5, no. 1 (January 1995): 57.

21. Michael Keeley, "The Trouble with Transformational Leadership," *Business Ethics Quarterly* 5, no. 1 (January 1995): 67.

22. I should say here that I am indebted to Jay Conger's work on charismatic leadership, although my analysis is quite different from his and I do not give "charisma" the centrality that he does.

23. Robert Wilson, ed., *Character Above All* (New York: Simon and Schuster, 1996).

24. New York: Free Press, 1995.

25. Niklas Luhmann, *Trust and Power* (New York: John Wiley, 1980), 80; Benjamin Barber, *Logic and Limits of Trust* (New Brunswick: Rutgers University Press, 1983), 2, 71.

26. Laurence Thomas, *Living Morally* (Philadelphia: Temple University Press, 1989); Annette Baier, *Moral Prejudice* (Cambridge: Harvard University Press, 1994).

27. The concept of the "background" comes from Heidegger and his analyses of human practices in general, but it is also explained in a more analytic framework by John Searle in his book *Intentionality* (Cambridge: Cambridge University Press, 1983).

28. Of course, there can be banter and all kinds of "speech," but the number of "speech acts" that simply break down is mind-boggling, and not only those that depend on trust that the other person is telling the truth.

29. In Diego Gambetta, *Trust* (Oxford: Blackwell, 1988), 73.

30. I have argued this analysis of anger at much greater length in my book *The Passions* (New York: Doubleday, 1976; Indianapolis: Hackett, 1993), and in numerous articles, for example, "Getting Angry," in Richard Schweder and Robert LeVine, eds., *Culture Theory* (Cambridge: Cambridge University Press, 1984).

31. Burns, September 1996. "Empowerment for Change" (unpublished paper).

32. Thus, Dunn also insists that trust is a "modality" as well as a human passion. See Gambetta.

33. I have discussed this sort of self-deception as an active and necessary ingredient of social relations in "Self, Deception and Self-Deception," in Roger Ames, ed., *Self and Deception* (New York: SUNY Press, 1997).

34. The last definition follows Talcott Parsons, to whom Barber is obviously indebted. See Parsons on trust as a consequence of commitment in his *Politics and Social Structure* (New York: Free Press, 1969), 4.

35. Barber seems to conflate "trust" with "confidence," a distinction he borrows from Luhmann, who talks about trust in "the market."

36. The difference between practical trust and theoretical distrust is a fascinating topic in its own right, especially in leadership studies. It is often noted, for example, that Americans now claim to distrust their government at the same time that their demands and expectations of government are at an all-time high. Attitudes toward banks and banking—except for those rare eccentrics who prefer to keep their cash under the mattress—is another case in point. "In God We Trust" is printed on American money. The awkward truth, however, is that "In Government We Trust" is the necessary precondition of the value of any currency.

37. The Bank of New Zealand scare of 1990 threatened to undermine that entire economy, not to mention the current difficulties of the big Tokyo banks.

38. Alexander Cockburn, *The Nation*, February 1996.

Puzzles and Perils of Transformational Leadership

6

The Trouble with Transformational Leadership: Toward a Federalist Ethic for Organizations

Michael Keeley

Following the American War of Independence, a variety of local conflicts broke out within the loosely united states. New York taxed ships bound for New Jersey, which retaliated by levying lighthouse fees. Maryland fishermen fought Virginians over oysters taken from Chesapeake Bay. Moneyless farmers in Massachusetts banded together to stop courts from convening and sending debtors to prison. Such events brought state delegates to Philadelphia in the summer of 1787 to plan a new organization: a federal government to coordinate their joint affairs and protect their individual rights. The resulting plan, the Constitution of the United States, was shaped in large part by James Madison—who set the stage for the Philadelphia convention with a speech about a classic organizational problem.

Madison told the delegates that all societies were divided into different interest groups, or factions: "rich and poor, debtors and creditors, the landed, the manufacturing, the commercial interests, the inhabitants of this district, or that district, the followers of this political leader or that political leader, the disciples of this religious sect or that religious sect" (June 6, 1787; quoted in Padover 1953, 17–18). Madison went on to observe that throughout history different factions have tried to take advantage of one another: "In Greece and

Rome the rich and poor, the creditors and debtors, as well as the patricians and plebeians alternately oppressed each other with equal unmercifulness . . . . We have seen the mere distinction of color made in the most enlightened period of time, a ground of the most oppressive dominion ever exercised by man over man." Madison concluded that a key problem in designing a system of government was how to manage factional tensions, given the readiness of groups to pursue their own interests at others' expense.

Two hundred years later, this is still a key problem—in the management of governments, corporations, and organizations of all sorts. The general issue is how to deal with the diverse interests that are prevalent in any complex social system: how, for example, to reconcile the expectations of various lobbies, lawmakers, taxpayers, and other constituents of public agencies; how to satisfy the frequently competing claims of investors, employees, customers, dealers, and other stakeholders of private firms; how, more specifically, to control in-fighting among corporate divisions, to gain union cooperation in meeting foreign competition, to contain executive salaries and perks, to keep insiders from exploiting privileged information, and so on.

Lately, writers on management have voiced real concern about such things. In both popular and academic reports, a common complaint is that many of our organizations are going to ruin because those in charge have let private interests (their own included) run amok. Zaleznik (1989, 11), for instance, contends that "business in America has lost its way" due to mediocre management, whose major fault has been complicity in self-serving organizational politics as opposed to productive work. John Gardner (1990, 94–95) adopts a Madisonian perspective and sees "the mischiefs of faction" throughout the fabric of American society, which is at best "loosely knit, at worst completely unraveled"; to Gardner, "it is a mystery that [this society] works at all," as group after group pursues parochial aims and grievances in a "war of the parts against the whole." From a global standpoint, Bennis and Nanus (1985, 2) argue that "a chronic crisis of governance—that is, the pervasive incapacity of organizations to cope with the expectations of their constituents—is now an overwhelming factor worldwide."

What is interesting about recent attempts to deal with the problem of faction is that these writers, and many others, offer a cure that Madison in 1787 considered worse than the disease. The suggested remedy is a type of leadership that transforms self-interest and unites social systems around common purposes (often termed "transformational" leadership). So opposed was Madison to this prescription that he insisted on Constitutional devices to counteract it in the American system of government. The American experiment was to be a government of laws, not of men or women or charismatic leaders.

Perhaps Madison was shortsighted; perhaps his concerns have little applicability to nongovernmental organizations; perhaps they are no longer relevant at all. But possibly he recognized something important that has been overlooked by modern leadership theorists. The purpose of this chapter is to compare Madison's views and emerging theories of leadership, especially as these bear on the problem of controlling self-interested organizational behavior.

TRANSFORMATIONAL VERSUS TRANSACTIONAL LEADERSHIP

Much of the current interest in transformational leadership stems from a study of governmental leaders by political scientist-historian, James MacGregor Burns (1978). Burns differentiates two sorts of leadership: transactional and transforming. The more common, he notes, is transactional leadership. This involves the exchange of incentives by leaders for support from followers—in politics, for instance, jobs for votes, or subsidies for campaign contributions. The object of such leadership is agreement on a course of action that satisfies the immediate, separate purposes of both leaders and followers.

Transforming leadership, in contrast, aims beyond the satisfaction of immediate needs. According to Burns (1978, 4), "the transforming leader looks for potential motives in followers, seeks to satisfy higher needs, and engages the full person of the follower." Here, the object is to turn individuals' attention toward larger causes (political reform, revolution, national defense, etc.), thereby converting self-interest into collective concerns. The distinguishing feature of transforming leadership is a common goal; the purposes of leader and followers, "which might have started out as separate but related, as in the case of transactional leadership, become fused" (Burns 1978, 20).

Burns goes on to develop the basic normative theme of the paradigm: Transforming leadership is generally superior to transactional—indeed, the latter is hardly leadership at all. For Burns, transforming leadership is motivating, uplifting, and ultimately "*moral* in that it raises the level of human conduct and ethical aspiration of both leader and led" (1978, 20). A textbook example is Gandhi's elevation of the aspirations and life chances of millions of Indians who followed him toward independence. Transactional leadership, on the other hand, is characterized as immobilizing, self-absorbing, and eventually manipulative in that it seeks control over followers by catering to their lowest

114   Ethics, the Heart of Leadership

needs. Burns's examples of transactional figures include Tammany Hall bosses bent on trading political favors for preservation of the status quo. In Burns's view, transactional politicians are questionable "leaders" because they focus on mutually tolerable behavior, rather than jointly held goals—on means, rather than ends—and "leadership is nothing if not linked to collective purpose" (Burns 1978, 3).

This line of analysis has been extended to organizations by a number of theorists. Bass (1985) finds elements of transactional leadership at the root of popular organizational theories (such as exchange, expectancy, and path-goal models) and common management practices (such as contingent reinforcement and management-by-exception). These theories and practices imply that organizations consist of agreements between managers and subordinates to fulfill specific obligations for mutual advantage; they further imply that leaders should make these agreements even more specific in order to increase subordinates' satisfaction and performance. Bass argues, however, that any satisfaction or performance gains from transactional leadership are apt to be small. He claims that much larger effects are produced by "transformational" leaders, as suggested by Burns.

THE VISION THING

Bass builds on Burns's framework by identifying three main components of transformational leadership. The first and most important component, charisma, is displayed by leaders "to whom followers form deep emotional attachments and who in turn inspire their followers to transcend their own interests for superordinate goals" (Bass 1985, 31). The second component, individualized consideration, is shown by leaders who mentor and enhance the confidence of followers. The final component, intellectual stimulation, occurs as leaders arouse awareness of shared problems and foster visions of new possibilities.

Bass associates these three aspects of transforming leadership with extraordinary levels of effort and high degrees of organizational effectiveness. Though he stops short of insisting that transformational administrators are always more moral than transactional types, he follows Burns in portraying the former as true leaders who raise attitudes and behavior to a "higher plane" of maturity, the latter as mere managers mired in "compromise, intrigue, and control." According to Bass (1985, 187), transactional managers act like "everyone has a price; it is just a matter of establishing it"; whereas transformational leaders motivate individuals to put aside selfish aims for the sake of some greater, common good.

Other theorists have concentrated on particular features of transformational leadership. Conger and Kanungo (1988), for instance, try to give a more precise account of charisma as a dimension of leader behavior. The authors describe charismatic transformation as a three-stage process in which leaders first identify deficiencies in the status quo; second, formulate and articulate a vision of ideal goals that highlight present deficiencies; and, third, devise innovative means of achieving the vision. Throughout this process, charismatic leaders exhibit a variety of distinctive behaviors: They actively search out existing or potential needs for change, set bold (even utopian) goals, and employ unconventional or countercultural tactics. They build enthusiasm for their vision through symbols, rhetoric, and other forms of impression management. Finally, they set examples by performing heroic deeds involving self-sacrifice and personal risk (a consummate act being Lee Iacocca's taking charge of troubled Chrysler and reducing his first year's salary to one dollar). Conger and Kanungo hypothesize that these charismatic behaviors result in high emotional attachment of followers to leaders, high commitment to shared goals, and high task performance.

Though somewhat speculative, the approach of Conger and Kanungo is very representative of recent work on transformational leadership. In line with their approach, most theorists assume that charisma is a key aspect of the phenomenon (Howell 1988; Zaleznik 1989). Many recognize the same leader behaviors affecting organizational transformations (Kouzes and Posner 1987; House, Woycke, and Fodor 1988). Some researchers provide case studies of executives, like Iacocca, that demonstrate the general stages in the transformational process, as well as the special importance of a strategic vision (Tichy and Devanna 1986; Westley and Mintzberg 1988). Others offer empirical evidence for the motivational effects attributed to transformational leadership (Hater and Bass 1988; Howell and Frost 1989). The paradigm emerging from this work is now sufficiently defined that it is finding its way into mainstream texts on organizations (White and Bednar 1991; Ivancevich and Matteson 1993)—and transformational leaders are appearing as archetypes of good management in applied literature of all kinds, from business ethics (Camenisch 1986) to labor relations (Spector 1987).

ADMINISTRATIVE IMPLICATIONS

Among students of transformational leadership, there is hardly consensus on all issues, but there does seem to be broad agreement on the following basic ideas: It is a fact of organizational life that participants get preoccupied with their own aims and interests. This has certain negative consequences, such as unproductive conflict and depletion of resources. To avoid these consequences, it is necessary to unify organizational members by refocusing their attention on collective goals. This is no job for the faint of heart. Extraordinary leaders are required to transform members' self-interested tendencies—leaders who can create exciting visions, communicate these in compelling ways, and energize others to achieve them, despite personal costs. Bass (1990, 21) summarizes the administrative ideal: "Superior leadership performance—transformational leadership—occurs when leaders broaden and elevate the interests of their employees, when they generate awareness and acceptance of the purposes and mission of the group, and when they stir their employees to look beyond their own self-interest for the good of the group." The policy implication is that "transformational leadership should be encouraged" (25). Bass supplies examples. At the individual level, factors associated with transformational leadership "should be incorporated into managerial assessment, selection, placement, and guidance programs." At the organizational level, institutional constraints on managerial behavior should be reduced to allow transformational leaders more freedom of action: "Organizational policy needs to support an understanding and appreciation of the maverick who is willing to take unpopular positions, who knows when to reject the conventional wisdom, and who takes reasonable risks" (26).

Proponents of transformational leadership suggest that without it organizations are just marketplaces for self-serving transactions, subject to drift and disintegration. With no leaders to transform them, corporations become disabled by bureaucracy and mediocrity, because positions of authority fall to transactional managers who simply muddle through, much like their governmental counterparts described by Burns (1978, 405):

[They] grope along, operating "by feel and by feedback." They concentrate on method, technique, and mechanisms rather than on broader ends or purposes. They protect, sometimes at heavy cost to overall goals, the maintenance and survival of their organization because they are exposed daily to the claims of persons immediately sheltered by that organization. They extrude red tape even as they struggle with it. They transact more than they administer, compromise more than they command, institutionalize more than they initiate. They fragment and morselize policy issues in order to better cope with them, seeking to limit their alternatives, to delegate thorny problems "down the line," to accept vague and inconsistent goals, to adapt and survive. Thus they exemplify the "satisficing" model, as economists call it, far more than the "maximizing" one.

Who would want to settle for leaders of this type? Who would not find transformational leadership more interesting to study and more deserving of encouragement?

Possibly, James Madison.

THE FRAMERS' VISION

Many of the governmental practices that bother leadership theorists, such as James MacGregor Burns, are the legacy of Madison and the other framers of the United States Constitution. Burns, in particular, has very grudging respect for this legacy. In 1963, he characterized the American political process as *The Deadlock of Democracy*, an allusion to "the system of checks and balances and interlocked gears of government that requires the consensus of many groups and leaders before the nation can act" (6). Burns states that this system exacts a "heavy price of delay and devitalization" and that it was "designed for deadlock and inaction" from the start—by Madison and those delegates to the Constitutional Convention who shared his fear of strong leadership.

The framers' implicit theories of leadership, however, were far from naive; and their explicit plan of government, with all its interlocking checks and balances, was not irrational. The framers were people of practical affairs—planters, lawyers, traders, above all politicians—and so, perhaps, transactional leaders in Burns's terms. Yet they were also educated people, who were aware of the heights to which leaders could aspire in the ideal world of political theory. They obviously never read John Gardner or used the jargon of transformational leadership. But they read similarly inclined writers, like Plato; they knew of related protagonists, like philosopher-kings. And they rejected the lot.

What's more, the framers shied away from transformational leadership knowing, firsthand, maybe the finest example of it. At their meeting in Philadelphia, they drafted their plan of divided government under the supervision of one of the most revered leaders in history. Look for a moment at the background of the convention's chief executive.

CHIEF EXECUTIVE OF THE CONVENTION

The unanimous choice to preside over the Constitutional Convention was George Washington—father of the country, symbol of virtue, and a larger-than-life monument even in 1787 (Cunliffe 1982). Much of Washington's fame stemmed from his ability to transform a fractious lot of rebels into a victorious army in the American War of Independence. No small feat: Rank-and-file Americans were not eager to risk *their* lives and fortunes fighting for the sacred honor of Congress. Volunteers from some states wanted nothing to do with militia from others. Farmers and merchants were reluctant to take Continental currency and provide food or supplies to Washington's forces. His staff included quarrelsome, treasonous, and simply useless officers. (Short of good officers, for instance, Washington had a surplus of unemployed European officers sent by friends abroad; Morison (1965) notes that, "since Americans disliked serving under foreigners, there was nothing for most of them to do except serve on Washington's staff, and tell him in French, German, or Polish as the case might be, that his army was lousy" (230).

Washington's army lost most of the battles, yet somehow won the war. Flexner's (1967) account of Washington's behavior as commander in chief describes a transformational leader in every sense of the term. From the outset, Washington displayed heroic acts. Upon accepting command of the Continental Army, he informed Congress that he would take no salary, a selfless and inspiring gesture in an age when it was customary for military officers to enrich themselves at public expense. (Two centuries later, Iacocca's deferral of compensation at Chrysler seems cheap by comparison). Throughout the war, shortages of money and equipment drove Washington to devise unconventional means of motivating his troops. British and other professional soldiers of the time were paid to carry out orders without concern for what the struggle was all about—European kings and generals did not want their armies thinking about which way to point their weapons! Lacking the funds to employ such compliant professionals, Washington united and motivated a bunch of rugged individualists by refocusing their attention on higher ends: "Washington labored to inspire his soldiery with confidence in the value and the nobility of the cause" (Flexner 1967, 542–43). This military innovation—encouragement of combat by appeals to nationalism—transformed not only the Continental Army, but the very nature of modern warfare.[1]

Such was the man selected to serve as president of the Constitutional Convention. If ever there existed a role model of transformational leadership, here it was right in the midst of the delegates as they went about designing a system of government.

What's interesting is that the framers recognized and appreciated individual greatness—but they refused to count on it. Despite the pressing social problems that brought them together, they decided not to bet their future, and ours, on model leaders like George Washington. Rather, they chose to protect us from the misdeeds of scoundrels and the frailties of ordinary men and women. The fates of nations whose political systems are more open to strong leadership (say, China or the former Soviet Union) suggest that the choice was a fortunate one. The historical record suggests it was also an informed choice.

MADISON'S PLAN

Madison's analysis of the issues is the most famous. Recall his opening point that all societies are divided into different interest groups or factions: rich and poor, debtors and creditors, inhabitants of various regions, disciples of one religion or another, followers of this leader or that, and parties to all sorts of commercial dealings. These factions tend to pursue their own welfare at others' expense, resulting in conflict. Unless managed in some way, conflicts get settled by force: Policies are made by those with the most power at the time. This leads, ultimately, to injustice and instability. How, then, to manage factional conflict and minimize its potential for harm?

In *Federalist* No. 10, Madison examined alternative strategies. According to Madison, there are two ways of curing the mischiefs of faction: one, by removing its causes; the other, by controlling its effects. There are, in turn, two ways of removing the causes of faction: the first, by suppressing the freedom of persons to advance their own interests; the second, by persuading persons to share the same interests.

Madison questioned both methods of avoiding the causes of faction. The first, denying personal freedom, he considered unwise. It stifles initiative, destroys political life, and is even worse for individuals than the condition it is meant to remedy. The second, inducing common interests, Madison considered impractical. Although some people may share some interests for some time (for instance, the coalition of militants who waged the American War of Independence), commonality of purpose is fragile at best (as shown after the war, when those who fought and wound up impoverished turned against those who profited). Madison argued that, if nothing else, the varying abilities and fortunes of individuals will divide them into haves and have-nots, whose interests diverge in matters of social policy. He added that "different leaders ambitiously contending for pre-eminence and power" will be more apt to inflame and exploit such societal divisions than to reconcile them. Madison, therefore, opted to control the effects of faction, instead of its causes. He proposed to use government to help factions check and balance one another, thus limiting the capacity of the strong to take advantage of the weak.

In subsequent *Federalist* papers, Madison explained how the framers' plan of government would handle the effects of faction. A key feature of this plan is division of governing powers among autonomous, semi-functional bodies: a federal executive, legislature, judiciary, and their state counterparts. These bodies are not tied to any given social interests but represent all kinds of constituents (a departure from prior "mixed" regimes, whose institutions represented kings, lords, and commoners). Their functions are not cleanly separated, but different bodies and branches of government compete in similar activities, such as lawmaking (Huntington 1981). Most importantly, throughout the system, authority is not centralized—nor merely decentralized—but power is noncentralized. Decentralization, as in "organic" types of organizations, implies an ultimate authority who delegates, at pleasure, responsibility to others. In contrast, noncentralization of authority, as entailed in the American political system, means that power is diffused and shared, by right, among independent agents (Elazar 1981). These independent agents of government are, at the same time, the dependent agents of private interest groups.

The basis of the system is what Dye (1990) calls "competitive federalism": rivalry among federal, state, and local units of government to offer constituents better services at lower perceived costs. In the framers' scheme, government was designed to manage factional interests much as a market responds to consumer preferences—through enterprising public officials, of whom there are many thousands elected or appointed to offices and agencies at various levels of government. These federal, state, and local officials exchange their political influence and expertise for the support of particular groups, thereby advancing both their own careers and the causes of their constituents. A neglected group creates an opportunity for officials to build a base of support or add to their current base. A dissatisfied group can shift allegiance to numerous contenders for it. In theory, then, virtually any interest group has a way of achieving representation, but no one group is likely to capture enough centers of power to subjugate opponents.

In sum, the framers' task was to "enable the government to control the governed; and in the next place oblige it to control itself" (*Federalist* No. 51, 322). The trick was to preclude tyranny, which Madison equates with the accumulation of power in the same hands—whether few or many, whether self-designated or elected. Consolidation of power, or tyranny, he says, cannot be prevented by formal, legal restrictions, by mere "parchment barriers," but only by "rival and opposite interests." So, the framers set about dividing power, devising checks and balances. Power was first divided between "two distinct governments," state and federal, which vie to control one another. Within each government, power was then subdivided among "distinct and separate departments," which have wills of their own, stemming from the desires of member-officials to maintain or enlarge their personal authority. Madison commented that "ambition must be made to counteract ambition.

The interest of the man must be connected with the constitutional rights of the place. It may be a reflection on human nature that such devices should be necessary to control the abuses of government. But what is government itself but the greatest of all reflections on human nature? If men were angels, no government would be necessary" (*Federalist* No. 51, 322).

Further divisions were created, Madison continues, because "it is not possible to give each department an equal power of self-defense" against encroachments by others. (Because Congress was considered likely to dominate, for example, federal legislative power was divided again between two houses.) Still other checks and balances, such as an executive veto, were added as backup devices for preserving, in practice, the departmental independence prescribed on paper.

This compounding of separations has seemed excessive to some critics (for example, Dahl 1956; Burns 1963; Sundquist 1986), who complain that it weakens national resolve, hampers unified action, or thwarts majority wishes. But Madison and the framers accepted consequences of this sort in order to avoid more serious ones. Their constitutional system was arranged to protect individuals in minority factions from being bulldozed by members of majority factions bent on pursuing some alleged common goal. In this regard, the framers—and Madison especially—showed insights into social behavior and ethics that elude modern advocates of transformational leadership.

MADISONIAN AND
TRANSFORMATIONAL-LEADERSHIP MODELS
COMPARED

To better appreciate Madison's approach, compare his views of human nature with the motivational assumptions of transformational leadership as outlined by Burns (1978). Like Madison, Burns begins with conflict, which provides the "seedbed" of leadership: "Every person, group, and society has latent tension and hostility. . . . Leadership acts as an inciting and triggering force in the conversion of conflicting demands, values, and goals into significant behavior" (Burns 1978, 38). In this process, leaders can appeal to a variety of motives for cooperation. The type of motive triggered is critical, argues Burns. Here he invokes a theory of psychological development borrowed, in part, from Freud, Maslow, Kohlberg, and others—which, all together, looks a lot like Herzberg's (1966) two-factor theory of motivation.

Burns differentiates "lower" needs, such as physical survival and economic security (similar to Herzberg's hygiene factors), from "higher" needs, such as moral purpose and "participation in a collective life larger than one's personal existence" (similar to Herzberg's motivators). The lower needs are addressed by transactional leaders, who may at best defuse conflict by meeting the parochial demands of their different constituents. The higher, more "authentic" needs are engaged by transforming leaders who can refocus attention—with much greater effect—on common goals that have transcendent value. The greater the goal, the greater the energizing force: "The leader who commands compelling causes has an extraordinary potential influence over followers. Followers armed by moral inspiration, mobilized and purposeful, become zealots and leaders in their own right" (Burns 1978, 34).

Madison could have accepted most of this; he was certainly not ignorant of the transforming potential of leadership. But he thought beyond it, to the problems that zealots—armed by moral inspiration, mobilized, and purposeful—might create for persons who disagreed with them. Madison concentrated on a fact about human motivation that proves troublesome for transformational-leadership theories: Not everyone is attracted to the same goals or leaders. This fact has been well established by research on both motivation and leadership. Not all workers, for example, are motivated as Herzberg and Burns suggest; some (especially academics and other professionals) do appear to be driven by "higher" needs and transcendent goals, but others seem to prefer fulfillment of the bread-and-butter flavor (Schein 1980; Steers and Porter 1987). With respect to leadership, even champions of the transformational approach acknowledge the fact of individual differences, that "some employees may not react well to a leader even though most view the leader in a positive way and as transformational" (Avolio, Waldman, and Yammarino 1991, 15). To Madison, such individual differences make all the difference in the world.

Madison reminds us that, because people differ, minority ideas about the value of particular goals and interests are likely to exist within large social groups—even where leaders are able to transform many individual views into a majority vision. In a letter to Thomas Jefferson soon after the Constitutional Convention, Madison wrote that popular theories supposed "that the people composing the Society enjoy not only an equality of political rights; but that they have all precisely the same interests, and the same feelings in every respect" (October 24, 1787; in Padover 1953, 40–41). Were this really the case, Madison noted, "the interest of the majority would be that of the minority also; [public policy] decisions could only turn on mere opinion concerning the good of the whole, of which the major voice would be the safest criterion." But, he pointed out to Jefferson, "no society ever did or can consist of so homogeneous a mass of Citizens." Madison cited his famous examples of different economic interests (rich and poor, farmers and merchants, etc.) and differences of belief (political, religious, and so forth), emphasizing that these persistent distinctions matter very much to ordinary people if not to social theorists. "However erroneous or ridiculous these grounds of dissension and faction may appear to the enlightened Statesman or the benevolent philosopher," Madison says, "the bulk of mankind who are neither Statesmen nor Philosophers, will continue to view them in a different light. It remains then to be enquired whether a majority having any common interest, or feeling any common passion, will find sufficient motives to restrain them from oppressing the minority."

Here we come to the crux of things. If not all social participants have the same goals, if transformational leaders are not able to persuade everyone to voluntarily accept a common vision, what is the likely status of people who prefer their own goals and visions? Judging from the rhetoric of management experts like Bennis (1989)—who complain of individuals marching stubbornly to their own drummers—or communitarian writers like Etzioni (1988)—who sound alarms about persons selfishly asserting their rights against society—it may be perilous indeed. Nonconformists have been targeted for criticism by leadership theorists since Plato (see his *Republic*), and many have been subjected to real injury by historical leaders with single-minded majorities on their side. (A brutal illustration is the persecution of Chinese dissidents in the Cultural Revolution inspired by Mao Zedong, one of James MacGregor Burns's transforming heroes.)

Madison posed to Jefferson: What if two persons share an interest that is disagreeable to a third; would the rights of the third be secure if decisions were left to a majority of the group? "Will two thousand individuals be less apt to oppress one thousand or two hundred thousand one hundred thousand?" (October 24, 1787; in Padover 1953, 41). What, after all, will stop majorities from taking advantage of anyone who opposes them? Madison considers possible restraints, such as concern for the public good, fear of negative public opinion, and personal moral standards. He rejects each as ineffective: The public good is no use, because majorities (and their leaders) define it for themselves. Similarly, public opinion supports their actions, by definition. And personal morality falls victim to groupthink: "The conduct of every popular Assembly, acting on oath, the strongest of religious ties, shews that individuals join without remorse in acts against which their consciences would revolt, if proposed to them separately in their closets" (42).

The conclusion drawn by Madison is a flat-out repudiation of transformational leadership. He reasons that, if differences in individual interests exist within society, and if a majority united by a common interest cannot be restrained from harming minorities, then the only way to prevent harm is to keep majorities from uniting around common interests—the reverse of what transformational leaders are supposed to do. In other words, unless leaders are able to transform everyone and create absolute unanimity of interests (a very special case), transformational leadership produces simply a majority will that represents the interests of the strongest faction. Sometimes this will is on the side of good—as in Gandhi's case. Sometimes it is on the side of evil—as in Hitler's. In any case, might is an arbitrary guide to right, as Madison clearly understood.

This, then, is why the Madisonian system of government divides power and purpose, why it frustrates majority wishes, and why it checks leadership in the pursuit of "collective" goals. It was designed to work this way in order to protect the basic interests of the weak from the self-interest of the strong. Without such protection, any response to the problem of faction is no solution: Social life can remain as imagined by Burns and others who would transform it—dog eat dog.

ORGANIZATIONAL IMPLICATIONS

Warren Bennis, a veteran observer of organizational leadership, sounds a familiar theme. Asking *Why Leaders Can't Lead* (1989, 40), Bennis points to increasing selfishness in American society and organizations. He notes that "everyone insists on having his or her own way now," from young urban professionals, to corporate executives, to the president of the United States. The trouble is that there is no agreement or commitment to the public good, no common vision, no mutual purpose:

As the world has divided into factions, so has America, and so consensus is harder and harder to come by. Each faction marches stubbornly to its own drummer, has its own priorities and agenda, and has nothing in common with any other faction—except the unbridled desire to triumph over all the others. The Peruvians call this *arribismo*. It means, "You've got yours, Jack, and now I'm going to get mine." It means "making it," carried to the *n*th power. This fragmentation and fracturing of the common accord occurred for good reason, because, in America, those on top have traditionally tried to keep everyone else down, but it makes leadership a chancy undertaking at any level. (Bennis 1989, 144)

Bennis's solution: "People in authority must develop the vision and authority to call the shots" (154).

Huh? Entrust those greedy individuals on top with even greater power to pursue "the common good" as they envision it? In fairness to

Bennis, there's a bit more to his argument; but it's difficult, in theory, to get from selfish public and corporate officials to selfless transformational leadership—perhaps even harder, in practice. Madison foresaw this. Moreover, his view is just as applicable to "private" organizations as governmental ones, because the same problems arise in their design. Among the most fundamental are problems of controlling factions and ambitious leaders.

THREATS POSED BY LEADERS

Madison suggests to us that in any kind of social system, inspired leadership can do as much harm as good. Lately, journalists and insiders have documented ample damage done by corporate folk-heroes once hailed as transformational leaders (such as F. Ross Johnson, who led barbarians to the gate at RJR Nabisco [Burrough and Helyar 1990]). Some advocates of transformational leadership allow that there is a "dark side," that the risks can be as large as the promises (Howell and Avolio 1992). Yukl (1989) remarks that history is full of charismatic leaders who caused death, destruction, and misery or who ruled over firms like tyrants and egomaniacs. However, Madison remains exceptional in taking the matter seriously.

In proposing social structures that would impact people's daily lives, Madison recognized a responsibility to build in protections against abuses of power. Contemporary leadership theorists are more inclined to shrug off the issue—and to depict protective devices (for example, checks and balances and right-conferring rules) as bureaucratic hindrances that reduce the autonomy and transforming potential of leaders. Bass (1990, 24–25), for example, grants that some transformational leaders have "authoritarian tendencies," that "some fulfill grandiose dreams at the expense of their followers;" yet, he still prescribes more "flexible" organizational structures to encourage determined leadership. Others offer timid advice to treat transformational leadership with caution. Roberts and Bradley (1988) compare charisma to an unpredictable genie in a bottle; they ask whether it should be set free to transform organizations; then, they leave the question hanging. Howell and Avolio (1992) go a bit further and urge top managers to screen corporate leaders more carefully to weed out unethical charismatics; but they fail to indicate just what to screen for, how to control those doing the screening, or what to do about opportunists who slip through the net. Howell and Avolio hold out a lot of hope for voluntary ethical codes and executives who function as positive role models. Although such things are not necessarily worthless, Madison knew enough not to rely on them. He felt that flesh-and-blood persons who might suffer from misconduct by public officials deserved better than parchment barriers and hypothetical defenses. Persons vulnerable to corporate officials do too.

But Madison's challenge goes far beyond showing the dangers of charismatic leaders, or the moral obligation to control them. It cuts to the very heart of transformational leadership theories, to the value of collective goals. Individuals are at risk, Madison argued, not only from self-interested leaders but from self-interested majorities acting in the name of some "common purpose." In modern organizations, no less than in the colonial assemblies of Madison's experiences, focused groups can act in ways that their members would not dream of, alone in their closets.

THREATS POSED BY FACTIONS

Grenier (1988) tells a relevant story of a company named (really) Ethicon. A suture-making subsidiary of Johnson & Johnson, Ethicon built an innovative plant in New Mexico that was designed to "de-bu-reaucratize" the work environment: Jobs were organized around teams—quality circles—in a flexible, participative organizational structure. "The designers of the Ethicon work environment were trying to present a new vision of work in contemporary America, a vision of unity, cooperation, purpose, and inspiration" (xiii).

Grenier studied teams in operation and found some grim facts behind the vision. In Ethicon's explanation of quality circles to employees, "the concept was likened to a sports team, where all participants worked together for a common goal and had a voice in how that goal would be reached" (Grenier 1988, 26). In theory, company supervisors (the team coaches) served as facilitators of communication, and workers discussed means of achieving production goals, including decisions about hiring, firing, evaluating, and disciplining other team members. In reality, "many workers referred to the team system as the 'rat system'" because it pit workers against one another to root out "counterproductive behavior." Counterproductive behavior turned out to be any expression of discontent with Ethicon or support for the Amalgamated Clothing and Textile Workers Union, which began an organizing campaign soon after the plant opened. A key issue among union supporters was their low wage in New Mexico, compared to company workers elsewhere. For Ethicon, the lower wage was a reason for locating in New Mexico in the first place, and a reason for trying to stay nonunion.

From the start, Grenier reports, management carefully screened employees to select "team players" and exclude union sympathizers. A subsequent strategy used teams to control workers who developed pro-union attitudes. The team strategy relied on peer pressure "to deprive the pro-union employees of status and identify them as losers" (Ethicon psychologist, quoted in Grenier 1988, 90). Facilitators were trained not only to bring "negative attitudes" to the group's attention in team meetings, but to encourage the anti-union majority to denounce their pro-union colleagues (with remarks like, "If you're not happy with the company, why don't you resign? If it were up to me I'd fire you" [77]). Workers singled out for public censure compared the feeling to being attacked by a pack of wolves; and some union activists were, indeed, fired. According to Grenier, such things went on because facilitators won approval from management, team members in turn won recognition from facilitators, and new hires won acceptance from the group by showing support for the company. Seeing the fate of "losers," the majority of workers just conformed. "The issue was who had the power to do more for the workers, and management had convinced most of the workers that management could do more, good and bad, than the union" (Grenier 1988, 147).

In the end, the pro-union minority lost the election (141–71). The victors gloated. And their opponents filed unfair-labor-practice charges (some of which were later settled in favor of union supporters discharged or denied jobs during the campaign).

The moral of the story is that Ethicon's efforts to achieve unity of purpose produced, instead, a sharply divided workforce motivated by fear. Ethicon's approach was to eliminate the causes of faction (1) by enlisting persons to share the same interests and (2) by suppressing dissent among those who failed to go along—the very cures that Madison said were worse than the disease. And the result, as Madison might have predicted, was not the peaceful absence of conflict, but a bitter truce between the victorious majority and a resentful, powerless minority.

TOWARD A MADISONIAN VIEW OF ORGANIZATIONS

What, if anything, might reduce this type of conflict and improve such an organization? Consider typical prescriptions of Burns, Bass, and Bennis.

Might a transformational leader help to inspire more commonality of purpose? Possibly—but, practically, leaders are unlikely to transform everyone, as noted earlier. In organizations like Ethicon, transformational leaders are liable to intensify commitment of the malleable majority. They are less apt to motivate a wary minority to give up their economic concerns for the sake of "higher" organizational goals. Consequently, a transformational leader could win high approval ratings, among most followers (as Bass claims), yet inspire little tolerance for different views, and actually incite more factional conflict (as Madison warned).[2]

Nonetheless, might a flexible organizational structure help to enhance opportunities for uplifting leadership to emerge? Possibly—but, ethically, this is risky. It also expands opportunities for exploitation by authorities, not to mention garden-variety capriciousness. It was precisely a flexible, antibureaucratic work environment that freed management from restrictive rules and enabled them to dole out jobs, perks, and pink slips to manipulate the work force at Ethicon.

Might, then, an institutional ethical code help to protect individuals against unprincipled leaders? Possibly—but, realistically, this is a thin line of defense, as Ethicon workers found out. It so happens that the Johnson & Johnson family of companies is famous for just such a code, the founder's corporate Credo of ethical responsibilities. The Credo states, with respect to employees, that "Everyone must be considered as an individual"—deserving of dignity, a sense of job security, "fair and adequate" compensation, freedom to voice complaints, and management that is "just and ethical" (Campbell and Nash 1992, 141). Campbell and Nash maintain that the Credo is a lived document whose principles have a powerful influence on decision making and behavior throughout the Johnson & Johnson companies. Clearly, however, there were lapses at Ethicon. And Madison's advice not to expect too much from paper codes is well taken.

Madison's suggested alternative steers us in another direction: away from belief in unity of purpose to dispel the causes of faction, and toward reliance on rival and opposite interests to control the effects of faction. How a Madisonian approach might apply to organizations is illustrated at another Ethicon site mentioned by Grenier (1988), a twin plant in New Jersey. Here, diversity of interests was acknowledged, such as differences between workers' and management's economic concerns. Here, governing power was divided to look after these separate interests. Here, rules were contracted that specified proper and improper behavior and restricted managers as well as workers. And, here, employees talked with pride about the company and how they performed their jobs. Though management might have preferred the wage Ethicon paid in New Mexico (about 45 percent less, on average), New Jersey workers were able to voice their preference that competitive cost savings come from items other than production salaries (often, a small proportion of the cost of manufactured goods to begin with). The essential difference, of course, was that workers in New Jersey had elected union representation.

The point is not that unions should represent every worker or win every election. Unionized majorities can be oppressive, too. The point, rather, is that some device for dividing power and purpose can be as appropriate in organizations as in Madison's plan of government—to ensure that all participants' interests are given due consideration and that factional differences are not settled merely by might. As in the case of government, no one organizational mechanism is likely to be the magic bullet for warding off tyranny. All kinds of checks and balances are potentially applicable: including due-process procedures, multi-constituent boards, individual employment contracts, staff councils, tenure systems, legal and even constitutional regulation of corporate affairs where managers insist on undivided power (more on this shortly). Exactly which power-sharing devices are most appropriate in what situations is a question for further research. In the United States, legislated agents (EEOC, OSHA, etc.) have tended to supplant labor unions as advocates of workers' interests. Which are more effective is an interesting issue, but a topic for another study. The issue here is whether, in organizations, a Madisonian strategy of deliberately dividing power and purpose—through whatever means—is legitimate at all. I contend that it is, because this strategy addresses (better than trans-formational leadership theories) basic problems that can arise in any type of social system: namely, problems of controlling factions and ambitious leaders.

In sketching the outline of a Madisonian view of organizations, I've focused on its implications for workers. Others have called attention to the advantages of a federalist model, for different corporate constituencies. European business authority Charles Handy (1992), for example, points out that shareholders profit from the federal organizational structure of radically noncentralized companies, such as British Petroleum. In global firms, strong central administrations may have negative added value, because their transaction costs can surpass their contributions: "That is why in many businesses the breakup value of the operations exceeds the market value of the total enterprise" (62). Federal firms like BP recover some of this breakup value by dispersing power among component businesses, which are linked together under a sort of contracted constitution. Handy's explanation of the underlying principle is decidedly Madisonian: "Federal states have constitutions, negotiated contracts that set the boundaries of each group's powers and responsibilities. Organizations need contracts too. It has to be clear who can do what, how power is to be balanced, and whose authority counts where. Leave all this to chance or personal goodwill and the powerful will steal more than they should and unbalance the whole" (Handy, 1992, 24).

O'Toole and Bennis (1992) suggest that other stakeholders can benefit from a federal system of organization. Consumers, for instance, have voted in large numbers (with their dollars, marks, and yen) for goods of the "United States of Benetton," a federation of independently owned manufacturers and franchised retailers.

Still, there is room for debate over how much power is really shared by top management in organizations like Benetton.[3] And there is room to question whether O'Toole, Bennis, or Handy are advocating true federalism or just another form of decentralization, under which "the central authority establishes the why and the what; the units are responsible for the how" (O'Toole and Bennis 1992, 79). Ultimately, these writers seem to pull back from the full-fledged federalism of Madison. Handy claims that common goals are a chief ingredient of federalism, needed to hold organizations together. O'Toole and Bennis add the necessity for visionary leadership. But Madison's insight was to see federalism as an alternative to dependence on common purposes and unifying leaders. Organization theorists continue to have difficulty with this view. Let me further clarify and defend Madison's strong brand of federalism by answering some possible objections.

OBJECTIONS

One might argue that a Madisonian view of organizations misses an important distinction between "public" governments, where Madisonian political principles might apply, and "private" associations, where they do not. However, such an argument carries the burden of showing just what the relevant distinction is. It is hard to sustain the common managerial distinction that private organizations seek specific, shared goals, whereas governments do not. As an empirical generalization, this is simply false: Lack of common goals, after all, is the big complaint of transformational leadership theorists about organizations of all kinds. It is also hard to sustain the common economic distinction that membership in private organizations is voluntary, whereas membership in government is not. Voluntariness is problematic in each case (Keeley 1988): Both Madisonian government and modern organizations resemble social contracts of adhesion, that is, working agreements on rights and obligations that may or may not be altogether voluntary. Finally, it is hard to sustain the common legal distinction that there is some fundamental theoretical or political axiom restricting constitutional principles to acts of government. The fact that private employers enjoy some immunity from constitutional provisions, such as freedoms granted to public employees under the U.S. Bill of Rights, doesn't mean that they should enjoy these immunities.

Recall that the framers' constitutional plan had two objectives: first, to enable government to control the governed; and, second, to oblige it to control itself. Critics like Burns note that the constitutional machinery for dividing power has been more effective in the second regard, in restraining government, than the first. The reason is that Madison's checks and balances were directly aimed at preventing governmental tyranny, and only indirectly at controlling oppression by nongovernmental factions (Carey 1978). To control the governed, Madison relied on a "multiplicity of interests" to provide social checks and balances in an expanded republic. These emergent social checks, he supposed, would prevent one interest group from completely dominating the republic. Yet, they do not prevent a group from dominating others in part of the republic—for example, plantation owners who held slaves until the Civil War—which can be nearly as bad.

The framers' plan seems incomplete, then, insofar as constitutional protections of individual rights apply only to acts of government, and not acts of factional majorities, such as "private" organizations. This limited protection was not something demanded by federalist political theory, but by antifederalist political pressures in 1787 (including slaveholders). Moreover, it was not a compromise that Madison took great pride in. Questioning the proposed Bill of Rights (aimed, as well, at governmental tyranny), he confided to Jefferson that the real power in the community and the main threat to rights "lies in interested majorities of the people rather than in usurped acts of the Government" (October 17, 1788; quoted in Padover 1953, 255). Jefferson replied that "half a loaf is better than no bread. If we cannot secure all our rights, let us secure what we can" (March 15, 1789; quoted in Rutland 1983, 197). And so they did, with Madison leading in drafting the Bill of Rights, which guaranteed some important rights against the federal government but left future generations to fight for the rest of the loaf: security of individual rights against other powerful groups.

Just as private organizations were eventually prohibited from slaveholding by the Thirteenth Amendment in 1865, just as the reach of the Bill of Rights was finally extended from federal to state governments in 1925, constitutional rights protecting individuals from majority factions might logically be extended to participants in nongovernmental organizations and corporations of all sorts in the future. Arguing for such an extension of constitutional rights, legal scholar Charles Reich (1991) says,

Freedom today means freedom in relationship to organization. Most people are not going to find freedom in the woods, like Thoreau. They must find freedom in the word-processing room, freedom in the conference room, freedom in the registrar's office, and freedom in the factory. It is . . . unrealistic to expect freedom after a long day at work. Freedom must be exercised in prime time, not as an afterthought. Freedom cannot be limited to leisure. We must look for freedom in the belly of the beast. (1427)

Again, whether this freedom is best brought about by legal means (for example, application of the Bill of Rights to organizations), by private means (for example, the corporate constitutions cited by Handy), or by both (for example, conventional collective bargaining) is not the issue. The point is that all of these may be appropriate.

RIGHTS VERSUS GOALS IN ORGANIZATIONAL THEORY

Many ordinary people might agree wholeheartedly with proposals to secure basic individual interests and freedoms against infringement in the workplace. Many might welcome, for example, guarantees of rights to due process in termination decisions (rights that tenured faculty members, of both public and private institutions, take for granted). Leadership theorists, on the other hand, express much less enthusiasm about protecting individual rights that could conflict with organizational goals. Things like freedom in the factory, unions, and constitutional checks on corporate policies are not generally what theorists have in mind when speaking of worker "empowerment." In the leadership literature, the meaning of the term is more like the interpretation at Ethicon–New Mexico: a Hegelian notion of freedom to serve the goals of the organization. (For a classic statement of this position, see Selznick [1957]; for a more recent version, see Kanungo [1992].)[4] Reich's idea of empowering workers to seek their own goals in organizations is apt to seem a little too, well, free. In such ethical matters, however, the opinions of Reich, Madison, and ordinary people may be better guides than traditional theories of organization.

Organizational theorists have historically found individual rights and freedoms less appealing than collective goals, not only in organizations but in society at large. On the heels of the American and French Revolutions, a pioneering organizational theorist, Henri de Saint-Simon, criticized Madisonian tendencies in the French Constitution:

[Lack of collective purpose] is the great gap in the Charter. It begins, as do all the constitutions dreamed up since 1789, by putting forward the rights of Frenchmen, which can only be clearly determined when the purpose of society is established in a positive way, since the rights of every associate can only be based upon the abilities which he possesses and which contribute toward the common goal. (In Ionescu 1976, 167)

It cannot too often be repeated that society needs an active goal, for without this there would be no political system. . . . The maintenance of individual freedom cannot be the goal. . . . People do not band together to be free. Savages join together to hunt, to wage war, but certainly not to win liberty. (158)

Saint-Simon was wrong—and Madisonian thinking prevailed in the reformation of many Western governments. Two hundred years of political history have shown that people do join together in societies to advance personal freedom and individual rights. People have joined organizations (especially labor organizations) for similar reasons.

Social theorists have remained uncomfortable about all this. Auguste Comte, Saint-Simon's disciple and the founder of modern sociology, challenged workers to consider themselves servants of society and its goals rather than "insisting on the possession of what metaphysicians call political rights, and engaging in useless discussions about the distribution of power" (in Lenzer 1975, 368). Later, Henri Fayol (1916), who laid much of the groundwork for a theory of management, expressed dismay that individuals refused to subordinate their interests to a common goal, either of business or nation: "Ignorance, ambition, selfishness, laziness, weakness and all human passions tend to cause the general interest to be lost sight of in favor of individual interest and a perpetual struggle has to be waged against them" (60). More recently, Henry Mintzberg (1983), a prominent organizational theorist, has likened organizations without common goals to "a bucket of crabs, each clawing at the others to come out on top" (421) just as in society at large, where pulling toward private ends (a pluralist "political arena") "will be found in the breakdown of any form of government, under conditions typically described as anarchy or revolution" (462).

Mintzberg echoes the persistent belief—shared by early sociologists, their Parsonian successors, modern communitarians and transformational-leadership theorists—that common ends (goals, goods, values, etc.) are the essential glue that holds social systems together. This belief has a long history, but that doesn't make it true. Organizational theorists have tried to defend it in various ways.

Some have tried to argue that "organization[s] would not exist if it were not for some common purpose" (Hall 1977, 83). Because they do exist, organizations must have the glue—or goals. This "goal paradigm" is still found in mainstream textbooks on organization (for example, Daft 1986), but it has prompted growing criticism in more analytical works (for example, Cyert and March 1963; Silverman 1970; Georgiou 1973; Keeley 1980; Weick 1985). The main objection is that it is easy to talk about common, organizational goals in the abstract, yet difficult to find them in the real world. Certainly, organizations produce real, objective consequences (for example, profits, deficits, wages, pollutants, all kinds of goods and costs). However, participants frequently disagree about the value of these consequences, about which of them are actual goals of the organization. In a firm, for instance, owners might view profits as goals, and wages as costs; workers might view wages as goals, and profits as costs; others might view both profits and wages as goals (say, top managers), or costs (say, consumers). It seems that people participate in organizations for a variety of purposes. It seems arbitrary to take some participants' purposes, or goals for an organization, to represent goals of the organization as a whole. And, for the most part, it seems that organizations look little like the organic, goal-seeking entities of management folklore.

Operational difficulties in identifying organizational goals are disappointing but not quite fatal for the goal paradigm. Theorists have developed a second line of defense, which interprets goal diversity not as evidence of a bad paradigm but bad organizations. In other words, if organizations don't in fact have common goals, then they lack the glue that holds social systems together. And thus, of course, they don't resemble functionally integrated organisms but, rather, disintegrating "buckets of crabs" or "houses divided against themselves" (Mintzberg 1983), wars of parts against the whole (Gardner 1990), fragmented and fractured communities of You've-got-yours-Now-where's-mine egoists (Bennis 1989), and so on. As we've seen, the implication of these images is that social systems without common goals are falling apart and need something, like a transformational leader or spirit of community, to supply the missing glue of collective purpose.

What we can learn from Madison, on the other hand, is that no such purpose or glue is necessary. For two centuries, his system of competitive federalism has held together—as a system of laws, not of leaders or public purposes. To this day, it works better than suggested by the disparaging images of transformational-leadership theorists. For instance, Burns's (1978) depiction of pluralist public agencies as pork barrels tended by transactional bureaucrats—who muddle along, spewing red tape, passing the buck, and dragging the system down with them—just doesn't square with the facts (Wilson 1989). Despite sensational reports of government waste, public bureaucracies such as the Social Security Administration have served clients with fairness and efficiency (relative to resources: see Mashaw 1983; Goodsell 1983). Despite media criticism of governmental gridlock, divided government has enacted decent legislation, such as the Americans with Disabilities Act and the Civil Rights Act of 1991 (Mayhew 1991). As Lindblom (1965) has stressed, Madisonian government works not because participants agree on goals, but because they can agree on specific activities (as in acts of legislation) that address their different goals. So, too, in "private" organizations, like corporations, the glue that holds them together need not be consensus on ends but can be simply consent to means—agreement on rules, rights, and responsibilities that serve the separate interests of their participants.

Some organizational theorists have appreciated the point and concluded that organizations generally look neither like social organisms nor asocial free-for-alls, but more like political coalitions (Cyert and March 1963) or markets (Pfeffer and Salancik 1978), sets of contracts (Keeley 1988) or stakeholders (Freeman and Gilbert 1988). Empirically, models of this sort more fairly reflect the possibility that in organizations, as in society, participants may be less concerned with collective goals than individual rights (for example, contractual rights to a paycheck or return on investment, legal rights to equal opportunity or workers' compensation, moral rights to information about the risks of products or services). Madison's model indicates why these participant concerns are appropriate ethically.

The fundamental issue is that notions of a "common goal," "general interest," "public good," and so forth, are theoretical concepts (every bit as metaphysical as natural rights). Any real social consequence used to operationalize these theoretical terms is apt to impact persons in different, often arbitrary, ways. That's why participants find it hard to agree on "organizational goals." Collective consequences like profits, wages, even organizational survival, may greatly benefit some participants (say, employees of tobacco firms) but ultimately disadvantage others (say, tobacco customers who develop smoking-related illnesses). Even participants who share an interest in a particular organizational consequence may be affected very differently by it: Employees with a joint interest in higher wages may care less about an organization's overall salary pool—which could be distributed capriciously—than about *Who gets what?*

Organizations and their leaders can deal with distributional concerns either by seeking fairness of outcomes to individuals (a Madisonian strategy), or by changing the subject. In the tradition of Saint-Simon, transformational leadership aims to get people's thoughts off distributional questions and refocus them on common goals, or communal interests. This may sound moral to James MacGregor Burns and like-minded theorists (as well as some critics: Rost 1991). But the ethical justification for diverting attention from individual to communal interests is unclear, given the hypothetical nature of the latter. If the operational consequences taken to represent collective ends are, in fact, weighted in favor of some persons' interests, it seems deceptive to win other persons' support by calling these weighted—perhaps biased—consequences, common goals, goods, interests, and so on. Many people are quick to perceive such deception (as demonstrated in public ridicule of trickle-down economics). Other people are more trusting and vulnerable (as shown by supporters of televangelists' visions). In any event, reliance on extraordinary leaders to define collective purposes just

papers over the problem of faction and, as Madison saw, puts participants at risk of manipulation, or worse.

In sum, contrary to the claims of theorists like Burns, common goals
are no more imperative ethically than they are empirically. As Madison
realized, people can still care for one another, if not for some alleged
common good. As he explained in *Federalist* No. 10, factional mischief
does not follow directly from diversity of interests; rather, it occurs
when some people try to impose their interests on others. In other
words, the problem of faction is not that individuals pursue separate
interests, but that some are stronger, smarter, or richer than the rest and
may use their power to take unfair advantage of other persons. Thus,
Madison proposed a safer way to prevent factional mischief than transforming individuals and eliminating diversity of interests. His solution
was to deter advantage-taking: to devise an impartial system of rules,
checks, and balances that can accommodate personal ambitions while
protecting each person's basic interests from impairment by others—
especially leaders who function in the name of the community.

This was the guiding idea, however imperfectly it may have been
executed, of the Philadelphia Constitution (Parent 1992). In designing
their system of government, Madison and the framers acted on the
belief that there are some interests of individuals that ought not be
sacrificed for the sake of an imagined public purpose. They expressed
this priority in the language of individual rights, which trump public
policies. Many participants in organizations today act and talk much
the same way, claiming rights that trump corporate policies. Maybe it
is time for leadership theorists to accept instead of oppose this priority,
to cease prescribing the old remedy of collective purpose, and to take
more seriously the distinctiveness of individual persons (as in Rawls
1971). Maybe, then, we could debate more significant questions. For
instance, which individual interests deserve absolute protection against
infringement in organizations (like constitutional prohibitions against
slavery)? Which are not veto-proof but still important enough to deserve redress for violations (like workers' compensation for job-related
injuries)? And which just deserve consideration in organizational pol-
icy-making (like employee voice in plant closing procedures)?

CONCLUSION

Let me conclude by illustrating what difference a Madisonian perspective might make in a familiar kind of organization. The views of
Saint-Simon, Mintzberg, Burns, and later leadership theorists are typi-
fied by Bennis (1977) in a classic article about his experiences as president of the University of Cincinnati. Wondering "Where have all the

leaders gone?," Bennis sees factional misbehavior all about him. The university, he writes, "has blunted and diffused its main purposes" (7) through a proliferation of interest groups. It is besieged by "external" constituencies, such as alumni, parents, and lawmakers. It is "fragmented" by internal pressure groups of all sorts:

We have a coalition of women's groups, a gay society, black organizations for both students and faculty, a veterans' group, a continuing education group for women, a handicapped group, a faculty council on Jewish affairs, a faculty union organized by the American Association of University Professors, an organization for those staff members who are neither faculty nor administrators, an organization of middle-management staff members, an association of women administrators, a small, elite group of graduate fellows. (8)

These groups, Bennis complains, go their own separate ways—marking the end of community.

Like Bennis, many of us work in complex universities with diverse aims, interest groups, and external dependencies. However, unlike Bennis, few might find such diversity objectionable. What, exactly, is wrong with women's groups or black groups or disabled groups or staff associations or other groups that flourish on our campuses?

Why do differences among these groups—in viewpoints, interests, and goals for the university—make us less a community, or just a bucket of crabs?

By invoking the ritual formula that organizations should have common purposes—and by painting organizations without them as snake pits—theorists perpetuate the illusion that there is something perverse about people who behave differently. Bennis, for example, portrays participants who assert their legal rights in universities as "bellyachers" who take advantage of the system, waste the organization's time and money in court, and prevent the proper authorities (especially presidents, like himself) from exercising real leadership. He is critical of persons who bring suits for injuries, malpractice, civil rights violations, or who are just "fed up with being ignored, neglected, excluded, denied, subordinated" (8). To counter those who might be tempted to file complaints under consumer protection laws, he adds, "At my own and many other universities . . . we are now in the process of rewriting our catalogs so carefully that it will be virtually impossible for any student [read: consumer] to claim that we haven't fulfilled our end of the bargain. At the same time, because we have to be so careful, we can never express our hopes, our dreams, and our bold ideas of what a university could provide for the prospective student" (13–14).

This is the rub, then. Leaders can't do what they want, because constituents have bold ideas of their own about what the organization should provide in return for their cooperation, and because "the courts are substituting their judgments for the expertise of the institution" (10). "Time was," Bennis says wistfully, "when the leader could decide—period. A Henry Ford, an Andrew Carnegie, a Nicholas Murray Butler, could issue a ukase—and all would automatically obey" (7). But no longer. Thanks to government, unions, lawyers, and their recalcitrant clients.

Thanks, also, to Madison and the framers. Were it not for the system of law they set in motion, individuals in harm's way of organizations might have little recourse at all. Bennis evokes a timeless undercurrent of leadership theory that Madison struggled against in 1787: a longing for "the philosophical race of kings wished for by Plato" (Federalist, No. 49, 315). Leaders, in this view, are to fabricate a vision of collective purpose—if necessary, a unifying myth. Followers are to put aside personal interests in its pursuit. (Madison, no doubt, read Plato's parable of the poor carpenter who fell ill and was advised by a doctor to look after himself for a time before carrying out his assigned duties to the community; Plato remarks that the worker must be inspired to ignore such advice, to "go back to his normal routine, and either regain his health and get on with his job, or, if his constitution won't stand it, die and be rid of his troubles." [Republic, 406].) Modern theorists are more sensitive to personal entitlements than the ancient Greeks, but the very concept of transformational leadership implies that individual interests are less legitimate than collective ends. Why else would they require transformation? Accordingly, participants who do not subordinate their interests to "organizational" goals—as envisioned by leaders or majorities—are disparaged, even when their expectations seem quite reasonable. In a university, for instance, what is so unreasonable about students expecting to be treated like consumers? or expecting accurate information in a college catalog? or expecting the university to fulfill its end of the bargain? It is nonsense to suggest that leaders cannot meet such basic expectations and still express their hopes and dreams. And it is presumptuous to suppose that these expectations are less valid than the visions of people in power.

In a recent study of academic leadership, Birnbaum (1992) responds appropriately to Bennis's (1977) plaintive question, Where have all the great leaders of the past gone? "They are dead," says Birnbaum, "along with the simpler times in which formal leaders could wield unbridled power to get what they wanted. In today's world of greater participation, shared influence, conflicting constituencies, and assorted other complexities, heeding the current vogue of calls for charismatic presidents who can transform their institutions would be more likely to lead to campus disruption than to constructive change" (xii–xiii).

Birnbaum's conclusions are based on a five-year longitudinal study of how college and university presidents exercise leadership. His research challenges a number of myths about effective leaders.

Myth 1—Presidents need to create a vision for their organization that transcends individual interests. Birnbaum (1992) found otherwise. Successful leaders and acceptable visions reflected the diverse interests of constituents rather than the leader's goals for the institution. One effective president advised: "Do a lot of listening. And when you do that, solicit the dreams and hopes from the people. Tell the people the good things you are finding. And in three to six months, take these things and report them as the things you would like to see happen" (26).

Myth 2—Presidents should be transformational leaders. Birnbaum discovered that transformational leadership, which changes participants' values and goals for the organization, is abnormal in universities. "Good leaders," he reports, "help change their institutions, not through transformation and the articulation of new goals or values, but through transactions that emphasize values already in place and move the institution toward attaining them" (30). Transformational efforts to initiate grand schemes "inflict leadership" on constituencies and cause more factional strife than they resolve.

Myth 3—Charisma is an important aspect of leadership. Birnbaum found only a few institutions where presidential charisma helped rather than hindered the organization. He proposes that charisma has more to do with impression management than with the hard work of running an institution. It allows presidents to substitute glitz for substance, and it encourages both leaders and followers to act on faith, as opposed to an understanding of the situation. Most importantly, reliance on presidential charisma tends to diminish the authority of other decision-makers and weakens the formal administrative structure of the university. The focus on a leader's persona diverts attention from the long-term job of building an "institutional infrastructure" of mutually accepted practices, rights, and responsibilities.

Birnbaum (a former college president himself) views the support of multiple constituencies as central to presidential effectiveness. His data indicate that the kind of imperial presidency suggested by Bennis is not effective. Among institutions studied, a primary cause of presidential failure was unilateral action that furthered presidential goals but was perceived to violate constituents' (particularly faculty) rights. In contrast, effective academic leaders in Birnbaum's sample seem downright Madisonian. The president of one successful institution described his college as "a political system: a 'pluralistic democracy,' with himself as

a 'governor,'" which meant treating faculty, union leaders, and other administrators as colleagues, instead of subordinates (Birnbaum 1992,
127). In general, successful academic leaders respected diversity (appre-
ciating, not deprecating, different values). They respected participants'
own goals for the institution (building on them, versus correcting them).
They respected individuals' right-claims (placing the needs of people
before system requirements). And they respected shared leadership
(dispersing power, not just decentralizing it). All clearly Madisonian
priorities.

There is a final point. I suspect that most of us work in universities
with some Madisonian characteristics, whether top administrators encourage them or not. It is interesting that academic professionals create
and seek employment in organizations with such institutionalized
checks and balances as self-supporting departments, faculty senates,
unions, tenure policies, grievance processes, and committees representing every interest imaginable. If this sort of federalist system is what
we choose for ourselves, if we claim academic freedom as our right, why
should we prescribe any less freedom for others?

NOTES

This chapter was originally published by *Business Ethics Quarterly* (Vol. 5, No. 1).

1. Washington's inspirational effect on his compatriots is well illustrated by an
incident at the close of the war. As hostilities with Britain diminished, so did
cooperation between the states with regard to honoring war debts. American
soldiers were owed years of back pay; officers had been promised pensions if they
served for the duration; and now state representatives were reluctant to pay the bill,
hoping the army would just go home. The army instead grew resentful at the lack
of public gratitude for members' sacrifices in the cause of independence. A mass
meeting of officers was called to discuss ways of securing their rights. Proposed
actions included refusing to lay down arms or disband, marching on Congress, and
even forming a military community on unsettled land. Some officers wanted
Washington to lead the movement against civil authorities, but he appeared at their
meeting and argued for restraint. His audience remained unpersuaded—until
Washington pulled from his pocket a piece of paper, a conciliatory letter from
Congress. Flexner (1967, 507) describes the scene:
    The officers stirred impatiently in their seats, and then suddenly every heart
missed a beat. Something was the matter with His Excellency. He seemed unable
to read the paper. He paused in bewilderment. He fumbled in his waistcoat
pocket. And then he pulled out something that only his intimates had seen him
wear. A pair of glasses. With infinite sweetness and melancholy, he explained,
"Gentlemen, you will permit me to put on my spectacles, for I have not only
grown grey but almost blind in the service of my country."

With tough veterans moved to tears, Washington read the letter and left. Passions cooled, officers drifted off, and plans for insurrection were abandoned.

2. Much of the empirical research on transformational leadership relies on retrospective attributions to demonstrate its existence and effects. A common procedure asks research subjects to rate the past performance and leadership qualities of managers, coworkers, or historical figures (Bass 1985; Hater and Bass 1988; Avolio, Waldman, and Einstein 1988). Correlations have been found between ratings of successful performance, charisma, and transformational behavior. Such correlations, however, do not prove that leadership causes success, or anything else. Attributions of successful performance may prompt attributions of leadership, as well as the reverse. In any event, performance attributions remain mere perceptions. The fact that some workers and college students think their bosses or popular leaders made things happen doesn't make it so (Meindl 1990). And popularity polls of the kind used in leadership research do not speak to the minority concerns that interested Madison.

3. See Lorenz (1992). Once again, effective separation of power may require multiple checks and balances, such as boards of truly independent, outside directors. Steps in this direction are illustrated in GM's new board "constitution," which gives outside directors substantial checks on corporate management (Dobrzynski 1994).

4. Selznick believes that leaders should motivate followers to think for themselves—so long as this contributes to institutional survival and integrity. Similarly, Kanungo tends to equate empowerment with motivation. He rejects notions of empowerment as sharing power or resources. He prefers a view of empowerment as an "enabling" force that "heightens the motivation for task accomplishment" (418). So conceived, "the behavioral effects of empowerment ... results [sic] in workers both initiating and persevering in work behavior."

REFERENCES

Avolio, Bruce J., David A. Waldman, and Walter O. Einstein. 1988. "Transformational Leadership in a Management Game Simulation." *Group & Organization Studies* 13: 59–80.
Avolio, Bruce J., David A. Waldman, and Francis J. Yammarino. 1991. "Leading in the 1990s: The Four I's of Transformational Leadership." *Journal of European Industrial Training* 15: 9–16.
Bass, Bernard M. 1985. *Leadership and Performance beyond Expectations.* New York: Free Press.
———. 1990. "From Transactional to Transformational Leadership: Learning to Share the Vision." *Organizational Dynamics* 18: 19–31.
Bennis, Warren. 1977. "Where Have All the Leaders Gone?" *Technology Review* 79: 3–12. Reprinted in William E. Rosenbach and Robert L. Taylor, eds. *Contemporary Issues in Leadership,* 2nd ed. Boulder, Colo.: Westview Press, 1989, pp. 5–23.
———. 1989. *Why Leaders Can't Lead.* San Francisco: Jossey-Bass.
Bennis, Warren, and Burt Nanus. 1985. *Leaders: The Strategies for Taking Charge.* New York: Harper and Row.

142   Ethics, the Heart of Leadership

Birnbaum, Robert. 1992. *How Academic Leadership Works*. San Francisco: Jossey-Bass.
Burns, James MacGregor. 1963. *The Deadlock of Democracy*. Englewood Cliffs, N.J.: Prentice Hall.
———. 1978. *Leadership*. New York: Harper and Row.
Burrough, Bryan, and John Helyar. 1990. *Barbarians at the Gate*. New York: Harper and Row.
Camenisch, Paul F. 1986. "Moral Leadership in Business: Some Preliminary Considerations." *Business & Professional Ethics Journal* 5: 98–110.
Campbell, Andrew, and Laura L. Nash. 1992. *A Sense of Mission*. Reading, Mass.: Addison-Wesley.
Carey, George W. 1978. "Separation of Powers and the Madisonian Model: A Reply to the Critics." *American Political Science Review* 72: 151–64.
Comte, Auguste. *System of Positive Polity*. Translated by J. H. Bridges. In Gertrud Lenzer, ed. *Auguste Comte and Positivism*. New York: Harper and Row, 1975 (Original, 1851–54), pp. 307–476.
Conger, Jay A., and Rabindra N. Kanungo. 1988. "Behavioral Dimensions of Charismatic Leadership." In Jay A. Conger, Rabindra N. Kanungo, and Associates. *Charismatic Leadership*. San Francisco: Jossey-Bass, 78–97.
Cunliffe, Marcus. 1982. *George Washington: Man and Monument*. New York: New American Library.
Cyert, Richard M., and James G. March. 1963. *A Behavioral Theory of the Firm*. Englewood Cliffs, N.J.: Prentice Hall.
Daft, Richard L. 1986. *Organization Theory and Design*, 2nd ed. St. Paul, Minn.: West.
Dahl, Robert A. 1956. *A Preface to Democratic Theory*. Chicago: University of Chicago Press.
Dobrzynski, Judith H. 1994. "At GM, A Magna Carta for Directors." *Business Week*, April 4.
Dye, Thomas R. 1990. *American Federalism*. Lexington, Mass.: Lexington.
Elazar, Daniel J. 1981. "Is Federalism Compatible with Prefectorial Administration?" *Publius* 11: 3–22.
Etzioni, Amitai. 1988. *The Moral Dimension*. New York: Free Press.
Fayol, Henri. *General and Industrial Management*. Translated by Constance Storrs. London: Pitman, 1949. (Original, 1916).
Flexner, James Thomas. 1967. *George Washington in the American Revolution*. Boston: Little, Brown.
Freeman, R. Edward, and Daniel R. Gilbert, Jr. 1988. *Corporate Strategy and the Search for Ethics*. Englewood Cliffs, N.J.: Prentice Hall.
Gardner, John W. 1990. *On Leadership*. New York: Free Press.
Georgiou, Petro. 1973. "The Goal Paradigm and Notes towards a Counter Paradigm." *Administrative Science Quarterly* 18: 291–310.
Goodsell, Charles T. 1983. *The Case for Bureaucracy*. Chatham, N.J.: Chatham House.
Grenier, Guillermo J. 1988. *Inhuman Relations*. Philadelphia: Temple University Press.
Hall, Richard H. 1977. *Organizations*, 2nd ed. Englewood Cliffs, N.J.: Prentice Hall.

Handy, Charles. 1992. "Balancing Corporate Power: A New Federalist Paper." *Harvard Business Review* 70 (November-December): 59–72.

Hater, John J., and Bernard M. Bass. 1988. "Superiors' Evaluations and Subordinates' Perceptions of Transformational and Transactional Leadership." *Journal of Applied Psychology* 73: 695–702.

Herzberg, Frederick. 1966. *Work and the Nature of Man.* New York: Crowell.

House, Robert J., James Woycke, and Eugene M. Fodor. 1988. "Charismatic and Noncharismatic Leaders: Differences in Behavior and Effectiveness." In Jay A. Conger, Rabindra N. Kanungo, and Associates, *Charismatic Leadership.* San Francisco: Jossey-Bass, 98–121.

Howell, Jane M. 1988. "Two Faces of Charisma: Socialized and Personalized Leadership in Organizations." In Jay A. Conger, Rabindra N. Kanungo, and Associates, *Charismatic Leadership.* San Francisco: Jossey-Bass, pp. 213–36.

Howell, Jane M., and Bruce J. Avolio. 1992. "The Ethics of Charismatic Leadership: Submission or Liberation?" *Academy of Management Executive* 6: 43–54.

Howell, Jane M., and Peter J. Frost. 1989. "A Laboratory Study of Charismatic Leadership." *Organizational Behavior and Human Decision Processes* 43: 243–69.

Huntington, Samuel P. 1981. *American Politics: The Promise of Disharmony.* Cambridge, Mass.: Harvard University Press.

Ivancevich, John M., and Michael T. Matteson. 1993. *Organizational Behavior and Management*, 3rd ed. Homewood, Ill.: Irwin.

Kanungo, Rabindra N. 1992. "Alienation and Empowerment: Some Ethical Imperatives in Business." *Journal of Business Ethics* 11: 413–22.

Keeley, Michael. 1988. "Organizational Analogy: A Comparison of Organismic and Social Contract Models." *Administrative Science Quarterly* 25: 337–62.

———. 1988. *A Social-Contract Theory of Organizations.* Notre Dame, Ind.: University of Notre Dame Press.

Kouzes, James M., and Barry Z. Posner. 1987. *The Leadership Challenge.* San Francisco: Jossey-Bass.

Lindblom, Charles E. 1965. *The Intelligence of Democracy.* New York: Free Press.

Lorenz, Christopher. 1992. "Fashionable Federalism." *Financial Times,* December 18, 9.

Madison, James. 1961. *Federalist* No. 10; *Federalist* No. 49; *Federalist* No. 51. In Clinton Rossiter, ed. *The Federalist Papers.* New York: Mentor, 77–84; 313–17; 320–25.

Mashaw, Jerry L. 1983. *Bureaucratic Justice.* New Haven, Conn.: Yale University Press.

Mayhew, David R. 1991. *Divided We Govern.* New Haven, Conn.: Yale University Press.

Meindl, James R. 1990. "On Leadership: An Alternative to the Conventional Wisdom." In Barry M. Staw and L. L. Cummings, eds. *Research in Organizational Behavior*, Vol. 12. Greenwich, Conn.: JAI Press, pp. 159–203.

Mintzberg, Henry. 1983. *Power in and around Organizations.* Englewood Cliffs, N.J.: Prentice Hall.

Morison, Samuel Eliot. 1965. *The Oxford History of the American People.* New York: Oxford University Press.

O'Toole, James, and Warren Bennis. 1992. "Our Federalist Future: The Leadership Imperative." *California Management Review* 34 (Summer): 73–90.

Padover, Saul K., ed. 1953. *The Complete Madison*. New York: Harper and Brothers.

Parent, William A. 1992. "Constitutional Values and Human Dignity." In Michael J. Meyer and William A. Parent, eds. *The Constitution of Rights*. Ithaca, N.Y.: Cornell University Press, 47–72.

Pfeffer, Jeffrey, and Gerald R. Salancik. 1978. *The External Control of Organizations*. New York: Harper and Row.

Plato. 1974. *The Republic*. Translated by Desmond Lee, 2nd ed. Harmondsworth, England: Penguin.

Rawls, John. 1971. *A Theory of Justice*. Cambridge, Mass.: Harvard University Press.

Reich, Charles A. 1991. "The Individual Sector." *Yale Law Journal* 100: 1409–48.

Roberts, Nancy C., and Raymond Trevor Bradley. 1988. "Limits of Charisma." In Jay A. Conger, Rabindra N. Kanungo, and Associates. *Charismatic Leadership*. San Francisco: Jossey-Bass, 253–75.

Rost, Joseph C. 1991. *Leadership for the Twenty-First Century*. New York: Praeger.

Rutland, Robert Allen. 1983. *The Birth of the Bill of Rights*. Boston: Northeastern University Press.

Saint-Simon, Claude-Henri de. "On the Industrial System." In Ghita Ionescu, ed. *The Political Thought of Saint-Simon*. London: Oxford University Press, 1976 (Original, 1821), pp. 153–81.

Schein, Edgar H. 1980. *Organizational Psychology*, 3rd ed. Englewood Cliffs, N.J.: Prentice Hall.

Selznick, Philip. *Leadership in Administration*. Evanston, Ill.: Row, Peterson.

Silverman, David. 1970. *The Theory of Organizations*. London: Heinemann.

Spector, Bert. 1987. "Transformational Leadership: The New Challenge for U.S. Unions." *Human Resource Management* 26: 3–16.

Steers, Richard M., and Lyman W. Porter, eds. 1987. *Motivation and Work Behavior*, 4th ed. New York: McGraw-Hill.

Sundquist, James L. 1986. *Constitutional Reform and Effective Government*. Washington, D.C.: Brookings Institution.

Tichy, Noel M., and Mary Anne Devanna. 1986. *The Transformational Leader*. New York: John Wiley.

Weick, Karl E. 1985. "Sources of Order in Underorganized Systems: Themes in Recent Organizational Theory." In Yvonna S. Lincoln, ed. *Organizational Theory and Inquiry*. Beverly Hills, Calif.: Sage, pp. 106–36.

Westley, Frances R., and Henry Mintzberg. 1988. "Profiles of Strategic Vision: Levesque and Iacocca." In Jay A. Conger, Rabindra N. Kanungo, and Associates. *Charismatic Leadership*. San Francisco: Jossey-Bass, pp. 161–212.

White, Donald D., and David A. Bednar. 1991. *Organizational Behavior*, 2nd ed. Boston: Allyn and Bacon.

Wilson, James Q. 1989. *Bureaucracy*. New York: Basic Books.

Yukl, Gary A. *Leadership in Organizations*, 2nd ed. Englewood Cliffs, N.J.: Prentice Hall.

Zaleznik, Abraham. 1989. *The Managerial Mystique*. New York: Harper and Row.

7

James Madison and the Ethics of Transformational Leadership

J. Thomas Wren

Transformational leadership has become one of the dominant paradigms of leadership studies since its first articulation by James
MacGregor Burns in 1978.[1] In recent years, however, this formulation
of leadership has come under criticism, to include the critique of its
ethical implications.[2] One of the most innovative and provocative of
such critiques is one by Michael Keeley in this book, grounded in his
close study of the political theory of James Madison.[3] Keeley argues that
Madison provides a model of leadership that opposes transformational
leadership and that avoids many of its ethical pitfalls. This chapter
suggests an alternative interpretation of Madison's theory and works;
one that places Madison's thought squarely in the historical intellectual
current that eventually yielded conceptions of transformational leadership. Moreover, I argue that Madison's continued concern with the
proper roles of leaders and followers suggests a remedy for the ethical
concerns over transformational leadership that Keeley and others so
rightly identify.

TRANSACTIONAL, TRANSFORMING, AND TRANSFORMATIONAL LEADERSHIP

The terms "transactional leadership," "transforming leadership," and "transformational leadership" entered our vocabulary with James MacGregor Burns's seminal book, *Leadership*. These terms are by now fairly well known. According to Burns, transactional leadership "occurs when one person takes the initiative in making contact with others for the purpose of an exchange of valued things." It is part-and-parcel of much of everyday leadership: the mutually advantageous exchange of economic or political or psychological assets between a leader and followers in the pursuit of a joint objective. It is important to note, however, what transactional leadership is not. It is not an enduring, or particularly uplifting, relationship. "The bargainers have no enduring purpose that holds them together," says Burns. "A leadership act took place, but it was not one that binds leader and follower together in a mutual and continuing pursuit of higher purpose."[4] Burns clearly acknowledges the reality of such leadership, but just as clearly he favors a more rewarding form of leadership relation.

The contrasting form of leadership he calls transforming leadership. "Such leadership occurs when one or more persons *engage* with others in such a way that leaders and followers raise one another to higher levels of motivation and morality." This sort of leadership has a powerful effect upon the leader-follower relation. "Their purposes, which might have started out separate but related, as in the case of transactional leadership, become fused." Thus leaders and followers are not incidental sojourners for the brief time that their independent purposes intersect (as in transactional leadership); there is a sense of an enduring "common purpose." Moreover, "transforming leadership ultimately becomes *moral* in that it raises the level of human conduct and ethical aspiration of both leader and led, and thus has a transforming effect on both."[5]

A closely related concept is that of transformational leadership. Although Burns sometimes uses the terms transforming and transformational leadership in his text interchangeably, the notion of transformational leadership is better identified with the work of Bernard Bass.[6] Drawing inspiration from Burns work, Bass adapted the concept of transforming leadership and applied it in the context of formal organizations. Under Bass's conceptualization of transformational leadership, leaders who demonstrate charisma, who give individualized consideration [by mentoring followers and the like], and who provide intellectual stimulation to followers, become transformational leaders. The results for the organization can be dramatic, yielding extraordinary levels of effort and organizational effectiveness.[7]

The Burns formulation and the Bass variation of transformational leadership are clearly distinct. Burns directly concerns himself with the morality of the leadership process; Bass has less of such a focus, although his contribution to this collection places him much closer to Burns than was heretofore the case.[8] For purposes of this chapter, the important point is the basic similarity between the two: both acknowledge leadership to be an important process dedicated to some common interest or common good (be it organizational or otherwise). Burns makes the point strongly: "leadership is nothing if not linked to collective purpose."[9] Similarly, Bass notes that "transformational leadership . . . occurs when . . . employees . . . look beyond their own self-interest for the good of the group."[10] That commitment to the common good links both formulations to the thought of James Madison.

In this chapter, the term "transformational" leadership is generally used to embrace both transforming and transformational leadership as portrayed here. "Transforming" leadership only appears when the moral overtones of Burns' work are at issue. Notions of "transactional" leadership come into play only in relation to the model posited by Michael Keeley.

THE KEELEY MODEL OF MADISONIAN LEADERSHIP, AND A REFUTATION

Keeley, in his intriguing essay entitled "The Trouble with Transformational Leadership: Toward a Federalist Ethic for Organizations,"[11] asserts that the existence of self-interested factions in society, organizations, and groups has been labeled by many leadership writers as dysfunctional. Leadership theories such as transformational leadership have been created, in part, to transcend such self-interest and restore a unified and productive focus to the leadership process. Keeley draws upon a close study of James Madison to suggest a different and better way to handle self-interested factions: One should embrace them (or at least acknowledge that they are inevitable) and construct a polity or organizational structure that allows for the free play of faction. In doing so, not only would one be likely to attain the best possible result, but this approach would also obviate the questionable ethics of transformational leadership, where dissenting individuals are coerced into accepting stances and values inimical to their personal beliefs.

To reach these conclusions, Keeley looks to some of Madison's most famous utterances—a key speech in the Constitutional Convention, some of his noted *Federalist* essays, and an almost equally celebrated private letter to Thomas Jefferson in the fall of 1787. From these sources, Keeley details both Madison's structural solutions to the problem of self-interested factions, as well as the underlying beliefs that led Madison to such a formulation. In order to faithfully assess Keeley's interpretation, it is important to isolate and identify the content of both the structural solution and the underlying assumptions that Keeley posits.

Madison's identification of and resolution to the problem of faction is among the most well known in American history. In numerous venues in the years surrounding the drafting of the Constitution, Madison had acknowledged the reality that society, far from being a unified whole, was instead composed of any number of self-interested "factions." Although this may seem a commonplace in today's diverse, individualistic world, Madison's insight was nothing short of revolutionary in a world still steeped in the classical republicanism of the eighteenth century. Moreover, Madison offered a variety of solutions to this new and troubling reality. The most famous of these he sketched in *Federalist* No. 10: The pernicious effects of self-interested faction could be lessened by making it more difficult for a "majority faction" (the only truly dangerous kind) to come into being. The method for doing so was to create a polity so "uncentralized"—to use Keeley's word—that majority factions would find it difficult to form. Keeley also argues that the Constitutional system of federalism and checks and balances also served the function of limiting domination by one faction.[12]

Of equal importance to Keeley's portrayal of the Madisonian solution are the essential underlying beliefs that he attributes to Madison. Several of these can be identified. They are set out here to facilitate extended discussion later in this chapter.

(1) Madison (according to Keeley) opposed any attempt to transcend or merge the various factions. This was unlikely to be successful, at best, and at worst could lead to tyranny. An assumption underlying this is that there is no "common good" around which to coalesce.[13]

(2) Madison had insufficient faith in leaders to rely upon them to remedy the situation. Although some leaders (such as George Washington) would undoubtedly benefit society's interests, leaders as a whole were a lot that was not to be trusted. It was much wiser to create a system of laws and structural protections against overweening leaders.[14]

(3) Likewise, Madison had little trust in the virtue of the people (followers). Much of Keeley's discussion of Madison's concern with faction suggests such a conclusion, which is supported by Keeley's remark that the framers "chose to protect us from the misdeeds of scoundrels and the frailties of ordinary men and women."[15]

With such assumptions concerning Madison's views to drive his analysis, it is little wonder that Keeley concludes that Madison embraced what we would come to know as transactional leadership. With no common good, and leaders and followers who could not consistently be trusted to do "the right thing," it is the only logical conclusion to be drawn from Madison's extensive commentary on the problem of factions. It makes little sense for leaders to do more than allow the factions to compete, and for the government or organization to, in Keeley's words, "manage factional interests much as a market responds to consumer preferences;" that is, to ensure a fairness in the competition. Notions of collective action are obviated by the underlying assumptions.

This analysis of Madisonian thought by Keeley is impressive in many ways. He draws upon several key documents of the Madisonian corpus, and his thesis is correct in many of its particulars. However, a reading of the entire corpus of Madison's writings spanning a long and prolific career also yields an alternative interpretation. When one views Madison's political writings in their entirety, a more complex and sophisticated picture emerges. Viewed from that perspective, a set of base assumptions contrary to those that Keeley posits appears. This modified interpretation of Madison's core beliefs, in turn, supports a quite different interpretation of his views of what constitutes appropriate leadership. The ensuing analysis, then, eventually leads us back to the concept of transformational leadership. The next sections of this chapter revisit the Madisonian assumptions posited by Keeley.[16]

JAMES MADISON AND THE COMMON GOOD

There can be no question that James Madison was mightily concerned with the impact of faction upon society, or that he constructed elaborate mechanisms to retard its impact. In doing so, however, Madison never embraced the notion that faction was a positive development, nor did he renounce belief in the possibility of transcending faction through the pursuit of some overarching common good. Indeed his very definition of "faction" inescapably implies the existence of some such permanent common interest. In his famous *Federalist* No. 10, Madison defined the term: "By faction I understand a number of citizens, whether amounting to a majority or minority of the whole, who are united and actuated by some common impulse or passion, or of interest, adverse to the rights of other citizens, or to *the permanent and aggregate interests of the community*" (emphasis supplied).[17] Thus Madison's elaborate attempts to balance factions can only be truly understood in terms of the real threat of faction to the common good. Madison embraced such a common good, and devoted much of his life to securing its ascendancy.

The proof of Madison's commitment to a common good need not be limited to such indirect evidence as the quotation from No. 10. Indeed, such a commitment was one of two driving forces (the other being a commitment to popular sovereignty) that shaped his entire career.

Madison's conception of the public good was unmistakable and had substantive implications. Madison was heir to the republican tradition, in which, according to historian Gordon Wood, "no phrase except 'liberty' was invoked more often . . . than 'the public good.'" Indeed, "the peculiar excellence of republican government was that . . . by definition it had no other end than the welfare of the people: *res publica*, the public affairs, or the public good."[18] As Madison put it, "the public good, the real welfare of the great body of the people, is the supreme object to be pursued, and . . . no form of government whatever has any other value, than as it may be fitted for the attainment of this object."[19]

Moreover, that public good was distinct, identifiable, and enduring. Madison referred to "the permanent and aggregate interests of the community"[20] and proceeded to outline what this encompassed. First and foremost, it involved "the necessity of sacrificing private opinions and partial interests to the public good."[21] In addition, a regime committed to the common good must embody liberty and justice. This, in turn, required the substantive protection of both personal and property rights. Madison, drawing from David Hume, argued that "justice is the end of government,"[22] and that this justice consisted, as historian Drew McCoy phrased it, "largely of a respect for the property rights of others." Indeed, "Madison believed, above all," McCoy went on, "in a permanent public good and immutable standards of justice, both of which were linked to the rules of property that stabilized social relationships and that together defined the proper ends of republican government."[23] "No government," Madison concluded, "will long be respected, without being truly respectable; nor be truly respectable, without possessing a certain portion of order and stability."[24]

In sum, Madison held to a conception of the common good characterized by a priority of the general interest over local or individual interests, and a polity devoted to liberty and justice in the form of the protection of individual liberty and rights of property. This, in turn, would lead to an orderly and stable regime. It was a threat to precisely these beliefs in the 1780s that spawned Madison's constitutional theorizing.

The developments of the 1780s are generally well known,[25] but Madison's "take" on these matters is important. "The symptoms . . . are truly alarming," he wrote Jefferson.[26] Although Madison was fully aware of the weaknesses of the Confederation government,[27] his real concern was at the state level: "No small share of the embarrassments of America is to be charged on the blunders of our [state] governments," he wrote.[28] In particular he was aghast at the instability caused by "new men" in government, the threat to creditors inherent in paper money and debtor relief legislation, and a general slide toward chaos.[29] Perhaps his concern is best captured by his report to Jefferson of conditions in Virginia on the eve of ratification: "Our information from Virginia is far from being agreeable. . . . The people . . . are said to be generally discontented. A paper emission is again a topic among them. So is an installment of all debts in some places and making property a tender in others. . . . In several Counties the prisons & Court Houses & Clerks offices have been willfully burnt. In Green Briar the course of Justice has been mutinously stopped."[30]

The fact of these developments was bad enough; much worse were the implications. The activities at the state level challenged standards of property and justice, and led to a lack of "wisdom and steadiness" in government.[31] As Madison put it, "complaints are everywhere heard from our most considerate and virtuous citizens, equally the friends of public and private faith, and of public and personal liberty, that our governments are too unstable; that the public good is disregarded in the conflict of rival parties; and that measures are too often decided, not according to the rules of justice, and the rights of the minority party, but by the superior force of an interested and overbearing majority."[32] That placed the issue in its starkest form: Popular sovereignty appeared to be undermining the public good.

Madison turned his considerable talents toward devising a solution. The key issue of the age was how to reconcile popular sovereignty and the common good. As Madison was to put it in the *Federalist*, "to secure the public good, and private rights against the danger of such a faction, is the great object to which our inquiries are directed." In his famous phrase, Americans must find "a republican remedy for the diseases most incident to republican government."[33] His solution was to be one of the most innovative and important developments in political history—America's Constitutional system.

Although it is unnecessary to explore all the details of this familiar document, it is important to explore the extent to which Madison hewed to his articulated priority of securing the common good. There can be little doubt that Madison continued to view the common good, as he defined it, as the ultimate objective. Madison was well aware that by 1787 conditions were such that the public was looking for relief from the existing conditions. As he wrote to Jefferson, "my own idea is that the public mind will now or in a very little time receive any thing that promises stability to the public Councils and security to private rights."[34] This concern with what Madison would label the public good would be his guiding light throughout the convention. On May 31, in one of his first addresses before the delegates, Madison assessed his charge: "He [Madison] would shrink from nothing which should be found essential to such a form of Government as would provide for the safety, liberty, and happiness of the Community. This being the end of all our deliberations, all the necessary means for attaining it must, however reluctantly, be submitted to."[35] This included, he added in remarks several weeks later, "the necessity of providing more effectually for the security of private rights, and the steady dispensation of Justice. Interferences with these," he added, "were evils which had more perhaps than any thing else, produced the convention."[36] Madison's efforts to preserve the common good were chiefly structural, and he kept his eyes on his ultimate objective at all times.[37] When he realized that a "pure democracy" was "no cure from the mischief of faction," and that "the public good is disregarded in the conflicts of rival parties," he recommended a representative republic, which would "refine and enlarge the public views . . . and be more consonant with the public good."[38]

The examples of Madison's commitment to what he considered to be a definitive and permanent common good throughout his long career can be multiplied almost without limit.[39] For purposes of this chapter, the important conclusion is that Madison did, indeed, believe in such a common interest, and in the value of attempting to achieve it. The next sections revisit his view of the nature of leaders and followers, and their roles in this quest. After those are ascertained, the implications for Madison's connection to transformational leadership become patent.

MADISON'S FAITH IN FOLLOWERS

Madison's view of the people—who constitute the followers in the polity—was complex and nuanced. There is no doubt that at certain points in his career—most notably in the 1780s and after 1820—he was deeply troubled by the seeming lack of wisdom demonstrated by the masses. The people could (and often did) become wrapped up in their perceived short-term, selfish interests, to the detriment of their own long-term common good. Madison recognized this fact and often lamented it. However, this did not at all mean that he had no faith in the people. To the contrary, the second of his two core beliefs (the first being his commitment to a common good) was his dedication to a government stemming from the people. If this seeming contradiction can be resolved, much of Madison's thought—and its relationship to transformational leadership—becomes clear.

One of the pole stars that guided all of Madison's thought and action was an unquenchable faith in government by the people—popular sovereignty. "The ultimate authority," he argued, "wherever the derivative may be found, resides in the people alone." All governments are "but agents and trustee of the people," he added, must be "dependent on the great body of citizens," and "derive all . . . powers directly or indirectly from the great body of the people." [40]

The era of the American Revolution had begun with the rather naive view that "the people" were a homogeneous community, peopled by "virtuous" citizens willing to sacrifice individual desires for the good of all. The events of the 1780s, with "new men" (non-elites) in politics scrambling to promote selfish interests, soon put the lie to such credulous notions.[41] That placed the issue in its starkest form: Popular sovereignty appeared to be undermining the public good.

This forced Madison to do some deep thinking about the roles and capabilities of the people and their leaders in a regime of popular sovereignty. He developed a sophisticated and nuanced conceptualization of the abilities of the people, one capable of legitimizing a multiplicity of adaptive responses to a series of challenges to the common good under the rule of the people.

Madison began by acknowledging the premise of popular sovereignty, but with a caveat. In responding to Jefferson's call for frequent conventions, Madison had agreed that "as the people are the only legitimate fountain of power, and it is from them that the constitutional charter . . . is derived; it seems strictly consonant to the republican theory, to recur to the same original authority" for any revisions. Quickly, however, he hastened to add: "but there appear to be insuperable objections against the proposed recurrence to the people."[42] The problem was that the people, as a whole, were not capable of such an undertaking. As he expressed in correspondence with Edmund Randolph, "Whatever respect may be due to the rights of private judgment, and no man feels more of it than I do, there can be no doubt that there are subjects to which the capacities of the bulk of mankind are unequal,"[43] and the making of a Constitution was one of them. It "certainly surpasses the judgment of the greater part of them," he added to Jefferson.[44]

The matter went back to the issue of the public good. To expect the people as a whole to keep in mind the overarching interests of the general population, and to respect the property rights of the minority, was too much to ask, particularly in the passions of the moment. "At present," Madison commented, "the public mind is neither sufficiently cool nor sufficiently informed for so delicate an operation."[45] "The *passions* therefore not the *reason*, of the public, would sit in judgment. But it is the reason of the public alone that ought to controul and regulate the government."[46] "Under all these circumstances," he wrote to George Turberville, "it seems scarcely to be presumable that the deliberations of the body could be conducted in harmony, or terminate in the general good."[47]

In one respect, then, Madison had doubts about the people as the source of the common good. "In a nation of philosophers," Madison wrote in *Federalist* No. 49, there need be no concern for achieving the common good. "But a nation of philosophers," he went on to say, "is as little to be expected as the philosophical race of kings wished for by Plato."[48] As he put it to Jefferson, while "enlightened Statesmen, or the benevolent philosopher" might be able to rise above faction and interest and majority passion, "the bulk of mankind . . . are neither Statesmen nor Philosophers."[49]

Nevertheless, those doubts were but one part of Madison's formulation. He joined his concerns about the people with a paradoxical yet ultimately complementary underlying faith that the people had sufficient virtue to support the public good. Madison was quite candid in this regard. "As there is a degree of depravity in mankind which requires a certain degree of circumspection and distrust," he acknowledged, "so there are other qualities in human nature, which justify a certain portion of esteem and confidence. Republican government," he asserted, "presupposes the existence of these qualities in a higher degree than any other form."[50] Indeed, "to suppose that any form of government will secure liberty or happiness without any virtue in the people is a chimerical idea."[51] Madison took solace from his own state of Virginia. "The case of Virga. seems to prove," he wrote to Jefferson, "that the body of sober & steady people, even of the lower order, are tired of the vicicitudes, injustice, and follies which have so much characterised public measures, and are impatient for some change which promises stability."[52]

Though these views of the people appear at first blush to be contradictory, in reality they were not, and it was Madison's view of the role of popular leaders that bridged the gap. Madison went on to articulate the nexus between such leaders and the people. Madison acknowledged his ambiguity concerning the capabilities of the people. Rejecting those in the Virginia ratifying convention who had no faith in the people, Madison stated, "I consider it reasonable to conclude, that they will as readily do their duty, as deviate from it." However, he was not naive. He could not "place unlimited confidence in them, and expect nothing but the most exalted integrity and sublime virtue." The saving grace lay in their relationship with their leaders. "I go on this great republican principle, that the people will have virtue and intelligence to select men of virtue and wisdom. . . . If there be sufficient virtue and intelligence in the community, it will be exercised in the selection of these men."[53] This was the nub of it. Popular sovereignty and the common good were indeed compatible, if only leaders and followers united their particular virtues in pursuit of the common good. Much of the remainder of Madison's career was devoted to just this endeavor (we return to this topic in the next section).

Before turning to Madison's view of leaders, however, it is important to recognize that Madison's own views of the role of the people shifted somewhat as times themselves changed. A brief example from the 1790s should suffice. By the 1790s, the challenge to the common good had been turned on its head. Rather than the threat of popular passion running amok (as in the 1780s), the problem now was that a group of elite leaders, headed by Alexander Hamilton, were pursuing their selfish interests at the expense of the majority of the people and, of course, the common good.

Because the source of the threat to the common good was now reversed—rather than from unruly state democracies, it now came from a "financial aristocracy, led and encouraged by an officer of the executive department, who had acquired a dominant influence,"[54] Madison was led to rethink the proper role of leaders and the people. He recognized that the great bulk of the people agreed with his position. "On the republican [Madisonian] side," he wrote, "the superiority of numbers is so great, their sentiments are so decided, and . . . there is a common sentiment and common interest" in favor of reversing the Hamiltonian trend.[55] This led him logically to turn to the people for assistance in redressing the problem. Having established a government based on the people, Madison now argued that "to secure all the advantages of such a system, every good citizen will be at once a centinel over the rights of the people; over the authorities of the confederal government; and over both the rights and the authorities of the intermediate governments."[56]

This stance involved a seeming departure from his position in the 1780s, when he had fully trusted the people only to have virtue enough to select proper leaders. And, indeed, Madison did rethink the nexus between leaders and followers that he had posited in the 1780s, yet his final conclusions were less contradictory than might at first appear. In confronting the challenge of the 1790s, Madison returned to the issue of leaders and followers in an essay entitled "Who Are the Best Keepers of the People's Liberties?" Here, he did not suddenly abandon his concerns about the capabilities of the people; "the people *may* betray themselves," he wrote, and the lessons of history—recent history—bore this out. Yet, as in the 1780s, his was not a totally negative view of the capability of the people. Then, he had acknowledged that the people had some "virtue," certainly enough to choose enlightened leaders. Now, facing a small group of leaders who were not pursuing the common good, Madison expanded his view of the obligations of the people. Rather than followers who "think of nothing but obedience, leaving the care of their liberties to their wiser rulers," Madison held that the new regime placed a larger responsibility upon the people. His answer, then, to the query "Who are the best keepers of the people's liberties?" was "The people themselves." He went on, "The sacred trust can be no where so safe as in the hands most interested in preserving it." But Madison attached an important addendum to his seeming reliance upon the people and their wisdom. "The people," he observed, "ought to be enlightened, to be awakened, and to be united" in their efforts at oversight.[57] And the logical candidates to guide this process remained leaders who retained a sense of the common good. Madison, then, in responding to the unexpected development of misguided leaders in control of the new polity, adapted his view of the role of the people in a regime of popular sovereignty, but did not abandon his core belief that the people needed to be directed by those who knew better. Much of Madison's activity in the 1790s reflected this belief.

In sum, far from despising the people and their capabilities, Madison was deeply committed to the long-term interests of the followers as the ultimate measure of the common good, and he maintained that the followers (the people) played an important role in securing that common interest. However, at all times the role of leaders in this quest was paramount. We now revisit the last of the assumptions about the beliefs of James Madison.

JAMES MADISON AND THE ROLE OF LEADERS IN SECURING THE COMMON GOOD

Madison's frequent outrage at leaders who placed their own interests above that of the long-term interest of their followers must not mask the important role he assigned to appropriate leaders in the pursuit of the common good. The key term is "appropriate leaders": those who could transcend their own self-interest, perceive the common good, and help followers to do so also. These leaders were the appropriate individuals to help followers rise above their immediate interests to embrace the good of society as a whole. Such leaders, who in another day and age might be called transformational leaders, were at the heart of Madison's political philosophy.

There can be no question that Madison often showed concern over the actions of the putative leaders of society. In a remarkable document written in early 1787 and titled "Vices of the Political System of the U. States,"[58] he detailed several of the abuses of the 1780s. More important, Madison contemplated the possible causes. One lay in the leaders of the era, who often placed "ambition [and] personal interest [above the] public good."[59] Yet society needed leaders; but these needed leaders must be of a different stripe.

Madison recognized the need for leaders, even (perhaps especially) in a regime grounded in the people. "There can be no doubt that there are subjects to which the capacities of mankind are unequal," he had said. In such cases, "they must and will be governed by those with whom they happen to have acquaintance and confidence."[60] It had ever been so. Looking back through the ages, Madison noted that "in every case reported by ancient history, in which government has been established with deliberation and consent, the task . . . has been performed by some individual citizen of pre-eminent wisdom and approved integrity."[61] More recently, the example of Virginia added further proof. "In Virginia," he observed, "the mass of people have been . . . much accustomed to be guided by their rulers on all new and intricate questions."[62]

In a regime of popular sovereignty, the nature of these leaders and their relationship to the people became all-important. Madison stated the general principle to Edmund Randolph: There must be "a fortunate coincidence of leading opinions, and a general confidence of the people in those who may recommend" such opinions.[63] But the specifics were critical. Appropriate leaders must be selected. Only "the purest and noblest characters" were appropriate; those who "feel most strongly the proper motives to pursue the end of their appointment."[64] And those "proper motives" went to the heart of the matter. "The aim of every political constitution," noted Madison, "is, or ought to be, first, to obtain for rulers men who possess most wisdom to discern and most virtue to pursue, the common good of society."[65] Moreover, his view of what constituted that common good remained consistent. Such leaders should be "individuals of extended views," who "will give wisdom and steadiness" to government, and who are "interested in preserving the rights of property."[66]

When Madison turned to create a new polity to resolve the perceived problems of the 1780s, he did much more than just erect a structure that would help mediate opposing factions. Such an interpretation underestimates the extent to which Madison counted upon the "right" sort of leaders to guide the new polity. Historian Gordon Wood has demonstrated the elite nature of Federalist constitutionalism, but Madison's own commitment to ensuring that the proper sort of leaders would be in place has been underappreciated.[67]

His chief vehicle for securing proper leadership was the republican form itself. By creating a representative republic, it became possible to actually improve upon popular rule. Under a republic, it was possible to "refine and enlarge the public views, by passing them through the medium of a chosen body of citizens [that is, leaders], whose wisdom may best discern the true interest of their country, and whose patriotism and love of justice, will be least likely to sacrifice it to temporary or partial considerations." Under such a system, Madison concluded, "it may well happen that the public voice pronounced by the representatives of the people, will be more consonant to the public good, than if pronounced by the people themselves."[68] Madison explained this startling conclusion by demonstrating that the leaders of a republic, particularly a large republic, would be "men who possess the most attractive merit, and the most diffusive and established characters,"[69] and thereby would keep the public good in view.

A closer look at Madison's explanation of the specific departments of the new national government reinforces his emphasis on securing proper leadership for the new government. The House of Representatives demonstrates nicely his nexus between the people and their leaders. The House, he said, "should rest on the solid foundation of the people themselves," and direct election of Representatives reinforced "a clear principle of free Government."[70] Despite its "dependence on . . . the people," the goal remained of "obtain[ing] for rulers men who possess most wisdom to discern, and most virtue to pursue the common good of the society."[71] This was to be achieved by the large election districts. "In so great a number," Madison noted, "a fit representative would be most likely to be found."[72]

The Senate, through its structure and the individuals who would make it up, was even more likely to uphold the common good. Indeed, that was its essential raison d'être. In speaking of the Senate, Madison suggested "that such an institution may sometimes be necessary, as a defence to the people against their own temporary errors and delusions. . . . In these critical moments, how salutary will be the interference of some temperate and respectable body of citizens, in order to check the misguided career, and to suspend the blow meditated by the people against themselves, until reason, justice and truth can regain their authority over the public mind?"[73] Such a body required appropriate leaders, so Madison called for more stringent qualifications for eligibility, to ensure "greater . . . stability of character."[74] This would also be ensured by the indirect election of that body.[75] Given these precautions, Madison was relatively sure that the actions of its members would correlate to "the . . . prosperity of the community."[76]

The executive and judiciary could also be expected to be inhabited by appropriate individuals, with a similar positive impact on the common good. Both the executive and judicial branches could be "useful to the Community at large as an additional check agst. a pursuit of . . . unwise & unjust measures."[77] Undoubtedly the president would be an individual "of distinguished character" and "an object of general attention and esteem,"[78] also elected indirectly. The executive could be expected to use his rather formidable powers in pursuit of the public good. "The independent condition of the Ex[ecutive] . . . will render him a just Judge," and help ensure "the safety of a minority in Danger of oppression from an unjust and interested majority."[79] The judiciary, to be nominated by that executive, who is "likely to select fit characters," will be "independent tribunals of justice [who] will consider themselves in a peculiar manner the guardians" of the public interest.[80]

In sum, throughout the new polity one could expect to find just the sort of leaders Madison had said were necessary for the accomplishment of the public good in a regime of popular sovereignty: men of broad views who would respect the property rights of the minority and seek the good of the whole, irrespective of factional politics.

Again, it is useful to make a brief foray into the 1790s to reinforce the staying power of Madison's commitment to good leadership. Recall that the challenge to the common good in these years was a small cadre of self-interested leaders who were attempting to foist selfish policies upon an unsuspecting citizenry. It was in these circumstances that Madison sought to invoke the latent power of the oppressed followers.

Given his views of the respective roles of leaders and the people, the concept of public opinion became key. Public opinion, which Madison defined as "that of the majority," "sets bounds to every government, and is the real sovereign in every free one."[81] Madison recognized that "all power has been traced up to opinion," and that "the most arbitrary government is controuled where the public opinion is fixed."[82] The problem was that "the Country is too much uninformed, and too inert to speak for itself."[83] "How devoutly is it to be wished, then, that the public opinion of the United States should be enlightened," Madison wrote. The solution was to turn to appropriate leaders. "In proportion as Government is influenced by opinion," Madison observed, "it must be so, by whatever influences opinion."[84] Leaders were just such an influence.

Madison's tactics can best be demonstrated by way of an example. In 1793, as the policies of the Hamiltonians seemed to have reached dangerous proportions, Madison wrote to Jefferson with a plan. "If an early & well digested effort for calling out the real sense of the people be not made," he wrote, "there is room to apprehend they may in many places be misled." Having consulted with a fellow Virginia leader (probably Monroe), Madison outlined their strategy. "We shall endeavor at some means of repelling the danger; particularly by setting on foot expressions of the public mind in important Counties, and under the auspices of respectable names." He gave an example. "I have written with this view to Caroline [county], and have suggested a proper train of ideas, and a wish that Mr. P[endleton] would patronise the measure. Such an example," he predicted, "would have great effect." Although drafted, proposed, and marshalled through by popular leaders, the result "would be considered as an authentic specimen of the *Country* temper." The only real problem with the plan was a lack of acceptable leaders. "The want of opportunities, and our ignorance of trust worthy characters," Madison concluded, "will circumscribe our efforts in this way to a very narrow compass."[85]

These examples suggest that Madison did perceive a need for leaders, but these were very special leaders indeed. They were men who could transcend their own private interests, perceive common interests salient to all members of the society, and who had the ability to arouse followers to recognize that common good and act accordingly. This sounds surprisingly like many things written about transformational leadership in our own day. It is to that connection that we now turn.

THE MADISONIAN LEGACY IN TRANSFORMATIONAL LEADERSHIP

Michael Keeley has argued that "popular media, communitarian writings, and recent management literature suggest that communities and organizations are rent by factional mischief: by individuals and groups who pursue their own selfish interests without regard for the common good. An emerging solution to this problem is 'transformational' leadership, which seeks to refocus individuals' attention on higher visions and collective goals."[86] This is true. James MacGregor Burns describes transforming leadership as occurring when the purposes of the participants in the leadership relation "become fused."[87] Bernard Bass characterizes transformational leadership as a process that causes "individuals to put aside selfish aims for the sake of some greater, common good."[88] Moreover, both Burns and Bass note the key role leaders play in this process. As Burns puts it, "the leader takes the initiative in making the leader-led connection. . . . Leaders continue to take the major part in maintaining and effectuating the relationship with followers and will have the major role in ultimately carrying out the combined purposes of leaders and followers."[89]

And Bernard Bass indicates that "transformational leadership . . . occurs when leaders broaden and elevate the interests of employees . . . and when they stir their employees to look beyond their own self interest for the good of the group."[90]

Having traced the central tenets of Madisonian thought, the paralellism between Madison and the modern writers on transformational leadership should be obvious. Indeed, it could be said that transformational leadership addresses a problem left unresolved by Madison. Throughout his career, Madison struggled with the tension that often existed between his two priorities of the common good and popular sovereignty. That had been at the heart of his elitist solution to the problem of majority tyranny in the 1780s (that is, the Constitution). His answer in the 1780s had been to create a polity that assured the wise leadership of those committed to the common good. Regrettably, at the end of his career (after 1820), with the overwhelming tide of majoritarian democracy sweeping all before it, Madison despaired of ever finding a lasting solution.[91] James Madison might have been comforted had his wide circle of correspondents included James MacGregor Burns. With his transforming leadership, Burns sought to identify a process to achieve the common good, even in a democracy—by raising the followers themselves to new levels of insight and commitment in pursuit of shared interests. In this sense, then, transformational leadership represents an advanced stage of Madisonian leadership, dedicated to the same end: achieving the common good.

An appreciation of Madison and the wellsprings of his thought also provides richness and depth to our understanding of the implications of transformational leadership. For example, though such writers as Burns and Bass have been instrumental in developing the concept (and numerous others have elaborated it), having a sense of Madison's experiences—such as his deeply held commitment to securing the good of all while facing the threats of faction and self-interest on one hand, and the dangers of overweening leaders on the other—permits a new perspective on one of the most important issues related to transformational leadership: its ethical implications. It is that to which we now turn.

JAMES MADISON AND THE ETHICS OF TRANSFORMATIONAL LEADERSHIP

Michael Keeley's study of Madisonian thought raises one other important issue that pertains to transformational leadership: the ethical danger of individual coercion in the interests of a perceived common good. Keeley's argument draws inspiration from his depiction of Madison's concern for oppressed minorities in the polity. The source of the difficulty remains the reality that there are different interests in society. Focusing on Madison's efforts to resolve "the problem of controlling self-interested organizational behavior," Keeley suggests that Madison's main concern was "the problems that zealots—armed by moral inspiration, mobilized and purposeful—might create for persons who disagreed with them."[92] Applying this insight to modern transformational leadership, Keeley concludes that "unless leaders are able to transform everyone and create an absolute unanimity of interests (a very special case), transformational leadership produces simply a majority will that represents the interests of the strongest faction."[93] Unethical individual coercion inevitably follows in the train of such leadership.

Keeley's ethical critique of transformational leadership extends beyond Madison. He argues that in today's world "there is no agreement or commitment to the public good, no common vision, no mutual purpose." "Transformational leadership," he asserts, "aims to get people's thoughts off distributional questions and refocus them on common goals, or communal interests." But "the ethical justification for diverting attention from individual to communal interests is unclear, given the hypothetical nature of the latter." Instead, organizational policies and stances are more likely to represent the personal interests of one or more stakeholders. That being the case, "it seems deceptive to win other persons' support by calling those [private agendas] . . . *common goals, interests*, etc."[94]

Although Keeley may have misinterpreted Madison to some extent,[95] the ethical critique of transformational leadership he articulates remains valid, perhaps more so today than ever before. It behooves us to consider that critique carefully, and to consider potential remedies. Ironically, perhaps, it is James Madison who provides the appropriate "jumping-off place"; he directs us toward a potentially viable solution.

Even though it is not necessary to fully accept Keeley's dismissal of the possibility of there being any common good in an organizational setting, the tremendous diversity in today's workplace and society cautions against a casual rejection of his concern about the coercion of individual interests and values in the name of a common societal or organizational cause. As Keeley suggests, to force group members to participate in pursuing objectives that do not mesh with their substantive needs has serious ethical implications. Given the diversity in constituent values, needs, and interests, perhaps the ultimate ethical challenge in today's organizations is to devise a process whereby the "common" objective to be pursued is congruent with follower needs and interests.

To be fair, James MacGregor Burns has never intended anything less, and Bernard Bass in this volume echoes Burns's stance. Burns has defined "moral leadership" as "a relationship . . . of mutual needs, aspirations and values. . . . Moral leadership emerges from, and returns to, the fundamental wants and needs, aspirations, and values of the followers."[96] Bass adds that "the truly transformational leader concerned with an ethical philosophy in managing an organization conceives of the organization's ultimate criterion of worth as the extent to which it satisfies all of its stakeholders."[97] The key question then becomes: Is it possible to achieve this in a diverse constituency?

Interestingly, it is James Madison himself who (albeit unknowingly) points to a potential solution. Throughout his career, Madison had struggled with the tension that often emerged between his dual commitments to popular sovereignty and the common good. In doing so, he often confronted a dilemma somewhat parallel to the concern voiced by Keeley: How could one secure the common good (in which Madison deeply believed) when the followers often misunderstood its nature and hence disagreed with Madison's perception of it? Throughout most of his career, Madison consoled himself with the knowledge that there was a unitary common interest to be had, and that appropriate leaders—if only they could be identified and placed in positions of influence—could lead the polity in securing it. To his increasing dismay, developments after 1820 thwarted Madison's preferred solution. By 1820, the sweep of mass democracy had made obsolete the role of elite leadership. Most individuals now agreed with Richmond newspaper editor Thomas Ritchie: "The day of prophets and oracles has passed; . . . we are free citizens of a free country, and must think for ourselves."[98]

Despite Madison's creative attempts to ensure stability, the protection of property rights, and justice in a majoritarian democracy, he gradually recognized that none of his proposed solutions was finding favor with the populace. Worse, events of the 1820s suggested that misguided popular passion was to be an ongoing reality. At the end of a long career devoted to seeking the congruence of rule by the people and the pursuit of the common good, Madison realized that a choice between these sometimes competing objectives needed to be made. When finally faced with this stark reality, Madison did not hesitate. As early as the 1820s, he had indicated his priority. In a letter to Jefferson, he had bemoaned the new reality, and noted that "the will of the nation being omnipotent for right, is so for wrong also." Nevertheless, "the will of the nation being in the majority, the minority must submit to that danger of oppression as an evil infinitely less than the danger to the whole nation from a will independent of [the majority]."[99] Thus, although the newly emergent majoritarian democracy held profound concerns for Madison, he chose to cast his lot with the perceived interests of the followers, even though at times this came at the expense of the common good.[100]

This focus on the supremacy of follower interests points the way to ethical transformational leadership. James MacGregor Burns, though acknowledging the important role that leaders must play, has also taken care to point out that for leadership to be moral, followers "in responding to leaders . . . [must] have adequate knowledge of all leaders and programs and the capacity to choose among those alternatives."[101] This is the key. If transformational leadership is to seek to attain a common interest among relevant stakeholders, the determination of what that good is must derive from the stakeholders themselves. Ethical transformational leadership requires no less.

Although the difficulty of achieving this lofty goal is legitimately daunting, modern leadership scholar Ron Heifetz suggests an approach to leadership that promises a solution. Heifetz introduces a creative process he calls "adaptive work," which he describes as "the activity of mobilizing a social system to face tough problems, or to adapt to challenges," or "the activity of mobilizing people to clarify their aspirations and adapt to challenges they face."[102] The key point in Heifetz's work is that the responsibility falls upon the followers to work through their differences in values, interests, and agendas. The role of the leader remains key; he or she has the obligation to keep the focus upon the central issues, to maintain a productive atmosphere for productive disagreement, and to ensure that all relevant stakeholders have a voice.[103] This move toward common ground will assuredly involve conflict, but if handled correctly, it will also yield a consensus concerning the acceptable direction of the organization. This consensus, as Bernard Bass explains, does not necessarily mean total agreement. "In true consensus," Bass says, "the interests of all are fully considered, but the final decision may fail to please everyone completely."[104] Even though not all may completely agree with the outcome, all have had their say and, ideally, are in agreement on fundamentals. If organizations have pursued such a process, ethical lapses are likely to be at a minimum.

This process of managed conflict, where leaders seek to help all stakeholders determine their own conception of the common interests to be pursued, is a far cry from a *laissez-faire* approach in which leaders merely serve as gatekeepers for contending factions who have no interest in a shared common purpose. This sort of transformational leadership fulfills Burns's notion of transforming leadership. "Every person, group, and society has latent tension and hostility," Burns acknowledges. "Leadership acts as an inciting and triggering force in the conversion of conflicting demands, values, and goals into significant behavior."[105] Thus conflict, properly managed, can lead to an acceptable version of the common good. Ethical transformational leadership, then, really involves leaders and followers working together to determine and achieve mutual interests. As leadership scholar Gill Hickman has stated, "rather than being unethical, true transformational leaders identify the core values and unifying purposes of the organization and its members, liberate their human potential, and foster plural leadership and effective, satisfied followers."[106]

CONCLUSION: JAMES MADISON, THE COMMON GOOD, AND THE ETHICS OF TRANSFORMATIONAL LEADERSHIP

Transformational leadership has become a central theme of modern leadership conceptions. As such, it deserves close and critical study. Therefore Michael Keeley has done us a great service in utilizing the thought of James Madison to fashion an ethical critique of this form of leadership and to repudiate its validity. My own explorations of Madison yield a somewhat different "take" on Madison and his relevance for transformational leadership. I see Madison's thought as a legitimate precursor to today's conceptions of transformational leadership, because both seek to realize the achievement of a common good. Indeed, James MacGregor Burns may have gone Madison one better; he proposes a type of leadership that has the potential to resolve a problem Madison gave up on as unsolvable: that of creating a nexus between the desires of followers and conceptions of the common good. If this is done correctly, transformational leadership can stand as a beacon for those interested in the pursuit of ethical leadership.

NOTES

1. James MacGregor Burns, *Leadership* (New York: Harper and Row, 1978).
2. For a summation of such critiques, together with a rebuttal, read Chapter 8, "The Ethics of Transformational Leadership," by Bernard Bass.
3. See Chapter 6, "The Trouble with Transformational Leadership: Toward a Federalist Ethic for Organizations," by Michael Keeley.
4. Burns, 19–20.
5. Ibid., 20.
6. Bernard Bass, *Leadership and Performance beyond Expectations* (New York: Free Press, 1985). For a cogent discussion of the contrast between Burns and Bass, see Richard A. Couto, "The Transformation of Transforming Leadership," in J. Thomas Wren, ed., *The Leader's Companion: Insights on Leadership through the Ages* (New York: Free Press, 1995), 102–7.
7. See generally Bass, *Leadership and Performance*.
8. Bass, "The Ethics of Transformational Leadership."
9. Burns, 3.
10. Bernard Bass, "From Transactional to Transformational Leadership: Learning to Share the Vision," *Organizational Dynamics* 18 (1990): 21.
11. See Chapter 6, p. 111.
12. Ibid., 121.
13. Ibid., 135.
14. Ibid., 117.
15. Ibid., 118 and *passim*. The quotation is taken somewhat out of context, that is, from Keeley's discussion of leaders, but the generalization seems justified.

16. Constraints of space require that the analysis here be rather severely truncated. Much of the analysis focuses only on Madison in the 1780s and 1790s. For a much more elaborate treatment of these issues, see J. Thomas Wren, "Leaders, the People, and the Common Good: James Madison and the Challenges of Popular Sovereignty" (Unpublished manuscript, University of Richmond, 1997). The best monographs on Madison are Drew McCoy, *The Last of the Fathers: James Madison and the Republican Legacy* (Cambridge: Cambridge University Press, 1989), and Lance Banning, *The Sacred Fire of Liberty: James Madison and the Founding of the Federal Republic* (Ithaca: Cornell University Press, 1995); but also see Jack N. Rakove, *Original Meanings: Politics and Ideas in the Making of the Constitution* (New York: Alfred A. Knopf, 1996). The best biography of Madison is Ralph Ketcham, *James Madison: A Biography* (New York: The Macmillan Company, 1971); but also consult Irving Brant, *James Madison*, 6 vols. (Indianapolis: Bobbs-Merrill, 1948–1961).

17. *Federalist* No.10, in *The Papers of James Madison, Congressional Series*, William T. Hutchinson et al., eds., 17 vols. (Chicago: University of Chicago Press, 1962–77; Charlottesville: University Press of Virginia, 1977–), 10: 264.

18. Gordon S. Wood, *Creation of the American Republic, 1776–1787* (New York: W.W. Norton & Company, 1969), 55.

19. *Federalist* No. 45, in *Papers*, 10: 429.

20. *Federalist* No. 10, Ibid., 264.

21. *Federalist* No. 37, Ibid., 364. See *also* Wood, 53–54.

22. *Federalist* No. 51, in *Papers*, 10: 479.

23. McCoy, 41–42.

24. *Federalist* No. 62, in *Papers*, 10: 540.

25. See generally Wood, 391–425.

26. Madison to Jefferson, 19 March 1787, in *Papers*, 9: 318.

27. Madison to Edmund Randolph, 25 February 1787, Ibid., 299.

28. *Federalist* No. 62, Ibid., 10: 538.

29. Ibid., 538–39. *Federalist* No. 44, Ibid., 421. "Notes for Speech Opposing Paper Money" [c. 1 November 1786], Ibid., 9: 158–59.

30. Madison to Jefferson, 6 September 1787, Ibid., 10: 164.

31. Madison to Caleb Wallace, 23 August 1785, Ibid., 8: 350.

32. *Federalist* No. 10, Ibid., 10: 264.

33. Ibid., 267.

34. Madison to Jefferson, 6 September 1787, Ibid., 164.

35. Speech in Constitutional Convention, 31 May 1787, Ibid., 21.

36. Speech in Constitutional Convention, 6 June 1787, Ibid., 32.

37. *Federalist* No. 37, Ibid., 360.

38. *Federalist* No. 10, Ibid., 264, 268.

39. See generally Wren, "Leaders, the People."

40. *Federalist* No. 46, in *Papers*, 10: 438–39. *Federalist* No. 39, Ibid., 379–80. See Marvin Meyers, *The Mind of the Founder: Sources of the Political Thought of James Madison*, rev. ed. (Hanover: University Press of New England, 1981), 408; Robert A. Rutland, *James Madison: The Founding Father* (New York: Macmillan Publishing Company, 1987), 33.

41. See generally Wood.

42. *Federalist* No. 49, in *Papers*, 10: 461.

43. Madison to Edmund Randolph, 10 January 1788, Ibid., 355.
44. Madison to Jefferson, 9 December 1787, Ibid., 313.
45. Madison to Jefferson, 10 August 1788, Ibid., 11: 226.
46. *Federalist* No. 49, Ibid., 10: 463. See also *Federalist* No. 50, Ibid., 471–72.
47. Madison to George Turberville, 2 November 1788, Ibid., 11: 331–32. Madison to Edmund Pendleton, 20 October 1788, Ibid., 307.
48. *Federalist* No. 49, Ibid., 10: 462.
49. Madison to Jefferson, 24 October 1787, Ibid., 213.
50. *Federalist* No. 55, Ibid., 507–8.
51. Speech in Virginia Ratifying Convention, 20 June 1788, Ibid., 11: 163.
52. Madison to Jefferson, 9 December 1787, Ibid., 10: 313.
53. Speech in Virginia Ratifying Convention, 20 June 1788, Ibid., 11: 163.
54. Madison to Jefferson, 8 August 1791, Ibid., 14: 69.
55. "A Candid State of the Parties," in *National Gazette*, 26 September 1792, Ibid., 372.
56. "Government," in *National Gazette*, 31 December 1791, Ibid., 179. See also "Charters," Ibid., 191.
57. "Who Are the Best Keepers of the People's Liberties?" in *National Gazette*, 20 December 1792, Ibid., 426.
58. *Federalist* No. 48, Ibid., 9: 348–57.
59. Ibid., 354.
60. Madison to Edmund Randolph, 10 January 1788, Ibid., 10: 355.
61. *Federalist* No. 38, Ibid., 365.
62. Madison to Jefferson, 9 December 1787, Ibid., 313.
63. Madison to Edmund Randolph, 10 January 1788, Ibid., 355–56.
64. "Vices of the Political System of the United States," Ibid., 9: 357. See also Speech in Constitutional Convention, 23 June 1787, Ibid., 10: 74.
65. *Federalist* No. 57, Ibid., 521. See Ralph Ketcham, "Party and Leadership in Madison's Conception of the Presidency," *Quarterly Journal of the Library of Congress* 37 (1980): 249.
66. "Vices," in *Papers*, 9: 355. Madison to Caleb Wallace, 23 August 1785, Ibid., 8: 350. "Observations on Jefferson's Draught of a Constitution for Virginia" [sent to John Brown, 15 October 1788], Ibid., 11: 287.
67. Wood, 471–518.
68. *Federalist* No. 10, in *Papers*, 10: 268.
69. Ibid.
70. Speech in Constitutional Convention, 31 May 1787, Ibid., 19. Speech in Constitutional Convention, 6 June 1787, Ibid., 32.
71. *Federalist* No. 52, Ibid., 484. *Federalist* No. 57, Ibid., 521.
72. *Federalist* No. 57, Ibid., 524.
73. *Federalist* No. 63, Ibid., 546.
74. *Federalist* No. 62, Ibid., 535.
75. *Federalist* No. 39, Ibid., 378.
76. *Federalist* No. 63, Ibid., 545.
77. Speech in Constitutional Convention, 21 July 1787, Ibid., 109.
78. Speech in Constitutional Convention, 19 July 1787, Ibid., 108.
79. Speech in Constitutional Convention, 4 June 1787, Ibid., 25.

80. Speech in Constitutional Convention, 21 July 1787, Ibid., 110. Speech in Constitutional Convention, 8 June 1787, in Gaillard Hunt, ed., *The Writings of James Madison*, 9 vols. (New York: G.P. Putnam's Sons, 1910), 5: 385.

81. Madison to Jefferson, 24 October 1787, in *Papers*, 10: 213. "Public Opinion," in *National Gazette*, 19 December 1791, Ibid., 14: 170.

82. "Charters," Ibid., 192.

83. Madison to Jefferson, 2 September 1793, Ibid., 15: 93.

84. "Public Opinion," Ibid., 14: 170.

85. Madison to Jefferson, 27 August 1793, Ibid., 15: 75. For similar examples, see Madison to Archibald Stuart, 1 September 1793, Ibid., 87–88; Madison to Jefferson, 2 September 1793, Ibid., 92–93.

86. Keeley, abstract of "The Trouble with Transformational Leadership," in *Business Ethics Quarterly* 5 (1995): 67.

87. Burns, 20.

88. Bass, *Leadership and Performance*, 187.

89. Burns, 20.

90. Bass, "Transactional to Transformational," 21.

91. Wren, "Leaders, the People"; McCoy, *The Last of the Fathers*.

92. See Chapter 6, pp. 140–41.

93. Ibid., p. 124.

94. Ibid., p. 129.

95. Although Madison had a deep and abiding commitment to the protection of individual liberties, he was less concerned with the problem of political minorities—unless that minority articulated the common good. Madison believed that there was a common good, permanent and identifiable. This was what must be protected against majorities and minorities. He was concerned with the treatment of minorities only insofar as they represented that common good. Other minorities could be dealt with "through the republican principle, which enables the majority to defeat [minorities that did not conform to common interests] . . . by regular vote." *Federalist* No. 10, in *Papers*, 10: 266.

96. Burns, 4.

97. See Chapter 8, p. 184.

98. Richmond *Enquirer*, 3 January 1829, in McCoy, 121. See Wren, "Leaders, the People."

99. Madison to Jefferson, 17 February 1825, in *Letters*, 3: 483.

100. Madison to Thomas Ritchie, 18 December 1825, Ibid., 507.

101. Burns, 4.

102. Ronald L. Heifetz, "Leadership with and without Authority" (unpublished ms., John F. Kennedy School of Government, Harvard University, 1992), 37, 39.

103. Ronald L. Heifetz, *Leadership without Easy Answers* (Cambridge: Harvard University Press, 1994), 127–28, 138–44.

104. See Chapter 8, p. 178.

105. Burns, 38.

106. Quoted in Bass, see Chapter 8, p. 188.

8

The Ethics of Transformational Leadership

Bernard M. Bass

INTRODUCTION

In the early 1980s, when an author submitted a manuscript for publication dealing with transformational leadership, one reviewer asked critically "What's different about transformational leadership? Isn't leadership completely covered by the two factors of initiation and consideration?" Since then, a host of empirical and theoretical articles and books have appeared using the transactional/transformational paradigm. They strongly support the efficacy of the conceptualization and utility of the contribution of transformational leadership to organizational performance. Nonetheless, an alarm has sounded by one critic over the "obsession" with transformational leadership (Gronn 1995) and its ethics have been questioned by several others such as Keeley (1995). And yet, it was conceived as leadership that involved the moral uplifting of followers (Burns 1978) and that required moral maturity (Kuhnert and Lewis 1987).

Critics fault the morality of transformational leadership for communications that may border on the unethical; for failing to consider the needs for countervailing power embodied in transactional exchanges, controls, and contracts; for appearing to the critics to be inconsistent with the democratic principles of the Organizational Development Movement; and for presumably being exploitative and manipulative in overriding the self-interests of followers in order to accommodate the self-interests of the leaders. So despite the array of meta-analytical evidence and generalizable findings that transformational leadership is more effective, productive, innovative, and satisfying to followers than is transactional leadership and that people's implicit theories of leadership are likely to be more transformational than transactional, some critics question its ethics. Although the criticisms overlap, I will attempt to refute each of them separately.

Declaring that ethics is at the heart of leadership, Ciulla (1995) concluded that "a culture's ethical values are what define the concept of leadership." Leadership is fundamental to ethical considerations. Again, Gini (1995) avowed that "without the continuous commitment, enforcement and modeling of leadership, standards of business ethics cannot and will not be achieved in organizations. . . . Badly led businesses wind up doing unethical things."

Kouzes and Posner (1993) noted that the credibility of leadership depended on its moral purpose, trust, and the hopes it engendered. Leaders are seen as obligated and responsible for the moral environment of their group, organization, or society (Greenleaf 1977). A major task for leaders is bringing together their followers around common values (Fairholm 1991). The leaders themselves, often are seen as the embodiment of such values (McCollough 1991). And just as when leaders are more competent, those they lead are more effective, so when leaders are more morally mature, those they lead display higher moral reasoning (Dukerich, Nichols, et al. 1990).

Contrary to the critics, it is the transactional leaders who are more likely to engage in unethical practices and transformational leaders who are less likely to do so. Transformational leaders concentrate on terminal values such as integrity and fairness. Whether the actions of leaders are seen as good, right, and proper or bad, wrong, and improper depends upon their stage of development. For Lichtenstein, Smith, and Torbert (1995), the least-mature leaders are transactional opportunists. Such "opportunists" practice manipulation, deception, and contingent reinforcement for utilitarian purposes. Their ethical awareness is to exchange "an eye for an eye." Similar to them in moral maturity are the "diplomats" for whom social norms determine what is right, good, and proper. At the other extreme in development are transformationally oriented leaders who see the responsibility for their organization's development and impact on society.

Burns (1978), Bass (1985), and Howell and Avolio (1992) specifically addressed the issue of the morality of transformational leadership. For

Burns, by definition, the transforming leader was morally uplifting. But Bass argued that transformational leaders could wear the black hats of villains or the white hats of heroes depending on their values. (Those who wear black hats are now seen as pseudotransformational.) Howell and Avolio described the values and traits that distinguish ethical from unethical transformational leaders. The former are socially oriented; the latter are self-oriented.

Burns (1978) discussed leadership as transforming, and on occasion as transformational. Both the leader and the led were transformed—sharply changed in performance and outlook. The change was not incremental. But transforming is just one of the effects of the leadership. We also need to examine the behaviors of transformational leadership and the attributions given to transformational leadership.

We will make much here of the distinction between transformational and pseudotransformational leadership to suggest that the criticism of the ethics of the former is really only relevant to the latter. Leaders are truly transformational when they increase awareness of what is right, good, important, and beautiful; when they help to elevate followers' needs for achievement and self-actualization; when they foster in followers higher moral maturity; and when they move followers to go beyond their self-interests for the good of their group, organization, or society. Pseudotransformational leaders may also motivate and transform their followers, but in doing so they arouse support for special interests at the expense of others rather than what's good for the collectivity. They foster psychodynamic identification, projection, fantasy, and rationalization as substitutes for achievement and actualization. They encourage "we-they" competitiveness and the pursuit of the leaders' own self-interests instead of the common good. They are more likely to foment envy, greed, hate, and conflict rather than altruism, harmony, and cooperation. In making this distinction between the transformational and pseudotransformational leader, it should be clear that we are describing two ideal types. Most leaders are neither completely saints nor completely sinners. They are neither completely selfless nor selfish. For example, Kemal Ataturk almost single-handedly willed and transformed the medieval Ottoman Empire into modern Turkey. He was ruthless in dealing with the Islamic establishment and his political opponents, yet it was for the common good that an illiterate country was made highly literate, the status of women was raised greatly, a modern infrastructure was built, and the new republic's borders successfully defended.

Let's be clear also about the differences between transformational and transactional leadership. For Bass and Avolio (1993), transformational leadership contains the interrelated components of charisma or idealized influence (attributed or behavioral), inspirational motivation, intellectual stimulation, and individualized consideration. Other theorists working in the same genre of the "new leadership," such as House and Shamir (1993) and Conger and Kanungo (1988), conceive of the same components falling under the rubric of charismatic leadership.

When leadership is charismatic, followers identify with the leaders' aspirations and want to emulate the leaders.[1] If the leadership is truly transformational, its charisma or idealized influence is characterized by high moral and ethical standards. Its inspirational motivation provides followers with challenges and meaning for engaging in shared goals and undertakings. Its intellectual stimulation helps followers to question assumptions and to generate more creative solutions to problems. Its individual consideration treats each follower as an individual and provides coaching, mentoring, and growth opportunities (Bass 1985).

In its simplest sense, transactional leadership is leadership by contingent reinforcement. Followers are motivated by the leaders' promises, rewards, and/or threats of disciplinary actions or punishments. The leaders' actions depend on whether the followers carry out what the leaders and followers have "contracted" to do. In constructive transactions, the leaders give out assignments, negotiate or contract/consult with followers, or they may participate in discussing what is to be done in exchange for implicit or explicit rewards and the allocation of desired resources. In corrective transactions or contingent rewarding, the leaders engage in active management-by-exception by monitoring follower performance and correcting their mistakes when and if they occur. Or, the leaders engage in passive management-by-exception by waiting passively for followers' mistakes to be called to their attention before taking corrective action with negative feedback or reprimand.

At one extreme, Carey (1995) has argued that it is possible to see transformational leadership as promoting the end values of justice, equality, and human rights, as well as endorsing the modal values of honesty, loyalty, and fairness as its basis for influencing change. But it can also be subverted to endorse perverse end values such as racial superiority, submission, and Social Darwinism. In the same way, transactional leadership is moral to the degree that promises are kept and negotiations are honest. At the same time, it is possible to locate the unethical excesses of transactional leadership. What we would regard as wrong, bad, and improper is seen in the transformational and transactional beliefs and behavior of Sir Charles Trevelyan. He espoused the principle of "natural causes" as the reason for the starvation of the Irish during the potato famines of 1845 to 1849. The British government's Treasury official in charge of organizing relief stated that if you fed the starving, they would come to depend on government handouts rather than working. Furthermore, government intervention with free food would lower the price of corn and wheat, thereby injuring traders and merchants. Therefore, food was provided only in county workhouses for work on useless projects for men who were often too weak to work. Benjamin Jowett heard a political economist say that he feared the famine in 1848 would not kill more than a million people, and that would scarcely be enough to do much good (Woodham-Smith 1991)!

THE ETHICS OF IMPRESSION MANAGEMENT

A first criticism of the ethics of transformational leaders is that they employ amoral puffery. To foster their influence and esteem among their followers, transformational leaders, particularly those leaders who want to bolster their charismatic and inspirational image, engage in impression management (Gronn 1994). Such leaders stretch the facts to make themselves appear more confident than they actually are, to exaggerate their mental accomplishments, to project an image of greater strength and decisiveness beyond their actual endowments, and to say more about their good points rather than their shortcomings. They may make themselves easier to identify with by focusing on their humble backgrounds and catering to the Horatio Alger fantasies of their followers. They appeal to the whims and fantasies of their followers. According to critics, such leaders espouse the values they feel fit the implicit theories that followers have about ideal leadership. To be more inspirational, they paint a vision of the future that is more fantasy than reality and exaggerate the meaningfulness of the followers' efforts.

Impression Management Needs to Remain Ethical

The criticism of impression management overstates the case and fails to appreciate the differences between absolute truth-telling, emotional and intellectual appeals, advocacy, gradations and shadings of the facts, and the big lies. The criticism fails to appreciate that credibility of the leaders suffers when the truth is stretched. Trust in the leader is risked, and that trust is the single most important variable moderating the effects of transformational leadership on the performance, attitudes, and satisfaction of the followers. This was the conclusion reached in a large-scale survey by Podsakoff, MacKenzie, Moorman, and Fetter (1990). Although the distant leader may be able to play with the truth longer than can the close, immediate leader (Bass 1993), the trust so necessary for transformational leadership is lost when the leader is caught in a lie, when the fantasy fails to materialize, or when hypocrisy and inconsistency are exposed.

A certain level of impression management has become the norm in our society of advertising, publicity agents, public relations consultants, and spin doctors seeking visibility and celebrity status. To the extent to which what is moral may be defined as what is customary and an accepted way of life, in the modern world some degree of puffery may be acceptable and controllable by the availability of full information and the concern of the leaders with maintaining their credibility and trust. Rhetorical skills that enhance appeals and impressions are seen as significant attributes of leaders who are at a distance from their followers but not as much so for those leaders close to their followers (Shamir 1995). It is the leaders who are close to their followers, in particular, who can lose all their reputation with just one episode of hypocrisy or shading of the truth.

The truly transformational leader who is seeking the greatest good for the greatest number and is concerned about doing what is right and honest is likely to avoid stretching the truth or going beyond the evidence, because he/she wants to set an example to followers about the value of valid and accurate communication in maintaining the mutual trust of the leader and his or her followers. Nonetheless, there are many instances when a moral leader may judge it best to "soften" the hard facts of a situation. Impression management can be hopeful and optimistic without being deceitful and treacherous. A transformational leader tries to keep hope alive in the face of bad news. As Franklin D. Roosevelt declared in his inaugural address in 1933, "The only thing we have to fear is fear itself." Presenting a prognosis of terminal illness may be delayed by a physician until the physician feels that the patient is ready to hear it (Heifetz 1994). Impression management can also avoid setting up negative self-fulfilling prophesies.

THE ETHICS OF CHECKS AND BALANCES

A second criticism points out that transformational leadership lacks the checks and balances of transformational leadership. Thus, Keeley (1995) looked to Madison's contention in the Federalist papers (1787) that a constitutional government required contending interests to be heard so that after rational debate, optimal decisions could be made. Otherwise, the many factions of society could be controlled by them and would abandon their own best interests if they were coerced into sharing the same interests. According to Keeley interpreting Madison, an unhealthy concentration of power and dictatorship by the majority at the expense of the minority results from inspired, transformational leadership, which succeeds in convincing people with truly diverse interests that they share common goals. The rules of governance must require the separation of powers of the executive, the assembly and the judiciary. Outcomes must depend on negotiation and the give-and-take of transactional leadership to avoid them depending on a majority representing the interests of only the strongest faction. When that happens, more factional conflict might emerge with less tolerance for minority views. Rival and opposing interests are best controlled if purpose and power are separated and negotiations, trade-offs, and exchanges produce compromises acceptable to all concerned. This is in contrast to the emphasis of transformational leadership on the sharing in a common vision and a common purpose.

The Best of Leadership Is Both Transformational and Transactional

In replying to the criticism that transformational leadership cannot be checked or balanced, I do not wish to quarrel with the framers of the U.S. Constitution. Rather, I believe that the all-or-none argument of Keeley misses the point that the best of leadership is both transformational and transactional. Transformational leadership augments the effectiveness of transactional leadership, it does not replace transactional leadership (Waldman, Bass, and Yammarino 1990). The checks and balances of the U.S. Constitution required a Civil War to end slavery and achieve the paramount sovereignty of the federal union over the individual states, but we are still living with much of the legacy of the conflict over states' rights and racial division. The Union survived due to Lincoln's transformational, coupled with transactional, leadership. He took many transforming executive decisions based on his own sense of timing (transactional). His sense of duty and what he personally thought was right, good, and proper propelled him into (transformational) executive decisions unapproved by Congress or not necessarily backed by public opinion. Thus he suspended habeas corpus in 1862 when faced with a capital almost surrounded by the Confederacy and yet, by his second inauguration, he was calling for a generous, forgiving settlement "with malice towards none."

The constitutional checks and balances can result in costly gridlock as partisan legislatures and the executive cannot agree. In strong democracies, civil service carries on unless budgetary impasses lead to costly shutdowns of government services. In weak democracies, gridlock sets the stage for military coups and dictatorships. When it comes to moral standards, transactional exchanges and negotiations are likely to be fraught with the potential for manipulation, withholding of information, acting confidently when unsure or lacking information, making political alliances, initiating actions but delaying their implementation, openly compromising but covertly diverting plans, bluffing, and timing the release of information for when it will do the most (Martin and Sims 1956). When the transformational leader sees himself/herself in a win-lose negotiation, he/she tries to convert it into a win-win, joint problem-solving situation. If this is not possible, then he/she can display the transactional skills necessary as an effective negotiator.

Curiously, Jefferson averred that the checks and balances would not be needed if the country shared common interests. His transformational vision was that of a United States of small, independent farmers and mechanics with common interests that could be discussed in rational debate to reach necessary decisions. Jefferson saw that this could be accomplished by the public education of an informed citizenry. J. S. Mill propounded the salutary effects of encouraging free speech to provide the marketplace for ideas. The best arguments supported by the most compelling evidence and convincing reasoning would prevail (Higgenbottom 1996).

ORGANIZATIONAL DEVELOPMENT

A third criticism suggests that transformational leadership may be antithetical to the philosophy and principles of the Organizational Development (OD) movement, which espouses shared values, equality, power sharing, consensus, and participative decision-making. OD grew out of sensitivity training that featured the spontaneous emergence of the different roles of leadership in initially ambiguous situations. Learning how to give and receive feedback provided the means for the group to progress. For organizations to improve themselves, the seeds of reform resided in the values, interests, and capabilities of their members. Organizations could improve if the members were empowered to try out their ideas and learn from feedback.

Critics argued that transformational leadership subverted OD. Thus, for example, Stevens, D'Intino, and Victor (1995) accuse transformational leaders of changing the values of the employees of an organization so that they will adopt them as their own. This process "fundamentally violates the democratic and humanistic values" of Organizational Development (125). Employees are induced by the leadership to forgo their own best interests for the sake of the organization. For White and Wooten (1986) the humanistic and democratic values of OD may conflict with the organizational values of productivity and efficiency. Faced with such value conflicts, the transformational leader may manipulate the employees into buying into organizational efficiency instead of the employees' more important personal needs (McKendall 1993) for security and income. Thus transformational leadership is seen as unfair and therefore unethical when it moves employees to set aside their own life plans for the good of the organization. There is no moral justification for why the vision of the CEO should become the future to be sought by the employees. Furthermore, humanism and democracy require that all change and development efforts be without coercion or dictation but rather result from participative leadership. Critics also argue that transformational leadership does not strive for the "fair settlement of values conflicts" (Stevens, D'Intino, and Victor 1995, 135), thus violating the ethical norms of OD.

Alignment of Interests Is Sought

What is completely ignored by some OD apologists is that the individual employee's interests do not have to be sacrificed in the transforming process for the good of the organization. Nor will those interests have to depend on democratic participation. The truly transformational leader concerned with an ethical philosophy in managing an organization conceives of the organization's ultimate criterion of worth as the extent to which it satisfies all of its stakeholders. In the case of business firms, this means aligning and balancing the interests of owners and shareholders, managers and employees, suppliers and customers, community and society. In the case of not-for-profit institutions and social movements, this means aligning and balancing the interests of the officers and directors, the rank and file, and the public (Bass 1952). Additionally, the leadership may need to take into account constituents' families, government regulations, technological advances, and future needs.

Also ignored by the OD enthusiasts is what happens when individual interests outweigh the common good and transformational leadership is absent. Whenever the same limited resource is freely available to all individuals apart from the costs and efforts to obtain the resource, what results is the "tragedy of the commons" (Siebold 1993). Thus, if the resource, the commons, is public grazing land, each nearby farmer can try to maximize its use in his/her self-interest. Soon the land becomes overgrazed and is able to feed fewer and fewer animals. Such is what happened to seventeenth-century Boston farmers. In the 1980s New England fishing boat owners invested heavily in new, high-technology vessels and proceeded collectively to overfish the Grand Banks and nearby fishing grounds. Marine biologists had predicted ten years earlier what would happen. The reproductive capabilities of the fisheries were seriously depleted. Owners were bankrupted; the fishing had to come to a near-halt. Missing was transformational leadership from government executive or legislature directing the regulation of a more rational policy. Missing likewise was transformational leadership from within the fishing industry to voluntarily promote cooperative guidelines for conservation. Transformational leadership could have stimulated agreements about priorities, shared values, perceived common goals, and meaningful purposes. The individual boat owners involved would have been moved to go beyond their self-interests for the good of the collective.

Recognizing the problem, envisioning the win-win solution to it, communicating and persuading others about the problem and possible solutions, and developing the cultural and organizational infrastructure could have prevented the tragedy of the commons. So the commons is now all the oceans of the world. Voluntary conservation at the local level is no longer enough because of the international poaching by the large factory ships with a global reach. Statesman-like transformational leadership is needed at a worldwide level to save the declining stocks of fish in all the oceans for agreements among local traditional fisherfolk, international factory vessels, conservationists, scientists, and governments (Parfit 1995).

Morality for the school of thought exemplified by Rost (1991) demands democracy, individual rights, and freedom of choice. Likewise, free choice is morally pleasing to OD ethicists; nonetheless, free choice can produce the tragedy of the commons. Moreover, people often appreciate leadership that points the way out of dilemmas, whether it comes from others within their own collective or from external authority. Political leaders as widely different as Mao Zedung and Shimon Peres agreed that the task of leadership was to sense the problems and wants of the polity and to provide solutions that satisfied its interests. Free choice can produce the Abilene Paradox (Burke, undated) in which each member of a group, in this case, a family, does not want to go to Abilene. With free choice and each believing that he or she is accommodating to the wishes of the others, without the needed leadership to test for consensus, the family proceeds to go to Abilene although no one wanted to go.

The transformational leader strives to achieve a true consensus in aligning individual and organization interests. However, some OD enthusiasts misunderstand the meaning of true consensus. In true consensus the interests of all are fully considered, but the final decision reached may fail to please everyone completely. The decision is accepted as the best under the circumstances even if it means that some individual members' interests may have to be sacrificed. In moving members beyond their self-interests, rather than being in conflict with the values and practices of OD, I believe, to the contrary, that for the most part, the theory and practice of transformational leadership is compatible with OD. Table 8.1 illustrates this by showing the parallels in principles, practices, and values of OD and transformational leadership.

Rost would have everyone a leader but no followers in the interests of true participative democracy. Nevertheless, when one sets up an initially leaderless group, the members compete with each other for leadership. The structure that emerges is one or more leaders, followers, and isolates (Bass 1954).

If trying to change the values of employees of a firm to move them into alignment with the organization's values for the good of all stakeholders is immoral, then it is immoral for correctional authorities to try to shift the values of prison inmates to become constructive, law-abiding citizens. And what is teaching all about if not trying to move pupils to internalize the values of good citizenship for the benefit of all of society? Libertarians would agree that one's life plans are paramount, but they are espousing anarchy, as are the OD extremists who charge immorality if the transformational leader intervenes in the individual follower's life plans. Thus it must be unethical to ever send a soldier into harm's way or to ask an employee to avoid disclosing trade secrets when the employee decides that his/her career will benefit by joining a competing firm.

Table 8.1
Compatibility of Organizational Development and Transformational Leadership

Organizational Development	Transformational Leadership
Human nature is good.	Human development is stressed.
Trust is essential.	Trust is the variable intervening between transformational leadership and its outcomes.
Aims to enhance self-worth and self-respect.	Individualized consideration.
Minimize status differences.	Walk-around management.
Develop the full potential of self and others.	Individualized consideration.
Joint success of organization and its individuals.	Alignment of individual and organizational goals.
Provide commitment to challenging work.	Inspirational motivation/ Intellectual stimulation.
Avoid manipulation and coercion.	Authenticity.
Avoid values-conflicts.	Resolve values-conflicts.

Organizational Development and Transformational Leadership Are More Alike Than Different

The OD critique of transformational leadership is a case of the pot calling the kettle black. The concepts and practices of OD grew out of sensitivity training. The trainer, often with much artifice, manipulated the trainees to abandon their concerns for the task and the content of their discussion. Trainees thought that they should try to get some work done. Often with much resistance, but ultimately for their own improved understanding of group dynamics and themselves, they were "seduced" into focusing their attention on the group processes, the roles they were playing, and their interpersonal influence. But we don't condemn sensitivity trainers for being unethical.

Democracy and freedom are fundamental to OD, nevertheless the consensus of individual interests may be false or forced by overzealousness. Individuals may not have formed opinions about an interest, value, or goal but may be asked to express an opinion or feel obligated to do so. As noted by White and Wooten (1986), data may be misused, and misrepresentations occur in the OD process. This would be akin to the inspirational leader oversimplifying his or her message or replacing rational facts with an excess of emotional appeals. In both instances, important details affecting individual interests might be glossed over in sins of omission or commission. But these lapses in authenticity do not, require us to view all of either as immoral.

INFLUENCING FOLLOWERS' VALUES AND SELF-INTERESTS

A fourth criticism sees transformational leaders as subversive because transformational leaders encourage members of an organization to go beyond their own self-interests for the good of the organization. As a consequence, according to the criticism, the members are led down a primrose path on which they lose more than they gain. Values-conflicts between leaders and followers are settled to the benefit of the leader and the detriment of the followers. Followers sacrifice their own best interests for the good of the collectivity or the leaders' visions. The faultfinders argue that it is unethical for leaders to change the hierarchy of values that are salient within the follower's self-concept to match the leaders' values. (Shamir, House, and Arthur [1993] see nothing immoral in this matching process.)

The corporation has been likened to a medieval fiefdom by Jackall (1988). The feudal lord (the CEO) offers his vassals (managers) and serfs (employees) transactional material benefits and advancement in exchange for services rendered. But the loyalty, teamwork, and trust involved in transformational leadership are also emphasized as well as politics and personality. Such feudal lords and CEOs may be practicing primarily transactional leadership and pseudotransformational rather than true transformational leadership. Many firms and agencies have sought employee commitment through asking employees to share the organization's goals above and beyond their personal, family, and community interests only for the employees to find themselves out of a job due to the downsizing of the organization. The CEO may feel morally justified by arguing that the downsizing was required for the organization's survival and the security of the remaining employees and other stakeholders. As much as possible, the previously devoted and now redundant employees are adequately prepared and assisted in finding new work.

The Value of the Congruence of Values and Interests

More generally, there is a moral justification for the transformational leader's efforts to achieve value-congruence between the leader and the led. When it is achieved, both are more satisfied emotionally (Meglino, Ravlin, and Adkins 1989). Much of this congruence may be a matter of acculturation because as employees are socialized into an organization, there is an increase in the congruence of their values and the values of the organization (O'Reilly, Chatman, and Caldwell 1991). Such congruence results in leaders being seen by followers as more considerate, competent, and successful and followers being more satisfied with their jobs (Weiss 1978).

Fairholm (1991) has formulated a model of value-centered leadership calling for shared vision and values, mutual trust and respect, and unity in diversity. Value-centered leadership is required to transform employees and organization to make them competitive globally. Both leaders and followers must transcend their own self-interests if the collectivity is to thrive. Downsizing may not be beneficial to the firm and its owners nor to its employees and other stakeholders. Although immediate bottom-line profits may be obtained by downsizing, often these expected benefits to the organization may fail to materialize (McKinley, Sanchez, and Schick 1995). And the costs to personal, family, and community interests may far outweigh what was thought to be gained by the organization.

But the moral question remains as to whether, in achieving shared values, the followers are influenced to adopt the values of the leadership and the organizational culture or the leaders and organizational culture change to best reflect the followers' values. In any event, values of individuals must change if congruence is to be attained. The issue is really how the congruence is to be attained. OD theorists would argue that the congruence would be morally acceptable only if it came about from participative decision-making pursuing consensus between leaders and followers. But whether a leader is participative or directive is not a matter of morality. Rather, it is a matter of how much follower satisfaction and commitment outweigh all other objectives (Vroom and Yetton 1973), the naiveté or experience of the followers, and many other contextual considerations (Hersey and Blanchard 1969). Under various conditions. directive leadership is more appropriate and acceptable to all concerned than is participative leadership (Bass 1990).

As Heifetz (1994) theorized, leaders may need to use their authority as experts to mobilize followers to lessen the gap in their values-conflicts. Leaders must help followers to adapt in the face of competing value perspectives and creative tensions to generate new approaches. In the physician-patient relationship, the patient first depends on the physician's technical expertise to provide a directive diagnosis and proposed treatment. Subsequently, decisions about treatment are shared, and ultimately the patient becomes more responsible. Learning often requires considerable direction, structure, and guidance, which is expected and accepted by novices. With such direction, subsequent participation then can become more than a pooling of ignorance. In high-performing teams, a member who is an expert on a particular subject will be accepted by the other members and be authorized by them to instruct and to temporarily direct the team.

Horatio Nelson transformed the British Navy's tactics, the nature of the Napoleonic Wars, and the reputation of the British Navy between 1805 and 1915. Until he was killed at the Battle of Trafalgar in 1805, he almost always exhibited all the components of transformational leadership. He continuously showed—for his times, place and position—his individualized consideration for his sailors and officers; he displayed a great deal of intellectual stimulation in the revolutionary way he positioned his ships; he was highly inspirational and charismatic in his sense of mission.

OD apologists argue that for leadership to be ethical and effective, it must be participative. Nelson illustrated that transformational leadership can be right, good, and proper, yet clearly he himself made the decisions on how his fleet of ships were to be positioned at his three great victories of the Battles of the Nile, Copenhagen, and Trafalgar. Prior to making his decisions, he called all his ship captains aboard his flagship to ask for their opinions, but he didn't take a vote as in a democratic process, nor did the final dispositions of the ships reflect a consensus. The positioning of the ships was based on innovative ideas of his own that revolutionized naval warfare. After the ships were in position, the captains were free to carry the fight to the enemy as they saw fit without further instructions from Nelson. Rather than questioning the ethics of Nelson's order-giving, the captains, officers, and men strongly identified with him and his vision of the need to find and destroy Napoleon's fleet even at the cost of many of their own lives. They had been brought to a high degree of morale and readiness by Nelson's attention to continuous training, practice, and improvement while at sea along with Nelson's then-unusual practice of empathic conversing one-on-one with the lowliest seaman to the ranking captains. Moreover, he assiduously cultivated his personal image of courage and bravery. His legend fortified the British Navy for the century that followed (Walder 1978).

Increasingly, we are seeing the need for organizations to be structured around transitory, fluid teams of members to meet the ever-changing requirements of new technologies, markets, and work forces. How is this possible without agreements about objectives, methods, and values? Direction from higher authority does not have to be arbitrary and without reason and explanation. How can we have learning teams and organizations without their members transcending their self-interests to seek the objectives of such fluid organizations? Along with its checks and balances, democracy requires that its leaders also go beyond their own self-interests with a nurtured devotion to the public good. Both with respect to its leaders and followers, governance calls for guidance and control of the irrational aspects and the encouragement of the values of logic and rationality (Holmes 1991). Locke (1960) pointed out that although humans are naturally self-interested, they are capable of virtue. Self-interest antithetical to the common good can be offset by transactional controls or by the appeals of transformational leadership. Neither, of necessity, would be unethical unless coercion were involved. Acceptance of controls should not be without the consent of the governed, nor should shifting of values closer to those of the leadership be due to blind trust (Adkinson 1987; Locke 1960).

In rebutting the arguments that ethics requires democratic and participative decisions, and that followers lose more than they gain when they sacrifice their self-interests to please the transformational leader, we need to distinguish between the authoritarian personality and the directive leader. The authoritarian personality is rigid, submissive to authority, low in risk preference, conventional in thinking, and comfortable in highly structured situations. Directive leadership is leadership behavior that may be transformational or transactional. The leader tells what needs to be done usually with explanation. If in a position of responsibility and authority, or if an acknowledged expert working with novices, the leader may give orders, make decisions for self and others, but ordinarily give reasons for the decisions. Or, final decisions may be made by the leader following consultation with superiors, colleagues, and subordinates as well as clients, customers, and others.

Usually, in utilitarian organizations such as factories or hospitals, conflicts in values keep occurring around the issues of improving performance, reducing costs of operations, and concern for the well-being of constituencies. Some argue that what is right, good, and proper is to reduce costs and increase profits. "What's good for General Motors is good for the country." Others argue that morality requires maximizing the well-being of the operators. Transformational leaders attempt to find ways to align those interests into a win-win situation. Graham (1995) agrees. Like Kuhnert and Lewis (1987), she also uses Kohlberg's (1981) stages of moral development to show that transactional leadership that focuses on enforceable contracts and job descriptions is at a "pre-conventional" level of moral development. On the other hand, transformational leadership is at a "post-conventional" level of moral development as it looks to universal principles of justice and the costs and benefits for all stakeholders in the organization (as Bass [1952] had proposed in order to pursue the ultimate criteria of the worth of the organization).

TRANSFORMATIONAL VERSUS PSEUDOTRANSFORMATIONAL LEADERSHIP

As noted before, in their efforts to accent the positive, to make inspiring appeals, to maintain the enthusiasm and morale of followers, many leaders may be manipulative. They withhold the release of information, or they time its release for when it will do the most good. They give the appearance of confidence even when they are unsure about what they are doing and what they are telling followers to do. They initiate projects that they personally oppose and delay implementing them so that the projects never are completed. They publicly support but privately oppose proposals. They openly compromise but privately divert the implementation of the compromise (Martin and Sims 1956; Bass 1968). They may have the public image of a saint but privately be deceptive devils. Critics attribute such behavior to transformational leaders, but in fact they are describing pseudotransformational leaders—although Martin and Sims (1956) and Bailey (1988) hold that all leaders must be manipulative. And as was said about impression management, transformational leaders may have to be manipulative at times for what they judge to be the common good, but manipulation is a frequent practice of pseudotransformational leaders, not truly transformational leaders. What are the differences between the false and true ones?

A Catalog of Differences

A first difference between transformational and pseudotransformational leadership lies in their values. Bass (1985, 182–85) summed up the importance of the personal values held by a transformational leader in determining his or her actions. The observed behavior might seem the same, but if the objectives were morally uplifting, then the leader was transforming as posed by Burns (1978), who added that without such moral uplifting of followers, the leadership could not be considered transforming. But at that time, Bass argued incorrectly that the dynamics were the same if the leaders had virtuous or evil ends, if they wore white hats or black hats; the moral differences were a matter of their aims and values, not the dynamics involved in their influence. Transformational leaders wearing white hats are concerned about the good that can be achieved for the group, organization, or society for which they feel responsible.

As true transformational leaders, Mahatma Gandhi and Martin Luther King Jr. espoused universal brotherhood. On the other hand, although the Ayatollah Khomeini and Louis Farrakhan could also be transforming, they were pseudotransformational when they preached that only "our kind are good, superior and well-intentioned; and their kind were evil, inferior and out to destroy us." Love "us" but hate "them." One cannot argue about the transforming effects of Khomeini and Farrakhan, but conceive of them as pseudotransformational.

The difference also is seen in that true transformational leaders, who may have just as much need for power as pseudotransformational leaders, channel the need into socially constructive ways in the service of others. Pseudotransformational leaders use power primarily for self-aggrandizement and are actually contemptuous privately of those they are supposed to be serving as leaders (see Howell and Avolio 1993). Although this may not be expressed publicly, privately pseudotransformational leaders are concerned about their power and gaining more of it. Insiders who work closely with them know them to be deceptive, domineering, egotistical demagogues while their public image may be that of saviors. Pseudotransformational leaders are predisposed toward self-serving biases. They are right and good; others are wrong and bad. They are the reason things go well; others are the reason for things going wrong. They wear different masks for different occasions, believe themselves to be high in self-monitoring, but are betrayed by their nonverbal contradictory behavior. Pseudotransformational leaders welcome and

expect blind obedience. Followers accept more ambiguities and incon-
sistencies, opening the opportunities for the self-enhancement of char-
latans. They feed on the ignorance of their followers. "People like Rush
Limbaugh and Louis Farrakhan live well off ignorance. . . . They are
smart, ambitious men with great charisma, who look like giants to
people of minor intellect. They are snake oil salesmen. They are confidence men who exploit . . . ignorant, scared, angry, frustrated people
for personal gain in the name of doing good for the entire nation or race"
(Lockman 1995).

Pseudotransformational leadership can be subtle and disguised. It
can speak with a forked tongue offering followers empowerment, yet
continuing to treat them as dependent children (Sankowsky 1995). But
whether the charismatic leader is distant and not directly related or
closer and directly related to the follower affects whether he or she can
do so. According to Shamir's (1995) interviews with 320 Israeli students, distant leaders were more likely to foster blind obedience.

Whereas true transformational leaders are concerned about developing their followers into leaders, pseudotransformational leaders are
more concerned about maintaining the dependence of their followers.
Pseudotransformational leaders attempt to enhance their personal status by maintaining the personal distance between themselves and their
followers. They encourage fantasy and magic in their vision of the
attractive future, whereas true transformational leaders promote attainable shared goals. Narcissistic pseudotransformational leaders manipulate arguments about political choices with a "twist that achieves the
desired responses" (Bass 1989). Transformational leaders persuade others on the merits of the issues. Pseudotransformational leaders set and
control agendas to manipulate the values of importance to followers
often at the expense of others or even harm to them. True transformational leaders openly bring about changes in followers' values by the
merit and relevancy of the leader's ideas and mission to their followers'
ultimate benefit and satisfaction (Howell 1988). Pseudotransformational leaders may create the impression that they are doing the right
things but secretly fail to do so when doing the right things conflicts
with their own narcissistic interests. They are less likely to listen to
conflicting views and more likely to be intolerant of the differences of
opinion between their followers and themselves (Avolio and Bass 1995).
In short, whereas transformational leaders may fail to exhibit any one
to three of the four components (idealized influence, inspirational motivation, intellectual stimulation, or individualized consideration), the
component that ordinarily is missing in the personalized leadership of
the pseudotransformational leader is individualized consideration.
Thus many intellectually stimulating, inspirational leaders such as

Hyman Rickover, who brought the U.S. Navy into the nuclear age, were known for their self-aggrandizing, inconsiderate, abusive, and abrasive behavior (Polmar and Allen 1995). Furthermore, instead of earning idealized influence from their followers, the pseudotransformational leaders seek to become the idols (rather than the ideals) of their followers (Howell and Avolio 1993). The ethics of transformational leadership are subverted by the pseudotransformational leader's contempt for self and others, by learning to rationalize and justify their deceptions, and by their feelings of superiority. They see themselves as having an unconventional but higher morality (Goldberg 1995). Nevertheless, they are mistaken. O'Connor et al. (1995) contrasted the biographies of eighty-two world-class personalized and socialized charismatic leaders. The socialized charismatics were rated more highly in their morality than were the personalized, especially as they behaved during their rise to power.

In addition to what has already been said, Howell and Avolio (1993) point out the need of truly transformational leaders to promote within their organizations ethical policies, procedures, and processes. They need to be committed to a clearly stated, continually enforced code of ethical conduct that helps establish acceptable standards. They need to foster an organizational culture with high ethical standards by appropriate recruitment, training, and rewards to eventuate in the internalization in all the organization's members of shared moral standards.

In the last analysis, transformational leadership is in the eyes of the followers. Whether it is judged true or false depends on who does the judging. For the Iranian Islamic revolutionaries, Khomeini was a saint—a true transformational leader. For a large percentage of the German public, Hitler spoke for what they valued with honor and integrity. They believed he had their well-being at heart (Burns 1978). Nonetheless, given any sense of an absolute morality, Khomeini and Hitler were pseudotransformational. The British Treasurer, Charles Trevelyan, in dealing with the Irish potato famine between 1845 and 1849 understood that the potato blight would severely reduce the needed fourteen pounds of potatoes that were the daily diet of an Irish peasant. But he was concerned that if he ordered corn from the United States, he would need to ensure that it was sold at the market price so as not to interfere with free enterprise. But the peasants had little or no cash to pay for the corn, so they starved. However, he arranged to institute public works involving mainly useless heavy labor, but the starving men, women, and children had lost the strength to break rocks and dig ditches. His policies were applauded by the Tories for his conforming to the principles of free enterprise and equity for the merchants and traders. But it meant starving to death or dying from the resulting typhus and dysentery for those who were unable to purchase the minimum rations of food. Trevelyan transformed the Irish landscape, but the values he placed on economic principles over the realities of human welfare clearly made him pseudotransformational as well as highly transactional in philosophy. He was in reality what Charles Dickens in 1854 had fictionalized in the values of the Coketown manufacturer, Mr. Bounderby, and the bank clerk, Bitzer. In "Hard Times," Bitzer was taught by his mentor, Mr. Gradgrind, that it was a fundamental principle of political economy that everything had to be paid for. Nobody was ever on any account to give anybody anything or render anybody help without purchase. The whole social system is a matter of self-interest. What you must always appeal to is a person's self-interest. It's your only hold. And so, for Gradgrind, to transform and maintain the well-being of society and pursue his ideal of the greater good for all, leadership must always be transactional!

SUMMARY AND CONCLUSIONS

Critics argue that transformational leadership is unethical. They contend that its rhetoric may appeal to emotions rather than to reason. They contend that it lacks the checks and balances of democratic discourse and power distribution. They contend that it violates the principles of the Organization Development (OD) movement and that it manipulates followers into ignoring their own best interests.

The critics fail to consider the positive aspects of inspirational leadership. They ignore the shortcomings of democratic processes and OD. They fail to distinguish between transformational and pseudotransformational leadership. We agree with Gill Hickman (1993) that rather than being unethical, true transformational leaders identify the core values and unifying purposes of the organization and its members; liberate their human potential; and foster plural leadership and effective, satisfied followers.

Rather than being immoral, transformational leadership has become a necessity in the postindustrial world of work. As Cascio (1995) has pointed out, the traditional manufacturing or service job, a fixed bundle of tasks performed by an individual worker, has been replaced by a manufacturing or service process, completed by a flexible team with diverse skills, interests, and attitudes. As a consequence, "today's networked, interdependent, culturally diverse organizations require transformational leadership to bring out . . . in followers . . . their creativity, imagination, and best efforts" (930).

Self-aggrandizing pseudotransformational leaders can be branded as immoral. But truly transformational leaders who engage in the moral uplifting of their followers, who move them to share in the mutually rewarding visions of success, who enable and empower them to convert the visions into realities, should be applauded, not chastised, for their efforts.

NOTES

1. For some, to be a follower implies dependency, weakness. susceptibility, lowered status, and antidemocratic inequalities. For me, it only means that at a point in time someone influences and someone is influenced. The influencer is the leader, and the influenced is the follower. The roles may be shared, alternated, and exchanged. Unfortunately, we don't have in English the exact term "lead*ee*" to accompany lead*er*, but to be seen as democratic, we have to make do with ambiguous terms such as associates and collaborators.

REFERENCES

Adkinson, D. 1987. "The Federalist and Human Nature." *Journal of Political Science* 15: 48–59.

Argyris, C., and D. A. Schon. 1984. "Organizational Learning." In D. S. Pugh, ed. *Organizational Theory*. Hammondsworth: Penguin.

Avolio, Bruce J., and Bass, Bernard M. 1995. "Individual Consideration Viewed at Multiple Levels of Analysis: A Multi-Level Framework for Examining the Diffusion of Transformational Leadership." *Leadership Quarterly* 6, no. 2.

Bailey, F. G. 1988. *Humbuggery and Manipulation: The Art of Leadership*. Ithaca: Cornell University Press.

Bass, B. M. 1952. "Ultimate Criteria of Organizational Worth." *Personnel Psychology* 5: 157–73.

———. 1954. "The Leaderless Group Discussion." *Psychological Bulletin* 51: 465–92.

———. 1968. "How to Succeed in Business According to Business Students and Managers." *Journal of Applied Psychology* 52: 254–62.

———. 1985. *Leadership and Performance beyond Expectations*. New York: Free Press.

———. 1989. "The Two Faces of Charisma." *LEADERS* 12 (4): 44–45.

———. 1990. *Bass and Stogdill's Handbook of Leadership*. New York: Free Press.

———. 1995, May. "Universality of Transformational Leadership." Distinguished Scientific Awards Address, Society for Industrial & Organizational Psychology, Orlando, Florida.

Bass, B. M., and B. J. Avolio. 1993. "Transformational Leadership: A Response to Critiques." In M. M. Chemers and R. Ayman, eds. *Leadership Theory and Research: Perspectives and Directions*. New York: Free Press.

Burns, J. M. 1978. *Leadership*. New York: Harper and Row.

Burke, W. W. (undated). "Abilene Paradox." Unpublished.

Carey, M. R. 1995. "Transformational Leadership and the Fundamental Option for Self-Transcendence." *Leadership Quarterly* 3: 217–36.

Cascio, W. 1995. "Whither Industrial and Organizational Psychology in a Changing World of Work?" *American Psychologist* 50: 928–39.

Chatman, J. A. 1989. "Improving Interactional Organizational Research: A Model of Person Organization Fit." *Academy of Management Review* 14: 333–49.

Ciulla, J. B. 1995. "Leadership Ethics: Mapping the Territory." *Business Ethics Quarterly* 5: 5–28.

Conger, J., and R. N. Kanungo. 1988. *Charismatic Leadership: The Elusive Factor in Organizational Effectiveness*. San Francisco: Jossey-Bass.

Dukerich, J. M., M. L. Nichols, D. R. Elm, and D. A. Vollrath. 1990. "Moral Reasoning in Groups: Leaders Make a Difference." *Human Relations* 43: 473–93.

Engelbrecht, A. S., and W. D. Murray. 1995. "Work Values and Transformational Leadership: A Model for the Influence of Leader-Subordinate Value Congruence on Leadership Style and Effectiveness." *CLS Report*, No. 7. Binghamton, N.Y.: Center for Leadership Studies, Binghamton University.

Ezekiel, R. 1995, Spring. "One American World." *Carnegie Quarterly* 9–12.

Fairholm, G. W. 1991. *Values Leadership: Towards a New Philosophy of Leadership*. New York: Praeger.

Fisher, D. H., and S. B. Fowler. 1995. "Reimagining Moral Leadership in Business: Image, Identity and Differences." *Business Ethics Quarterly* 5: 29–42.

Gardner, W. L., and B. J. Avolio. 1996. "Charismatic Leadership: The Role of Impression Management." *CLS Report*, No. 2. Binghamton, N.Y.: Center for Leadership Studies, Binghamton University.

Gerstein, M. S., and R. B. Shaw. 1992. "Organizational Architectures for the 21st Century." In D. A. Nadler, M. S. Gerstein, and R. B. Shaw, eds. *Organizational Architecture: Designs for Changing Organizations*. San Francisco, Jossey-Bass.

Gini, A. 1995. "Too Much to Say about Something." *Business Ethics Quarterly* 5: 143–55.

Goldberg, C. 1995, October. "Psychologist Posits the Origins of Evil." *Monitor*. Washington, D.C.: American Psychological Association.

Graham, J. W. 1995. "Leadership, Moral Development, and Citizenship Behavior." *Business Ethics Quarterly* 5: 43–54.

Greenleaf, R. K. 1977. *Servant Leadership*. New York: Paulist Press.

Gronn, P. C. 1994. "Greatness Revisited: The Current Obsession with Transformational Leadership." *Leading & Managing* 1: 14–27.

Heifetz, R. A. 1994. *A Leadership without Easy Answers*. Cambridge, Mass.: Belknap/ Harvard University Press.

Hersey, Paul, and Kenneth H. Blanchard. 1969. *Management of Organizational Behavior: Utilizing Human Resources*. Englewood, NJ: Prentice Hall.

Hickman, G. 1993. "Toward Transformistic Organizations: A Conceptual Framework." Paper, American Political Science Association, Washington, D. C.

Higginbottom, G. 1996. "Public Broadcasting Is Good for the Public." *Binghamton* (N.Y.) *Press*, July 23, A-6.

Hollander, E. 1995. "Ethical Challenges in the Leader-Follower Relationship." *Business Ethics Quarterly* 5: 54–65.

Holmes, S. 1991, Fall. "The Liberal Idea." *The American Prospect*.

House, R., and Boas Shamir. 1993. "Toward the Integration of Charismatic, Visionary and Transformational Leadership Theories." In M. Chemers and R. Ayman, eds. *Leadership Theory and Research: Perspectives and Directions.* New York: Academic Press.

Howard, J. M. 1988. "Two Faces of Charisma: Socialized and Personalized Leadership in Organizations." In J. A. Conger and R. N. Kanungo, eds. *Charismatic Leadership.* San Francisco: Jossey-Bass.

Howell, Jane M. 1988. "Two Faces of Charisma: Socialized and Personalized Leadership in Organizations." In J. R. Conger and R. N. Kanungo, eds. *Charismatic Leadership.* San Francisco: Jossey-Bass.

Howell, J. M., and B. J. Avolio. 1993. "The Ethics of Charismatic Leadership: Submission or Liberation?" *Academy of Management Executive* 6(2): 43–54.

Jackall, R. 1988. *Moral Mazes: The World of Corporate Managers.* New York: Oxford University Press.

Keeley, M. 1995. "The Trouble with Transformational Leadership: Toward A Federalist Ethic for Organizations." *Business Ethics Quarterly* 5: 67–95.

Kohlberg, L. 1981. *The Meaning and Measurement of Moral Development.* Worcester, Mass.: Clark University Press.

Kouzes, J. M., and B. Z. Posner. 1993. *Credibility: How Leaders Gain and Lose It and Why People Demand It.* San Francisco: Jossey-Bass.

Kuhnert, K. W., and P. L Lewis. 1987. "Transactional and Transformational Leadership: A Constructive/Developmental Analysis." *Academy of Management Review* 12: 648–57.

Lackomski, G. 1995. "Leadership and Learning: From Transformational Leadership to Organizational Learning." *Leading & Managing* 1: 2.

Lichtenstein, B. M., B. A. Smith, and W. R. Torbert. 1995. "Leadership and Ethical Development: Balancing Light and Shadow." *Business Ethics Quarterly* 5: 97–116.

Locke, J. 1960. *The Two Treatises of Government.* P. Laslett, ed. Cambridge: Cambridge University Press.

Lockman, N. 1995. "American Ignorance American Hate." *Press & Sun Bulletin* (Binghamton, N.Y.), December 19, 9A.

Lowe, K., K. G. Kroeck, and N. Subrabramanian. In press. "Effective Correlates of Transformational and Transactional Leadership: A Meta-Analytic Review." *Leadership Quarterly.*

Madison, J. *Federalist* Nos. 10, 49, 51. In C. Rossiter, ed. *The Federalist Papers.* New York: Mentor, 1961.

Martin. N. H., and J. H. Sims. 1956. "Thinking Ahead: Power Tactics." *Harvard Business Review* 36(6): 25.

McCullough, T. E. 1991. *The Moral Imagination and Public Life.* Chatham, N.J.: Chatham House.

McKendall, M. 1993. "The Tyranny of Change: Organizational Development Revisited." *Journal of Business Ethics* 12: 104.

McKinley, W., C. M. Sanchez, and A. G. Schick. 1995. "Organizational Downsizing: Constraining, Cloning, Learning." *Academy of Management Executives* 9(3): 32–42.

Meglino, B., Lavlin, E. C., and Adkins, C. L. 1989. "A Work Values Approach to Corporate Culture." *Journal of Applied Psychology* 74(3): 424–32.

O'Connor, J. O., M. D. Mumford, T. C. Clifton, T. L. Gessner, and M. S. Connelly. 1995. "Charismatic Leaders and Destructiveness: An Historiometric Study." *Leadership Quarterly* 6: 529–55.

O'Reilly, C. A., J. Chatman, and D. F. Caldwell. 1991. "People and Organizational Culture: A Profile Comparison Approach to Assessing Person-Organization Fit." *Academy of Management Journal* 34: 489–516.

Parfit, M. 1995. "Diminishing Returns: Exploiting the Ocean's Bounty." *National Geographic Magazine* 188: 2–37.

Podsakoff, P. M., S. B. MacKenzie, R. H. Moorman, and R. Fetter. 1990. "Transformational Leader Behaviors and Their Effects on Followers' Trust in Leader, Satisfaction, and Organizational Citizen Behaviors." *Leadership Quarterly* 1: 107–42. San Francisco: Jossey-Bass.

Polmar, N., and T. B. Allen. 1995. *Code Name Downfall: The Secret Plan to Invade Japan and Why Truman Dropped the Bomb.* New York: Simon and Schuster.

Rost, J. C. 1991. "Leadership for the Twenty-first Century." New York: Praeger.

Sankowsky, D. 1995. "The Charismatic Leader as Narcissist: Understanding the Abuse of Power." *Organizational Dynamics* 23: 57–71.

Schwartz, S. H., and C. Sagiv. 1995. "Identifying Culture-Specifics in the Content and Structure of Values." *Journal of Cross-cultural Psychology* 26: 92–116.

Senge, P. M. 1990. *The Fifth Discipline: The Art and Practice of the Learning Organization.* New York: Doubleday.

Shamir, B. 1995. "Social Distance and Charisma: Theoretical Notes and an Exploratory Study." *Leadership Quarterly* 6: 19–47.

Shamir, B., R. J. House, and M. B. Arthur. 1993. "The Motivational Effects of Charismatic Leaders: A Self-Concept Based Theory." *Organizational Science* 4: 577–94.

Siebold, G. L. 1993, November. "Leadership as the Management of the Commons." Paper, 35th Annual Conference of the Military Testing Association, Williamsburg, Va.

Stevens. C. U., R. S. D'Intino, and B. Victor. 1995. "The Moral Quandary of Transformational Leadership: Change for Whom?" *Research in Organizational Change and Development* 8: 123–43.

Terry, R. W. 1993. *Authentic Leadership: Courage in Action.* San Francisco: Jossey-Bass.

Vroom, V. H., and P. W. Yetton. 1973. *Leadership and Decision-Making.* New York: Wiley.

Walder, D. 1978. *Nelson.* New York: Dial Press/James Wade.

Waldman, D. A., B. M. Bass, and F. J. Yammarino. 1990. "Adding To Contingent-Reward Behavior: The Augmenting Effect Of Charismatic Leadership." *Group & Organizational Studies,* 15: 381–94.

Weiss, H. M. 1978. "Social Learning of Work Values in Organizations." *Journal of Applied Psychology* 63: 711–18.

White, L. P., and K. C. Wooten. 1986. *Professional Ethics and Practice in Organizational Development: A Systematic Analysis of Issues, Alternatives, and Approaches.* New York: Praeger.

Woodham-Smith, C. 1991. *The Great Hunger: Ireland 1845–1849.* London: Penguin Books.

Index

About the Editor
and Contributors

BERNARD M. BASS is Distinguished Professor Emeritus of Management and Director of the Center for Leadership Studies, School of Management, State University of New York at Binghamton. He has published over four hundred articles and twenty-three books. Bass is the founding editor of *Leadership Quarterly* and coauthor of *Bass and Stogdill's Handbook of Leadership*. In 1994 he received the Distinguished Scientific Contributions Award of the Society for Industrial & Organizational Psychology.

JAMES MACGREGOR BURNS is a Senior Scholar at the Academy of Leadership at the University of Maryland, College Park. He has also served as Visiting Scholar at the Jepson School of Leadership Studies, University of Richmond, and as professor of political science at Williams College. He is the author of *Leadership* and a number of political biographies, including *Roosevelt: The Lion and the Fox*, which was awarded a Pulitzer Prize.

JOANNE B. CIULLA is the Coston Family Chair in Leadership and Ethics at the Jepson School of Leadership Studies, University of Richmond. She has held academic appointments at the Harvard Business

School, the Wharton School, Oxford University, and La Salle University. She has published in leadership studies, business ethics, and the philosophy of work. She is on the editorial boards of *Business Ethics Quarterly*, *The Journal of Business Ethics*, and *Business Ethics*.

AL GINI is associate professor of philosophy and adjunct professor in the Institute of Industrial Relations at Loyola University of Chicago. He is also Managing Editor of *Business Ethics Quarterly*, the journal of the Society for Business Ethics. His published work includes coauthorship of *Philosophical Issues in Human Rights*, *It Comes with the Territory: An Inquiry into the Nature of Work*, and *Case Studies in Business Ethics*.

EDWIN P. HOLLANDER is University Distinguished Professor in the Industrial/Organizational Psychology graduate programs at CUNY's Baruch College and Graduate Center. He was Provost of Social Sciences and Administration at SUNY Buffalo, and Director of the Social/Organizational Psychology Department there. His books include *Leaders, Groups, and Influence* and *Leadership Dynamics*. He has taught at Carnegie-Mellon, Washington University, and American University, with visiting appointments at Wisconsin, Harvard, Oxford, Istanbul (Fulbright), and London's Tavistock Institute (NIMH Senior Fellow).

MICHAEL KEELEY is Professor of Management at Loyola University of Chicago. He is the author of *A Social-Contract Theory of Organizations*, as well as numerous journal articles. He is currently writing a book on James Madison's management and organizational theories.

ROBERT C. SOLOMON is Quincy Lee Centennial Professor of Business and Philosophy and Distinguished Teaching Professor at the University of Texas at Austin. He is the author of *Above the Bottom Line*, *It's Good Business*, *Ethics and Excellence*, and *New World of Business*, as well as *The Passions*, *In the Sprit of Hegel*, *About Love*, *A Passion for Justice*, *Up the University*, and a *Short History of Philosophy*.

J. THOMAS WREN is Associate Professor of Leadership Studies at the Jepson School of Leadership Studies at the University of Richmond. He is the author of a number of articles on history and leadership and editor of *The Leader's Companion: Insights on Leadership through the Ages*.

ISBN 1-56720-175-X

90000>

HARDCOVER BAR CODE

LP212   96